Plagiarama!

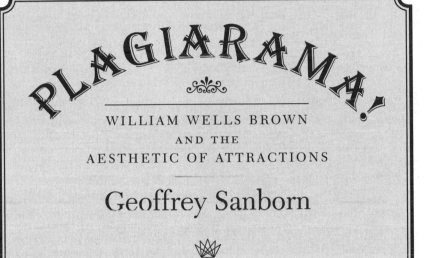

PLAGIARAMA!

WILLIAM WELLS BROWN AND THE AESTHETIC OF ATTRACTIONS

Geoffrey Sanborn

Columbia University Press
New York

Columbia University Press
Publishers Since 1893
New York Chichester, West Sussex
cup.columbia.edu

Library of Congress Cataloging-in-Publication Data
Sanborn, Geoffrey.
Plagiarama! : William Wells Brown and the aesthetic of attractions / Geoffrey Sanborn.
pages cm
Includes bibliographical references and index.
ISBN 978-0-231-17442-8 (cloth : acid-free paper) — ISBN 978-0-231-54058-2 (e-book)
1. Brown, William Wells, 1814?—1884—Criticism and interpretation. 2. Plagiarism—United States—History—19th century. 3. American literature—African American authors—History and criticism. 4. Abolitionists—United States—History—19th century. 5. American literature—19th century—History and criticism. I. Title.

PS1139.B9Z86 2015
813'.4—dc23

2015016643

Columbia University Press books are printed on permanent and durable acid-free paper.
This book is printed on paper with recycled content.
Printed in the United States of America

c 10 9 8 7 6 5 4 3 2 1

COVER IMAGE: Image of the author William Wells Brown from his book *Three Years in Europe: Places I Have Seen and People I Have Met.* From Project Gutenberg via Wikimedia Commons. Public domain.

COVER DESIGN: Philip Pascuzzo

To Sarah, Colin, Eli, and Calvin

Contents

Plagiarama!

Introduction

About forty miles east of Louisville, Kentucky, is a small town with the improbable name of Pleasureville. Plenty of villages, towns, and cities in the United States associate themselves with pleasantness—there are sixty-four Pleasant Valleys, thirty-three Pleasant Views, eighteen Pleasantvilles, eight Pleasantons, four Pleasant Points, a Pleasant Run, a Pleasant Branch, a Pleasant Ridge, a Pleasant Mountain, a Pleasant Lake, a Pleasant City, and a plain old Pleasant—but only two, as far as I have been able to tell, identify themselves with pleasure. It is not hard to see why. Most American municipalities define themselves in relation to stable values and easeful, long-lasting forms of happiness—in relation to *plaisir*, as Roland Barthes would have put it, rather than *jouissance*. A town with the word "pleasure" in its name is defined, by contrast, in relation to an experience that comes and goes, that "exceeds any (social) function and any (structural) functioning," that scandalizes consistency and order.[1]

The Kentucky Pleasureville—the other is in Pennsylvania—has a strange story attached to it. In the "Memoir of the Author" that introduces William Wells Brown's *The Rising Son* (1874), we are told that in 1871, during a trip to Pleasureville to promote an organization that he had founded, the National Association for the Spread of Temperance and Nightschools, Brown was kidnapped by the Ku Klux Klan.[2] Shortly after dark, while walking on a country road, he was waylaid by "some eight or ten men," bound, tied to a horse, and dragged down "what appeared to be a cow-path." "While on this road," he writes, "my hat fell off, and I called out to the man behind and said, 'I've lost my hat.' 'You'll need no hat in half an hour's time,' he replied."

As they neared a log house, a man came out and said, tremulously, "Jim's dying!" Upon hearing "the cries, groans, and ravings of the sick man," Brown instantly recognized it as "an extreme case of delirium tremens," a condition that he had previously treated, while practicing medicine in Boston, with an injection of morphine. Serendipitously, he had a syringe and a supply of morphine with him. "I know what's the matter with that man," he told his captors, "and I can relieve him in ten minutes."

The men untied him and brought him into the sick man's chamber. Having determined that he would "try to impress them with the idea that I had derived my power to relieve pain from some supernatural source," Brown said, "Now, gentlemen, I'll give this man complete relief in less than ten minutes from the time I lay my hands on him; but I must be permitted to retire to a room alone, for I confess that I have dealings with the devil, and I must consult with him." They complied. After loading the syringe and putting it in his vest pocket, Brown returned to the bedroom, waved his hands in the air, and said, "Gentlemen, I want your aid; give it to me, and I'll perform a cure that you'll never forget. All of you look upon that man till I say, 'Hold!' Look him right in the eye." They complied again. Brown took out the syringe, injected the man, put the syringe back in his pocket, and cried, "Hold!" Ten minutes later, Jim was at ease. The leader of the lynching party, a man called Cap, "gazed steadily at me, then at the sick man, and exclaimed,—'Big thing! big thing, boys, d—d if it ain't!'"

Brown then talked Cap into having some devil-aided work done on his sciatica—"I'll do anything you tell me," Cap promised him—and surreptitiously sedated him, singing, as he did so, "a noted Methodist hymn." After some consultation, all but one of the remaining men rode away, with the intention of returning before dawn to finish the lynching. The man left to guard Brown drank too much and fell asleep at the table. The last obstacle to Brown's departure, an angry dog, was brought to heel by Jim's wife, and, with a "grateful look" at her, Brown left the house. "Taking the road that I had come, and following it down," he writes, "I found my hat, and after walking some distance out of the way by mistake, I reached the station, and took the morning train for Cincinnati."[3]

Let's say, for the sake of argument, that none of this ever happened.[4] Why, at a time when white vigilante activities were a real and constant threat, would Brown make up a comic story about escaping from half-witted Klansmen? Why is the story flanked by, and implicitly paralleled with, an anecdote about refusing to put up with wet bedsheets in an English hotel and an anecdote about arranging to have a bag of flour dumped on the heads of hostile audience members in upstate New York? Why does he choose not to offer any concluding reflections on the event? And why—if it never happened and he could have situated it pretty much anywhere along the path of his travels in the rural South—did he set the story in the bizarrely named town of Pleasureville?

These are the kinds of questions that have spurred and respurred my interest in William Wells Brown over the last few years. Answers come to mind—the comedy is an affirmation of elasticity in the face of a stultifyingly oppressive racial violence; the bedsheet and flour-bag stories communicate to the Klan story a similarly affirmative lightness; the absence of a moral underscores the gratuitousness, the fundamentally aesthetic quality, of the story's extremely prolonged telling; Pleasureville is the interpersonal space of literary experience—but I am not inclined to pursue them very far. Under the inspiration, or spell, of Brown, I am inclined, instead, to remain in the space between the emergence of questions and the expression of answers, a space in which various types of uncertainty (did this happen? did he make it up? what are its politics? what are its aesthetics?) simply swirl. As a result of that swirling, a kind of apparitional shimmer is generated. Brown glistens. I experience a Barthes-like bliss.[5]

Here is another example of the quality that I am attempting to capture here, taken from a speech that Brown delivered at a meeting of the New York Anti-Slavery Society in May 1856:

> Some year and a half ago, I landed in this city from a British steamer, having just left England, after having been abroad in different countries in Europe for a number of years, where I was never once reminded that I was a coloured person, so that I had quite forgotten the distinction of caste that existed in democratic America. I walked into an eating-house. I had scarcely got my hat off when the proprietor told me I could not eat there. Said I, "I have got a good appetite, and if you will give me a trial, I rather think I will convince you that I can." "But," said he, "it is not allowable." I did not know what to make of it; I had been away five years, and had forgotten the great power of slavery over the North. I felt insulted.

> I walked into another eating-house. The proprietor asked me what I wanted. I said I wanted my dinner. "You can't get it here; we don't accommodate niggers." That was twice I was insulted. I went into a third, with a like result. I then went and stood by a lamp post for some five minutes. I thought of the nineteen years I had worked as a slave; I thought of the glorious Declaration of Independence; I looked around me and saw no less than seven steeples of churches; and I resolved I would have my dinner in the city of New York (applause). I went to another restaurant. I made up my mind what I would do. I saw a vacant plate at a table; I took aim at it. I pulled back the chair, and sat down, turned over the plate, and stuck my knife in something. I was agitated, and did not know what it was, until I got it on my plate, when I found it was a big pickle (laughter). At any rate I went to work at it. The waiter stared at me. Said I, "Boy, get me something to eat." He stared again, walked to the proprietor, and said something to him, came back, and helped me. When I got through my dinner, I went up to the bar, and handed the proprietor a dollar. He took it, and then said, "You have got the greatest impudence of any nigger I have seen for a great while" (laughter).[6]

What is the pickle doing in this story? Again, a series of answers could take the place of that question: it is a phallic symbol; by stabbing it, Brown symbolically assaults white male potency; by eating it, he symbolically lays claim to that potency himself. But all such answers, however credible they might be from a certain perspective, miss the point. The point of the pickle is, quite simply, to energize the audience by creating a pleasurable uncertainty about where this narrative of resistance to Northern prejudice is going. By dropping into the lecture, at a carefully prepared-for moment, an object that is simultaneously too banal and too symbolically overdetermined to be taken seriously, Brown causes his narrative to lift off, in part, from the solid ground of moral earnestness. He causes, as well, an at least temporary rerouting of attention from the story to the teller; he gives the audience a satisfyingly structured anecdote, and they give him, in his capacity as a performer, a burst of laughter. The pickle is fictionality; the pickle is theatricality; the pickle is purely gratuitous pleasure.

Until very recently, these were not the kinds of qualities that critics of early African American literature tended to emphasize. "Almost from the very beginning," J. Saunders Redding wrote in 1939, "the literature of the

Negro has been literature either of purpose or of necessity."[7] The power of that equation—African American literature = literature of purpose or necessity—has made it difficult to draw other dimensions of literature and literary experience into the discussion. It has made it difficult, moreover, to bring in more than a handful of texts. For most scholars and teachers, nineteenth-century African American writing boils down to Frederick Douglass and Harriet Jacobs, and, if time is short, it boils straight down to Douglass—which is to say, straight down to *Narrative of the Life of Frederick Douglass* (1845), not the expansive, dilatory, aesthetically ambitious *My Bondage and My Freedom* (1855). In the last decade or so, critics such as Daphne Brooks, Lara Langer Cohen, Theo Davis, Gustavus Stadler, and Elisa Tamarkin have offered important challenges to the long-standing tendency in literary studies to prioritize the biographical, political, and cultural-historical dimensions of early African American writing.[8] Over the same period, several critics have tried to extend the canon of nineteenth-century black writing "beyond Douglass," as Michael J. Drexler and Ed White put it in the title to a 2008 collection of essays (or "Beyond Douglass and Jacobs," as John Ernest puts it in the title of a 2007 essay).[9] But the status quo persists. The image of the early black author repeatedly reverts to the image of a man or woman forced by Necessity to write with a Purpose; the criticism of early black writing repeatedly reverts to a historicization of the Necessity and a highlighting of the Purpose in a handful of canonical texts.

The aim of this book is to contribute to the developing discussion of the more-than-necessary and other-than-purposive aspects of early African American writing and to argue for the centrality, in any such discussion, of Brown. In spite of having been, in his day, generally reckoned the second-most important black abolitionist—after Douglass, of course—and in spite of having authored the first published African American novel, the first published African American play, and more total volumes than any other nineteenth-century African American writer, Brown is virtually unknown to nonspecialists and barely represented in the standard anthologies of American literature. His best-known work, *Clotel* (1853), is frequently derided as an aesthetic failure. His next-best-known work, *Narrative of the Life of William W. Brown* (1847), is deep in Douglass's shadow. The rest of his major publications—*Three Years in Europe* (1852) (later expanded into *The American Fugitive in Europe* [1855]), *The Escape* (1858), *The Black*

Man (1863), *The Negro in the American Rebellion* (1867), *The Rising Son*, and *My Southern Home* (1880)—are mostly unread.[10] This is a horrible shame. Our overlooking of Brown is an overlooking of what so many literary critics and readers in general are in search of these days: a writer with an idiosyncratic aesthetic sensibility who ranges up and down the cultural register in pursuit of political change. If we want to move not only beyond Douglass and Jacobs but beyond purpose and necessity, there is no better place to start than Brown.

Consider, in this light, the following two passages. The first is Douglass's famous description of learning to write, from his 1845 *Narrative*:

> The idea as to how I might learn to write was suggested to me by being in Durgin and Bailey's ship-yard, and frequently seeing the ship carpenters, after hewing, and getting a piece of timber ready for use, write on the timber the name of that part of the ship for which it was intended. When a piece of timber was intended for the larboard side, it would be marked thus—"L." When a piece was for the starboard side, it would be marked thus—"S." A piece for the larboard side forward, would be marked thus—"L. F." When a piece was for starboard side forward, it would be marked thus—"S. F." For larboard aft, it would be marked thus—"L. A." For starboard aft, it would be marked thus—"S. A." I soon learned the names of these letters, and for what they were intended when placed upon a piece of timber in the ship-yard. I immediately commenced copying them, and in a short time was able to make the four letters named. After that, when I met with any boy who I knew could write, I would tell him I could write as well as he. The next word would be, "I don't believe you. Let me see you try it." I would then make the letters which I had been so fortunate as to learn, and ask him to beat that. In this way I got a good many lessons in writing, which it is quite possible I should never have gotten in any other way. During this time, my copy-book was the board fence, brick wall, and pavement; my pen and ink was a lump of chalk. With these, I learned mainly how to write.[11]

And here is Brown's much less famous description of learning to write, from the "Narrative of the Life and Escape of William Wells Brown" that appears in the opening pages of *Clotel*:

> How do you suppose I first commenced writing? for you will understand that up to the present time I never spent a day in school in my life, for I had no money to pay for schooling, so that I had to get my learning first from one and then from another. I carried a piece of chalk in my pocket, and whenever I met a boy I would stop him and take out my chalk and get at a board fence and then commence. First I made some flourishes with no meaning, and called a boy up, and said, "Do you see that? Can you beat that writing?" Said he, "That's not writing." Well, I wanted to get so as to write my own name. I had got out of slavery with only one name. While escaping, I received the hospitality of a very good man, who had spared part of his name to me, and finally my name got pretty long, and I wanted to be able to write it. "Now, what do you call that?" said the boy, looking at my flourishes. I said, "Is not that *William Wells Brown?*" "Give me the chalk," says he, and he wrote out in large letters "*William Wells Brown*," and I marked up the fence for nearly a quarter of a mile, trying to copy, till I got so that I could write my name. Then I went on with my chalking, and, in fact, all board fences within half a mile of where I lived were marked over with some kind of figures I had made, in trying to learn how to write.[12]

Unless, by some extraordinary coincidence, both Douglass and Brown really did learn how to write by luring white boys into alphabetic chalking competitions—and if so, it is equally extraordinary that Brown didn't bring it up in his 1847 *Narrative* or any other edition of his autobiography—what we have here is an exuberantly fictive instance of stylistic one-upsmanship.[13] Perhaps because Brown's paragraph is, to all appearances, transcribed from a lecture, it is full of the energies of verbal performance: the readers or listeners are close enough to be directly addressed; the sentences unfold in expansive, loose-jointed ways; the central encounter is dramatized through quick-moving dialogue; and the final sentences trampoline us into the regions of the tall tale. Douglass's paragraph is, comparatively speaking, stiff. There is something mechanical about his listing of all of the permutations of starboard, larboard, forward, and aft; most of his ensuing sentences are not only terse but roughly identical in length; and he never moves, as Brown does, from a past-tense account of what generally happened to a present-tense account of one incident in particular. He concludes the anecdote, moreover, not with a burst of extravagance but with a shapely rhetorical antithesis and an in-case-you-missed-it summary. Douglass seems to want, above all else, to be authoritative; Brown seems to want, above all else, to be interesting.

It is telling, in this context, that the payoff for tricking the white boys is so different in Brown's anecdote. Unlike Douglass, who parlays an ability to write four letters into an ability to write all twenty-six, Brown begins with no knowledge at all and parlays it into nothing more than an ability to write his own name. Theoretically, Brown could then take that knowledge of the eleven letters in his name and convert it into a mastery of the entire alphabet, but he clearly has no desire to take the anecdote in that direction. His story is about "getting up," as graffiti taggers say, about exhibiting a signifier of selfhood that is just one trick removed from a series of "flourishes with no meaning."[14] Writing and rewriting that cryptic signifier of identity is not an avenue to phallic mastery, as Douglass's comprehensive knowledge is. It is, instead, a campy travesty of mastery, an unserious hyperbolization of selfhood. Brown is telling a story about how one can, almost miraculously, by means of a redundant, extravagant, going-nowhere mode of signification, make the space between dispossession and possession unfold and expand. By ironically, fictively, pleasurably reiterating the barely more than material signifier of his identity, he exposes what Derrida would have called its *itérabilité*, its capacity to disappear and reappear, to be sensationally present without symbolically progressing.[15] He is, in this story, neither dominated nor dominating, neither on the bottom nor on top; he is, instead, an apparitional emergence, a lateral gliding, a sign of things to come. "Is not that," he asks the white boy, pointing toward the chalked flourishes on the fence, "*William Wells Brown*?"

The chapters that follow will trace out the implications of Brown's highly performative understanding of the self and its signifiers. I will begin with what is, undoubtedly, the most startling expression of that understanding in Brown's work: his lush, louche plagiarism. Over the course of his career—as I have discovered over the last few years, by means of various online databases—he plagiarized at least 87,000 words from at least 282 texts. He did not merely borrow ideas or creatively metabolize a major source text or two; he copied, for the most part, word for word. Neither did he replicate an accepted practice or unwittingly violate unwritten rules; in mid-nineteenth-century America and England, plagiarism came with a scarlet P, as Brown was forcefully reminded by Douglass in an 1852 article exposing one of his unlicensed transcriptions. Brown knew what he was doing and what he was risking by doing it and did it anyway.

At times, his motives for doing it seem to have been fairly banal. In *The Rising Son*, for instance, he saves himself a lot of time and pads his book with quite a few pages by importing massive chunks of text from Jonathan Brown's *The History and Present Condition of St. Domingo*. More often, however, he seems to have been animated by an edgy spirit of play. If the stigmatization of plagiarism is, as the critic Jonathan Elmer argues, a repression of the "disconcerting separability" of "selves and signs," then Brown's often outrageous textual appropriations—he plagiarizes at one point from the famous chapter on plagiarism in Washington Irving's *The Sketch-Book of Geoffrey Crayon*—might be seen as, in part, an expression of the pleasure he takes in that separability.[16] Because language belongs to no one, because its materials, protocols, and structures so dramatically exceed the proprietorship of its users, one is, in language, both oneself and anyone. To certain sensibilities, like Brown's, that is intoxicating.

But while plagiarism will be a crucial element of this book, it will function primarily as a starting point, a way into a range of different approaches to Brown's work. In chapter 2, I will turn to a different kind of textual borrowing: the appropriation of anecdotes from white popular culture. Like P. T. Barnum, whose 1855 autobiography is, to an extraordinary degree, a compendium of practical jokes, Brown has a fondness for comedies of advantage seizing and a preference for ones that have already been test marketed. Because there is often cruelty and sometimes a cringeworthy minstrel-show humor to what Brown calls "fun," critics have tended to keep their distance from it. But it is absolutely central to Brown's fictional enterprise, and without diminishing its disturbing qualities, we should recognize its analytical acuity and utopian thrust. What it suggests is that Brown concluded early in his career that white Americans strongly prefer narratives of self-making that are a little "off," in which something other than merit is at work. Officially, socioeconomic advancement depends on industriousness and honesty; unofficially, it depends on a spirit of capitalization, on shrewdness, on being able to take advantage of opportunities as they arise. Officially, too, one person's advancement sets no one else back; unofficially, it always comes at someone else's expense. In the spaces between those official and unofficial discourses, Brown senses a potential for interracial sociability, for the black-white enjoyment of an insider knowledge so fundamentally ironic in its structure that it is capable of being—he hopes—receptive to the ironies of race as well.

This will lead, in chapter 3, to one of the book's central arguments: that Brown's literary and extraliterary performances are animated by what the film historian Tom Gunning has described, with respect to early cinema, as an "aesthetic of attractions." Throughout his career as a lecturer, panorama showman, and playwright-actor, Brown seems to have detected in his mostly white audiences a desire for a certain variety-show aesthetic, in which factual assertions, moral appeals, sentimental flourishes, and low-cultural moments of humor take turns displacing one another. This now-you-see-it-now-you-don't aesthetic does not exist to the exclusion of narrative in Brown's works any more than it did in early cinema. It is, however, the dominant mode, the style of literary, visual, and dramatic entertainment toward which he leans. Without an appreciation of that mode, which has percolated, over the last century-plus, into slapstick, musicals, action movies, and other pop-cultural genres, it is hard to appreciate the form of most of Brown's works. Focusing primarily on *Clotel*, I will highlight the presence of that mode and suggest some of the possibilities that Brown seems to have glimpsed in it. It seems to have held out, for him, the prospect of a democratically non-narrative space, a stage on which various discourses and subjectivities might intermittently, clashingly appear. By providing his readers and audiences with a relief from the self-sameness of conventional narrative—a relief from characters who are in keeping with themselves, plots that obey Aristotelian unities, and events with easily formulated morals—Brown provides them, as well, with a sense of what a culture based on the pleasurableness of difference might feel like.

But not all kinds of pleasure open up this prospect. The racist's pleasure does not; the rapist's pleasure does not. With that in mind, I focus, in chapter 4, on the character type that has drawn the most attention in the scholarship on Brown: the young, beautiful, light-skinned slave woman. For most critics, Brown's foregrounding of this figure is either a damaging reinforcement of white standards of beauty or an implicit critique of the slave power/rape power that narcissistically produces and consumes such figures. There is, however, a third option. What I will argue in this chapter is that Brown's deployment of the figure of the beautiful slave girl is neither as static as the first of those readings suggests nor as lurid as the second suggests—that it is, instead, lightly, even self-parodically, fetishistic. By conjuring up scenarios starring this instantly recognizable figure, setting those scenarios in transitional spaces and times, and using the fascination of her beauty to prolong that in-betweenness, he keeps his distance, and encourages us to keep our distance, from the traumatic reality that she evokes. The intensity of his desire to draw our attention to that reality repeatedly returns him to these scenarios, but the equal intensity of his desire to preserve the dignity of this figure leads him to fetishize a strange, preliminary time: the time before slavery—an abusive, nonreciprocal pleasure taking that will repeat itself, if left to itself, endlessly—begins. Slavery presented itself as a done deal. Brown presents slavery as a deal that is not yet done.

That delaying tactic can be pursued, in a striking number of cases, all the way down to the level of syntax. Again and again, in sentences Brown imported from elsewhere and in sentences he wrote himself, beauty is registered by means of repletion, by means of sentences that expand inwardly through recursive repetitions of formal elements. In chapter 5, I consider the music of such sentences in relation to *The Escape*, a play with thirty-seven speaking parts that Brown performed in staged readings. There is a relationship, I argue, between the position that Brown occupies in such readings—between the speech-identities of others, speaking in his own voice only when announcing scene changes, tableaux, and movements—and the pauses within and between sentences that give passages of prose their peculiar rhythm. Just as Brown may be said to identify himself not with any one subject position but with the capacity to move between them, so may he be said to have an aesthetic preference for impersonal rhythms and flows, a preference that manifests itself both in his attraction to syntactic repletion and in his understanding of characters as vehicles, things to be provisionally occupied and moved from place to place. The pleasure that he takes in plagiarism is, I argue, best understood in relation to this preference. He likes speaking both as and not as himself, blending his voice with the voices of others, becoming no one thing in particular. In place of what Gillian Beer has described as "the desolate privacy of the Romantic ego," Brown offers sociable, mobile, jostling, boundary-disrespecting assemblages of quasi egos, in which he is amid others and others are amid him.[17] If he identifies, finally, with anything, it is with the endlessly reopening space from which all such identities emerge and to which they inevitably return.

In a 1974 introduction to his short story "Paraguay"—a traveler's tale of a journey to an imaginary, hyper-rationalized country, composed in part out of bits and pieces of other people's writing—Donald Barthelme writes that what he likes about the story "is the misuse of language and the tone." By "misuse," Barthelme seems to mean experimental cobbling, a practice that lies somewhere between the earnest use and the satirical abuse of language. The point of the misuse, Barthelme does not hesitate to say, is his own pleasure. "Mixing bits of this and that from various areas of life to make something that did not exist before is an oddly hopeful endeavor," he writes. "The sentence 'Electrolytic jelly exhibiting a capture ratio far in excess of standard is used to fix the animals in place' made me very happy—perhaps in excess of its merit. But there is in the world such a thing as electrolytic jelly; the 'capture ratio' comes from the jargon of sound technology; and the animals themselves are a salad of the real and the invented." This is "a highly specialized enterprise," he acknowledges, "akin to the manufacture of merkins, say—but it's what I do. Probably I have missed the point of the literature business entirely."[18]

Brown was not, of course, quite as free to miss the point of the literature business entirely. To make an impact, through his writing, on the abolitionist movement, Brown had to know how to turn out basic literary products, recognizable, market-tested genre pieces. And he did. But he also—intermittently, covertly, performatively—missed their point, in what was, I think, an "oddly hopeful" way. Knowing that we are not ourselves alone in language, believing that language is as much about display as it is about communication, Brown put on a wildly expropriative show, a plagiarama, that we are only now able to witness. What was the point of that strange, secret, scandalous show for Brown? What might it be for us? Something, perhaps, like the point that the vet tries to communicate to the narrator of *Invisible Man*. "Play the game, but don't believe in it," he says. "That much you owe yourself."[19]

CHAPTER

ONE

Plagiarama!

> I didn't create language, writer thought. . . . I'm constantly being given language. Since this language-world is rich and always changing, flowing, when I write, I enter a world which has complex relations and is, perhaps, illimitable. This world both represents and is human history, public memories and private memories turned public, the records and actualizations of human intentions. This world is more than life and death, for here life and death conjoin. I can't make language, but in this world, I can play and be played.
>
> —KATHY ACKER

It started small. A melodramatic flourish from a book by a Canadian political prisoner ("a shudder,—a feeling akin to horror shot through my frame"), imported into his first publication, the 1847 *Narrative of William W. Brown*, to describe his feelings upon being captured by slave catchers.[1] A transitional phrase from the abolitionist Stephen S. Foster's *The Brotherhood of Thieves* ("Dark and revolting as is the picture here drawn"), right after a quotation from a newspaper article about slave drivers (*C* 41).[2] Three sentences from an account of a slave auction, woven into the scene in the *Narrative* in which he says goodbye to his mother for the last time. ("She dropped her head upon her heaving bosom, but she moved not. Neither did she weep—her emotions were too deep for tears. . . . I could bear no more—my heart struggled to free itself from the human form" [*C* 39].)[3] Minor upgrades, brief samplings. Nothing that anyone would likely notice.

A year later, in the second edition of the *Narrative*, he took it a bit farther. In the opening section of the appendix, he drops in some lines from *Tribute to the Memory of Thomas Shipley*, a eulogy delivered in 1836 by the black abolitionist Robert Purvis ("You cannot keep the human mind forever locked in darkness. . . . For one day of freedom, oh! who would not die?").[4] Later on, he passes off the introduction and conclusion of Edward M. Davis's *Extracts from the American Slave Code*—the paragraphs beginning "The following are mostly abridged selections from the statutes of the slave states and of the United States" and "Reader, you uphold these laws *while you do nothing for their repeal*"—as his own writing.[5] Later still, he does the same with a transitional fragment ("Mr. Robert Wickliffe of Kentucky, in a speech published in the Louisville Advertiser, in opposition to those who were averse to the importation of slaves from the states, thus discourseth") from Lewis Tappan's *Address to the Non-Slave Holders of the South*.[6] He was now masquerading, in a book whose full title includes the phrase *Written by Himself*, as the author of at least six other people's written work.

But that, too, was nothing in comparison to what was about to come. At least 9 percent of Brown's 1852 travel narrative, *Three Years in Europe*, is plagiarized, and the 112 passages in question—passages in which at least eight consecutive words are copied from another text—are taken from fifty-two sources. His 1853 novel, *Clotel*, contains at least 102 plagiarized passages, many of them extremely lengthy, from fifty-five sources; they make up 23 percent of the novel as a whole. Each of the subsequent versions of the novel—*Miralda; or, the Beautiful Quadroon* (1860–1861), *Clotelle: A Tale of the Southern States* (1864), and *Clotelle; or, The Colored Heroine* (1867)—contains a substantial amount of plagiarism (10 percent, 8 percent, and 6 percent, respectively), and at least 14 percent of *St. Domingo: Its Revolution and Patriots* (1855), 9 percent of *The American Fugitive in Europe: Sketches of People and Places Abroad* (1855), 3 percent of *The Escape; or, A Leap for Freedom* (1858), 10 percent of *Memoir of William Wells Brown* (1859), 9 percent of *The Black Man: His Antecedents, His Genius, and His Achievements* (1862), 12 percent of *The Negro in the American Rebellion: His Heroism and His Fidelity* (1867), 22 percent of *The Rising Son; or, The Antecedents and Advancement of the Colored Race* (1873), and 8 percent of *My Southern Home; or, The South and Its People* (1880) were plagiarized as well. By the end of his career, Brown had plagiarized at least 87,000 words from at least 282 texts (see appendix A). The voices of at least 265 different writers resonate along with his own (see appendix B).

15
Plagiarama!

Plagiarism is often thought to be a sign of weakness, an implicit confession of imaginative and expressive limitations. But when the scale of the plagiarism is so vast, it can begin to seem as though it indicates the reverse: an unconstrained resourcefulness, a wide-ranging awareness of, and freedom with, the materials of one's culture. Although Brown frequently plagiarized from informational and polemical sources—antislavery journals, such as the *Liberator* and the *National Anti-Slavery Standard*; antislavery pamphlets, such as Sarah Grimké's *An Address to Free Colored Americans* and William Cooper Nell's *Services of Colored Americans in the Wars of 1776 and 1812*; documentary accounts of slavery, such as Theodore Weld's *American Slavery as It Is* and William Bowditch's *Slavery and the Constitution*; and histories of Africa and the black diaspora, such as Samuel Goodrich's *Lights and Shadows of African History* and John Reilly Beard's *The Life of Toussaint L'Ouverture*—he was by no means confined to them. He plagiarized from Samuel Johnson's *Lives of the English Poets*, for instance, as well as from William Hazlitt's *The Spirit of the Age* and Washington Irving's *The Sketch-Book of Geoffrey Crayon*. He plagiarized from Robert Willmot's *Pleasures, Objects, and Advantages of Literature* and David Macbeth Moir's *Sketches of the Poetical Literature of the Past Half-Century*, from Lydia Sigourney's *Pleasant Memories of Pleasant Lands* and Elizabeth Spence's *Summer Excursions*, from a captivity narrative and a pamphlet accompanying the exhibition of a panorama, from *Memorials of Early Genius* and *Gleanings from Pious Authors*, from a valedictory address in the *Eclectic Medical Journal* and a newspaper article about a tenement fire. He had an especial fondness for Louis-Marie de Lahaye Cormenin's *The Orators of France*, from which he plagiarized seventeen passages, and George Washington Bungay's *Crayon Sketches and Off-Hand Takings*, from which he plagiarized twelve. In his last extended series of plagiarisms, in the final chapter of *My Southern Home*, he takes four forceful passages from Robert Knox's virulently antimiscegenationist *The Races of Man* and weaves them into a paean to racial intermixture. "[Our] only hope is education, professions, trades, and copying the best examples," Brown writes midway through the chapter, "no matter from what source they come" (*C* 848).

The modes of his copying are equally diverse. In some places, he pastes in extremely lengthy clippings: in *Clotel*, he takes 673 consecutive words from Seth Gates's description of a woman's flight to and suicidal leap from the Long Bridge between Washington, D.C., and Alexandria, Virginia; in

The Negro in the American Rebellion, he takes 847 consecutive words from an anonymous tribute to Robert Gould Shaw; and in *My Southern Home*, he takes 1,282 consecutive words from a journalist's description of a Baptist sermon. Elsewhere, he uses other people's phrasings as grace notes or decorative accents: in his biographical sketch of the African American lawyer John Mercer Langston in *The Black Man*, to take only one example, he incorporates fragments of sentences from Cormenin's *Orators of France* ("in vigor of thought, in imagery of style, in logical connection, in vehemence, in depth, in point," "profound without being hollow, ingenious without being subtle") and Joel Tyler Headley's preface to the American edition of Cormenin's book ("a deep and majestic stream, he moves steadily onward, pouring forth his rich and harmonious sentences in strains of impassioned eloquence" [*C* 620]).[7] In some cases, he retains the structure of a sentence but switches out the nouns: an encomium to four French writers in Cormenin ("Who has better known the human heart than Moliere, better painted than old Corneille the grandeur of virtue, better sighed than Racine the subtle weaknesses of love? Who had ever a sounder taste, a more exact intellect, than Voltaire?") becomes, in *Three Years in Europe*, an encomium to four very different writers ("Who has better known the human feelings than Shakspere; better painted than Milton, the grandeur of Virtue; better sighed than Byron over the subtle weaknesses of Hope? Who ever had a sounder taste, a more exact intellect than Dante?")[8] In other cases, he keeps the nouns and changes everything else: a description of Madison Washington's wife in *The Black Man*—"Her well-moulded shoulders, prominent bust, black hair which hung in ringlets, mild blue eyes, finely-chiselled mouth, with a splendid set of teeth, a turned and well-rounded chin, skin marbled with the animation of life, and veined by blood given to her by her master, she stood as the representative of two races" (*C* 508)—is cobbled together from bits and pieces of a character's description in Alphonse de Lamartine's *History of the Girondists*: "a prominent bust . . . black and soft hair, blue eyes . . . splendid teeth, a turned and well-rounded chin . . . a skin marbled with the animation of life, and veined by blood."[9] If at times Brown's plagiarism appears to have enabled him to take a break from the labor of writing, at other times it appears to have expressed a distinctive literary aesthetics, at the heart of which was an intense, animating understanding of sentences as modifiable structures with nonsingular origins.

We are clearly in unfamiliar critical territory here. Although the existing scholarship on plagiarism can be of some use in this case, insofar as it can help us understand the cultural and historical contexts of the practice—it is important to know, for instance, that plagiarism was, throughout Brown's life, a scandalous thing, and that the reputations of writers like Coleridge were badly damaged by the discovery of their unauthorized copyings—it can do little to help us make sense of plagiarism on this scale.[10] Because Brown plagiarized from so many different texts, any effort to argue for a revisionary relationship to one of them, along the lines of Hannah Crafts's relationship to Dickens's *Bleak House* in *The Bondwoman's Narrative*, inevitably raises the question of his relationship to the other 281 on the list.[11] Because he plagiarized from those texts in so many different ways, moreover, any effort to characterize the mode of his plagiarism in familiar, stable terms—as, for instance, a partial metabolization of the original or as a selective importation of high-quality goods—is bound to seem unconvincing. It may well be that the critical territory we are entering here will rapidly expand; online databases, the means of my discovery of most of his plagiarisms—a few were already known—may eventually reveal that a great many writers used published texts in similar ways. In the course of phrase searching for instances of plagiarism in Brown's work, for example, I discovered that three writers, William Hunt, Wilson Armistead, and Pauline Hopkins, plagiarized either from Brown or from a common source text (more on this below). It may also be, however, that even in an expanded plagiaristic environment, the scope and style of Brown's use of other people's language will turn out to be singular. It may turn out to be, that is, that he is the sublimest of the nonsublime, the most original artist of nonoriginality in American literary history.

That evaluation will only take hold, however, if the popular and scholarly perception of plagiarism undergoes a significant change. In the minds of many, plagiarism is, in Thomas Mallon's words, "irredeemably sleazy."[12] It leads to court cases, job losses, withdrawals of books from circulation, and shame, shame, shame.[13] In the same issue of *African American Review* in which I first reported the extent of Brown's plagiarisms in *Clotel*, for instance, Erika Renée Williams castigates Nella Larsen, whose career was destroyed by a revelation of plagiarism, for repeating elements of the opening paragraph of John Galsworthy's "The First and the Last" in the opening paragraph of her first novel, *Quicksand*. "I believe that no rhetoric of formalist innovation can mitigate the error of an author's verbatim copying from another author," Williams writes. For her, Larsen's "illicit and derivative use of source texts exploits her fellow authors by enacting violence upon their texts, whose fragments she lifts only to bury in the confines of her own literary output."[14] In the end, Williams speculates, the plagiarist's violence is visited upon herself or himself as well, even if the plagiarism is not discovered. "By drawing considerably from Galsworthy for the opening passage of her novel, and then, passing as an originating author," she writes, "Larsen neglected to honor . . . her own text, and therefore, herself." The remedy, Williams concludes, is sunlight: "only by acknowledging Larsen's plagiarism, by daring not to, in Larsen's words, avoid 'mention' of untoward 'things' and thus, maintain the pretense that 'they do not exist,' might we mitigate the ethos of secrecy that sustains errors in judgment and acts of self-deception alike."[15]

This kind of moralism is, I think, misplaced. We have pluralized so much in contemporary American culture, yet we are still, for the most part, fundamentalists about plagiarism, responding to it in the same way no matter where or how it appears.[16] Surely we are capable of differentiating between plagiarism in a term paper, in which the point is for the student to display his or her mind at work on the materials of the course, and plagiarism in a work of literature, in which the author is being neither graded nor credentialed, in which his or her aim is, traditionally, to instruct and delight. Plagiarism defeats the purpose of a term paper; it only defeats the purpose of work of literature if that purpose is imagined to include something that it does not, in fact, necessarily include: the modeling of an autonomously creative subjectivity. Surely, too, we are capable of recognizing that there is, in Melville's words, "an aesthetic in all things" and that plagiarism is, in the final analysis, just a different way of generating, selecting, and marking the materials out of which verbal structures are composed.[17] To conceive of yourself as the sole owner and proprietor of your writing is to forget that, in Barack Obama's words, "you didn't build that." Just as successful small-business owners, the original subjects of Obama's 2012 remarks, could not have succeeded without the infrastructural aid of things like roads, bridges, dams, and public investment in education, so are successful writers dependent on the prior existence of infrastructural elements: the lexicon, the grammar, the history of genres, the printing press, the publishing system, and, these days, personal computers and the Internet. Every writer works with, and on the basis of, things that he or she did not originate. "You're not on your own," Obama reminds his audience. "We're in this together."[18]

Brown is capable of helping us not only feel this but feel good about it. In the remainder of this chapter, I will try to demonstrate the degree to which plagiarism, as a compositional practice, is motivated in Brown's work by what Paul Saint-Amour has called a "readerly hedonics." In the late nineteenth century, Saint-Amour writes, a significant number of "plagiarism apologists" argued, in an effort to "transfer literary value from priority to utility," that "the origins of ideas and expressions mattered less than their capacity to satisfy and edify the reader."[19] In doing so, the plagiarism apologists—who were, in fact, pressing their case as early as the 1840s—challenged "labor theories of value, which evaluated the conditions of literary production and esteemed the labor of original composition most highly," with "a readerly hedonics that countenanced plagiarism for the sake of pleasure."[20] That hedonism is, crucially, writerly as well as readerly; in addition to gratifying his or her audience, the plagiarist is implicitly gratifying himself or herself, both by extending an experience of reading into an experience of writing and by enjoying—to cite Melville again—the "pleasure which is wickedly said to be in sinning," even if it is, in the end, nothing more than "a literary sin."[21] With that in mind, instead of looking for the ways in which new writing faces off against old writing, struggling, in a zero-sum game, for primacy, we might begin to look, in the works of Brown and likeminded authors, for the ways in which writing perpetuates reading. We might begin to turn from the question of whether a piece of writing is original to the question of where its readers are, and where they can go, when a text gives them pleasure. "He tells such ridiculous stories," writes Charlotte Forten Grimké in her journal after an 1858 visit from Brown, "that although I believe as little as I please—I can't help being amused."[22]

In Kathy Acker's "Dead Doll Humility" (1990), an artist named Capitol makes a "writer doll" and invents a biography for her that resembles Acker's own. In her early twenties, having been taught by "prominent Black Mountain poets, mainly male," that "a writer becomes a writer when and only when he finds his own voice," the writer doll "tried hard to find her own voice. Couldn't. But still loved to write. Loved to play with language. Language was material like clay or paint. Loved to play with verbal material, build up slums and mansions, demolish banks and half-rotten buildings, even buildings which she herself had constructed, into never-before-seen, even unseeable jewels." Soon, the writer doll decided that "to find her own voice would be negotiating against her joy." What the typical male Black Mountain poet meant by the writer's voice was "a process, how he had forced the language to obey him, his will. The writer's voice is the voice of the writer-as-God." She didn't want that voice, because to her "wildness was writing and writing was wildness." She wrote "by using anyone's voice, anyone's text, whatever materials she wanted to use." Used "both good literature and schlock." Believed that "cleverness, one of the formal rules of good literature, can be a method of social and political manipulation. Decided to use language stupidly. In order to use and be other voices as stupidly as possible, decided to copy down simply other texts. Copy them down while, maybe, mashing them up because wasn't going to stop playing in any playground. Because loved wildness."[23]

It is not as far from Acker to Brown as it may seem, especially if we take a route that runs through Nathaniel West and Pauline Hopkins. Over a fifth of *A Cool Million*, West's comic evisceration of American optimism, is, as Douglas Shepard and Gary Scharnhorst have shown, plagiarized from the novels of Horatio Alger.[24] For the most part, West's plagiarisms have been read as satirical commentaries on their sources, much like Acker's copyings of Harold Robbins in *The Adult Life of Toulouse Lautrec* (1978), Dickens in *Great Expectations* (1983), and Hawthorne in *Blood and Guts in High School* (1984). But just as Acker's conscious political intentions are accompanied by a not-entirely-conscious love of language play for its own sake—a wildness, a stupidity, a joy—so is West's critique of Alger accompanied by connoisseurish fascination and private delight. One doesn't have to copy a text word for word in order to evoke its spirit, after all, as satirists everywhere know. When one follows so faithfully and so often the unfolding contours of another's prose, one is almost inevitably doing so not only out of a desire to make a point but also out of a desire to surrender one's point-making capacity, to stop uttering one's own discourse, to flow in and with someone else's. From one perspective, the light in which the passages from Alger are bathed is the bright white light of the interrogation room. From another, the one that I am emphasizing here, it is the sensuous, ambient light of department-store windows, an auratic, pleasure-heightening glow.

Take, for instance, the following passages from *A Cool Million*:

> All hail Old Glory! May you be the joy and pride of the American heart, alike when your gorgeous folds shall wanton in the summer air and your tattered fragments be dimly seen through clouds of war! May you ever wave in honor, hope and profit, in unsullied glory and patriotic fervor, on the dome of the Capitol, on the tented plain, on the wave-rocked top-mast and on the roof of this garage![25]

> The dress had a full waist made with a yoke and belt, a gored skirt, long, but not too long to afford a very distinct view of a well-turned ankle and a small, shapely foot encased in a snowy cotton stocking and a low-heeled black slipper. The material of the dress was chintz—white ground with a tiny brown figure—finished at the neck with a wide white ruffle. On her hands she was made to wear black silk mitts with half-fingers. Her hair was worn in a little knot on the top of her head, and one thick short curl was kept in place by a puff-comb on each side of her face.[26]

The first passage, spoken by the former president and future fascist organizer Shagpoke Whipple, is a reshuffling of the following sentences from Edward Everett's "An Address Delivered at Lexington":

> All hail to the glorious ensign! . . . May it for ever wave in honor, in unsullied glory, and patriotic hope, on the dome of the capitol, on the country's strong holds, on the tented plain, on the wave-rocked top-mast. . . . Alike, when its gorgeous folds shall wanton in lazy holiday triumph, on the summer breeze, and its tattered fragments be dimly seen through the clouds of war, may it be the joy and pride of the American heart.[27]

The second passage, a description of the way in which the novel's heroine is costumed in a house-of-all-nations brothel, is derived from the following paragraph in Martha Finley's *Elsie's Girlhood*:

> The dress had a full waist made with a yoke and belt, a gored skirt, long, but not too long to afford a very distinct view of a well-turned ankle and a small, shapely foot encased in a snowy cotton stocking and a low-heeled black slipper. The material of the dress was chintz—white ground with a tiny brown figure—finished at the neck with a wide white ruffle. On her hands she was made to wear black silk mitts with half-fingers.

> Her hair was worn in a little knot on the top of her head, and one thick short curl was kept in place by a puff-comb on each side of her face.[28]

Just as Everett's high-toned rhetoric enables West to induce, in the final phrase of Whipple's speech, a comic drop in cultural register ("on the roof of this garage!"), so do Finley's painstakingly exact observations enable West to mock archaic fashions, both sartorial and discursive, by inverting their context. ("While not exactly in period, [the costume] was very striking," his narrator tells us, "and I will describe it as best I can for the benefit of my feminine readers.")[29] But the value of these passages, for West, lies not only in what they are not but in what they are—not only in their vulnerability to satire, that is, but in the air of difference that sets them off from their immediate surroundings. The same may be said of many of the passages from Alger in *A Cool Million*, especially the ones drawn from the "man from Pike County" section of *Joe's Luck*, which do nothing to advance the novel's critique of entrepreneurial optimism and seem to have been included for the sake of their stylistic texture alone. ("'Jack, says I, 'don't provoke me. I kin whip my weight in wildcats.'"[30]) By modeling, in his externally generated stylistic variations, a capacity to be neither entirely himself nor entirely someone else, the narrator of *A Cool Million* provides us with what is missing from the world of the novel: an ability to aestheticize not the form of an unconsciously alienated self but the process of coming-to-selfhood. All that the characters in *A Cool Million* can do is be themselves, which is, in West's world, a kind of sickness, akin to the vaudevillian compulsive disorder of Harry Greener in *The Day of the Locust*. The narrator of *A Cool Million* is, comparatively, healthy, insofar as he can break up his speech identity at will with the imagined, remembered, and transcribed speech identities of others.

In *Of One Blood; Or, the Hidden Self* (1902–1903), a serialized novel in which at least 8,596 words, roughly 18 percent of the whole, are copied without attribution, Pauline Hopkins may be said to theorize, or at least thematize, that process-oriented, plagiarism-friendly aesthetic.[31] Among the twenty-eight texts from which she plagiarizes in *Of One Blood* are several that one might imagine she is deploying in implicitly critical ways, texts like H. Rider Haggard's *She*, Rudyard Kipling and Wolcott Balestier's "The Naulahka," and John Hartley Coombs's *Dr. Livingstone's Seventeen Years' Exploration and Adventure in the Wilds of Africa*. It is, however, nearly impossible to classify her replications of passages from those works as instances of, in Henry Louis Gates's terms, "motivated Signifyin(g)."[32] There are no signs of intertextual parody in her deployments of Haggard's description of moonlight on the ruins of a city ("Bright fell the moonlight on pillar and court and shattered wall, hiding all their rents and imperfections in its silver garment") or Kipling and Balestier's description of daybreak in the ruins of a city ("without warning or presage, the red dawn shot up behind him, and there leaped out of the night the city of the dead").[33] Neither is there anything like a critical edge in her nearly word-for-word repetition of Coombs's description of central Africa as "a gorgeous scene, decorated with Nature's most cheering garniture, teeming with the choicest specimens of vegetable and animal life, and refreshed by innumerable streams, not a few of which are of sufficient magnitude for the purposes of navigation and commerce."[34] To all appearances, she uses such phrasings because she likes them and, on a larger compositional scale, because she likes the effect that they create when she intersperses them with her own phrasings. In lieu of the "double-voiced" quality that Gates, drawing on Bakhtin, ascribes to the black literary tradition—a clashing of perspectives in a single utterance, as a result of a revisionary troping of the source—Hopkins offers, in *Of One Blood*, a series of passages with strange harmonic resonances, passages in which the tone of the source is subtly modified by its repositioning in Hopkins's narrative and in which Hopkins's narrative is subtly modified by the unannounced sampling of the source.[35] At the same time that someone else, without knowing it, falls silent as an author while continuing to speak as a writer, she falls silent as a writer while continuing to speak as an author.

Like the mergings of consciousness that occur so often in *Of One Blood*—via romantic love, intrafamilial love, and mixtures of the two, as well as mesmerism and a passion for music—such intertextual mergings seem to be, in certain cases, contingent on "mental affinity."[36] Watching Dianthe speak in a trance, Aubrey Livingston is himself "in a trance of delight . . . feeling the glamour of her presence and ethereal beauty like a man poring over a poem that he has unexpectedly stumbled upon, losing himself in it, until it becomes, as it were, a part of himself."[37] To the original version of those lines, which come from a story called "Alixe" in *Frank Leslie's Popular Monthly*, Hopkins adds only "ethereal" and "that he has unexpectedly stumbled upon."[38] The suggestion of the passage is that beauty, whether personal or literary, is both transmitted and received in a trance state—that "mental affinity" partially dissolves the boundaries between self and other. Not all of the plagiarisms in *Of One Blood* seem to have proceeded from affinities of this kind, and only rarely, as in the case of Emma Hardinge Britten's "The Improvvisatore," which occupies the majority of chapters 20, 22, 23, and 24, do the affinities seem to have been self-dissolvingly intense. Nevertheless, Hopkins does appear to have, on the whole, a remarkably dedifferentiated relationship to other people's language in *Of One Blood*. It is as if the "one blood" of the novel's title, our common, coursing element, is the psychic material circulating in our hidden selves, a material that can, under conditions of affinity, interflow.

This is not to say that Hopkins is opposed to autonomy or that she never signifies, in Gates's sense, on writers and discourses. She wrote most of the book herself, after all, just as she appears to have written nearly all of *Contending Forces* and most of *Winona* and *Hagar's Daughter* herself. And as many of her critics have observed, she pointedly repeats, with a critical difference, the contemporary discourses of race (particularly with respect to the essentialization of origins) and gender (particularly with respect to the expectations of submissiveness from women and autonomy from men). What I am arguing for is a relatively high degree of porousness between herself and her reading and a mostly nonconflictual relationship between the text she copies and the text she composes. Early in *Of One Blood*, as Dianthe sings at a party, another voice is heard singing along with hers, a "weird contralto, veiled as it were, rising and falling upon every wave of the great soprano, and reaching the ear as from some strange distance."[39] Those lines, and most of the rest of the party scene, are drawn from a story called "The Haunted Voice," in which a certain Lady Beatrice is accompanied, when singing at a party, by the baritone voice of her spurned and now-dead lover Rupert.[40] Just as Dianthe's voice bears along with it the voice of, as it turns out, her mother, so does Hopkins's voice bear along with it the voice of her source text's anonymous author. Or the reverse: just as Dianthe's voice is borne along by her mother's, so is Hopkins's voice borne along by the anonymous author's. Either way, a voice is haunted; either way, a nonsingular vocality resounds.[41]

In each of these three cases, then, plagiarism is intimately bound to Saint-Amour's "readerly hedonics." In spite of all of the obvious differences between them, Acker, West, and Hopkins share a mostly unspoken pleasure in the blurrability of texts and styles, a delight in the deauthenticating mobility of everything that it is possible to write or say. But it would be misleading to represent plagiarism solely in those terms. By way of contrast, consider the examples of William Hunt and Wilson Armistead, two little-known compilers of nonfictional texts. For Hunt, who tells us in the preface to *The American Biographical Sketch Book* that he was "born in a humble sphere, which precluded the advantages of a liberal education," plagiarism seems to have been nothing more than a performance-enhancing device, a means of competing with the privileged and learned.[42] As a rule, Hunt plagiarized from writers who were, in the words of another textual compiler, "sayer[s] of sententious things."[43] Later in the preface to *The American Biographical Sketch Book*, he imports, in the course of a single paragraph, the sententious sayings of William Cobbett ("To provide for a wife and children is the greatest of all possible spurs to exertion"), John Randolph ("To a young man, nothing is so important as a spirit of devotion [next to his Creator] to some virtuous and amiable woman, whose image may occupy his heart and guard it from the pollution which besets it on all sides"), and Benjamin Disraeli ("Whatever may be the harsher feelings that life may develop, there is no one, however callous and constrained he may have become, whose brow will not grow pensive at the memory of First Love").[44] Plagiarism seems to have been, for Hunt, anything but hedonic; it seems to have been, instead, an effort to lay claim to the cultural authority that pithiness and wide-ranging knowledge signify.

Although Armistead, a British Quaker and abolitionist whom Brown befriended in the early 1850s, enjoyed a higher level of social prestige than Hunt, he too seems to have plagiarized in a spirit of instrumentality alone, as a means of picking up what he understood himself to lack. In the 2,679-word introduction to his best-known compilation of biographical and historical materials, *A Tribute for the Negro* (1848), Armistead plagiarizes a total of 423 words (16 percent) from Thomas Clarkson's *History of the Rise, Progress, and Accomplishment of the Abolition of the African Slave Trade*, James Munson Phillippo's *Jamaica*, Richard Watson's *Sermons and Sketches of Sermons*, William Lloyd Garrison's preface to Frederick Douglass's *Narrative*, James Nourse's *Views on Colonization*, Susanna Moodie's introduction to *Negro Slavery Described by a Negro*, and Thomas Whittemore's *The Modern History of Universalism*. In the 1,408-word conclusion to *A Tribute*, Armistead plagiarizes a total of 755 words (54 percent) from James A.

Thome and J. Horace Kimball's *Emancipation in the West Indies*, an article in *Chambers' Edinburgh Magazine*, Lydia Maria Child's *Letters from New York*, and John Williams's *A Narrative of Missionary Enterprises in the South Sea Islands*.[45] Nowhere does Armistead show signs of any Ackerish joy; to all appearances, he is simply getting the job done, making text appear where text needs to appear. From predictable texts (abolitionist or Christian) he plagiarizes predictable passages (polemical or declamatory) in predictable ways (verbatim or lightly paraphrased).

As I have already noted, there are places in Brown's work in which his plagiarism could fairly be described in those terms. Far more often, however, his plagiarisms usher us into a radically different compositional realm. Here, for instance, is a passage from *Miralda*, describing Isabella's reaction to the discovery that her white lover is married:

> As she stood there, the full moon cast its bright rays over her whole person, giving her an angelic appearance and imparting to her flowing hair a still more golden hue. Suddenly another change came over her features, and her full red lips trembled as with suppressed emotion. The muscles around her faultless mouth became convulsed, she gasped for breath, and exclaiming, "Is it possible that man can be so false!" again fainted.[46]

And here is the source of the passage, a filler paragraph that appeared in at least thirty-three American newspapers and magazines between 1854 and 1860, usually under the title "Very Touching":

> After whirling for some time in the ecstatic mazes of a delightful waltz, Cornelia Adamanda and myself stepped out unobserved, to the balcony, to enjoy a few of those moments of solitude so precious to lovers. It was a glorious night, the air was cool and refreshing. As I gazed on the beautiful being at my side, I thought I never saw her look so lovely; the full moon cast her bright rays over her whole person, giving her almost an angelic appearance, and imparting to her flowing curls a still more golden hue. One of her soft hands rested in mine, and ever and anon she met my ardent gaze with one of pure confiding love. Suddenly a change came over her soft features, her full, red lip trembled as if with suppressed emotion, a tear-drop rested on her long, drooping lashes, the muscles around her faultless mouth became convulsed, she gasped for breath—and

> snatching her hand from the warm pressure of my own, she turned suddenly away, buried her face in her white fine cambric handkerchief, and—sneezed![47]

This, somewhat shockingly, is plagiarism as private joke. What do you get when you take the punchline out of a mass-cultural parody of sentimentalism? Brown asks, alone at his desk. Fine writing, he answers, and in it goes. Later, during the composition of *The Rising Son*, something similar must have occurred. What do you get when you take a description of syncretic Peruvian religious practices and recontinentalize the place names? A rampantly absurd Easter Monday in South Africa. (He changed "Cuzco" to "Noble," "the old Inca" to "an ancient," "America" to "Africa," and "Manco Capac" to "Mumbo Jumbo," but that's it.)

> The town of Noble is a settlement of modern times, sheltering forty thousand souls, close to an ancient city of the same name, the Rome of aboriginal South Africa. The religious ceremonies performed there are of the most puerile character, and would be thought by most, equally idolatrous with those formerly held in the same spot by the descendants of Mumbo Jumbo. On Easter Monday is celebrated the *Festa del Lenor de los Temblores*, or Festival of the Lord of Earthquakes. On this day the public Plaza in front of the Cathedral is hung with garlands and festoons, and the belfry utters its loudest notes. The images of the saints are borne out from their shrines, covered with fresh and gaudy decorations. The Madonna of Bethlehem, San Cristoval, San Bias, and San Jose, are borne on in elevated state, receiving as they go the prayers of all the Maries, and Christophers, and Josephs, who respectively regard them as patrons.[48]

And then there is Brown's description of the reading room of the British Library in *The American Fugitive in Europe*:

> It is a spacious room, surrounded with large glass cases filled with volumes, whose very look tells you that they are of age. Around, under the cornice, were arranged a number of old black-looking portraits, in all probability the authors of some of the works in the glass cases beneath. About the room were placed long tables, with stands for reading and

> writing, and around these were a number of men busily engaged in looking over some chosen author. Old men with grey hairs, young men with mustaches—some in cloth, others in fustian, indicating that men of different rank can meet here. Not a single word was spoken during my stay, all appearing to enjoy the silence that reigned throughout the great room. This is indeed a retreat from the world. No one inquires who the man is who is at his side, and each pursues in silence his own researches. The racing of pens over the sheets of paper was all that disturbed the stillness of the occasion.
>
> (*C* 277)

It is a dilated version of Washington Irving's description of the same room in "The Art of Book-Making," an essayistic sketch on the subject of plagiarism that first appeared in *The Sketch-Book of Geoffrey Crayon*:

> I found myself in a spacious chamber, surrounded with great cases of venerable books. Above the cases, and just under the cornice, were arranged a great number of black-looking portraits of ancient authors. About the room were placed long tables, with stands for reading and writing, at which sat many pale, studious personages, poring intently over dusty volumes, rummaging among mouldy manuscripts, and taking copious notes of their contents. The most hushed stillness reigned through this mysterious apartment, excepting that you might hear the racing of pens over sheets of paper.[49]

It is hard, for me anyway, not to admire the chutzpah of this. A writer who plagiarizes from a famous essay on plagiarism is a writer who likes testing the limits of his enterprise, a writer who plagiarizes, at least in part, for the fun of it.

But this is not the only kind of pleasure that Brown takes from plagiarism. On several occasions, he constructs sentences out of fragments that he has extracted from two different texts. In *Clotel*, for instance, he joins a slightly adjusted phrase from a newspaper article entitled "Prospects of Slavery" ("The once unshorn face of nature now blooms with splendid harvests") and a slightly adjusted phrase from Helen de Kroyft's *A Place in Thy Memory* ("where Lombard poplars lift their tapering tops almost to prop the skies; the willow, locust, and horse-chestnut spread their branches, and flowers never cease to blossom") to create a description of a Mississippi plantation ("The once unshorn face of nature had given way, and now the farm blossomed with a splendid harvest, the neat cottage stood in a grove where Lombardy poplars lift their tufted tops almost to prop the skies; the willow, locusts, and horse-chestnut spread their branches, and flowers never cease to blossom" [*C* 87]).[50] In *The Black Man*, he snaps off the beginning of a sentence from Moir's *Sketches* ("With acute powers of conception, a sparkling and lively fancy, and a quaintly curious felicity of diction, the grand characteristic of Leigh Hunt's poetry is *wordpainting*") and the end of a sentence from *Memorials of Early Genius* ("Under [poetry's] light and warmth we wake from our torpor and coldness to a sense of our capabilities") and fastens them together to create a description of William J. Wilson's writing ("With acute powers of conception, a sparkling and lively fancy, and a quaintly curious felicity of diction, Mr. Wilson wakes us from our torpidity and coldness to a sense of our capabilities" [*C* 619]).[51] And in *The Rising Son*, he merges a sketch of Percy Bysshe Shelley ("His eyes were large and lively; and the whole turn of his face, which was small, was graceful and full of sensibility") with a sketch of John Keats ("His features were well-defined, and delicately susceptible of every impression"), thereby creating a sketch of the poet Elijah W. Smith ("his eyes are lively, and the urn [*sic*] of his face is graceful and full of sensibility, and delicately susceptible of every impression").[52] Far from trying to "find [his] own voice," far from "forc[ing] the language to obey him," Brown is, in Acker's words, "having fun with texts." Sentences like these are indications of the degree to which he loves "to play with language," the degree to which he thinks of language as "material like clay or paint."[53]

The same may be said of his larger-scale experiments with textual suturing. Take, for instance, the twenty-sentence tribute to the African American polymath Benjamin Banneker in *The Black Man* (*C* 491–492). In his construction of this passage (reproduced below in roman type), Brown made use of sixteen sentences plucked from four different sources (reproduced below in italics):

> He well knew that every thing that was founded upon the admitted inferiority of natural right in the African was calculated to degrade him and

bring him nearer to the foot of the oppressor, and he therefore never failed to allude to the equality of the races when with those whites whom he could influence.

Every measure, as has been intimated, that is founded upon admitted inferiority of natural right in the African, is calculated to degrade him, and bring him nearer to the foot of the oppressor.
(D. Brown 17)

He always urged self-elevation upon the colored people whom he met. He felt that to deprive the black man of the inspiration of ambition, of hope, of health, of standing among his brethren of the earth, was to take from him all incentives to mental improvement. What husbandman incurs the toil of seed time and culture, except with a view to the subsequent enjoyment of a golden harvest?

Deprive him of the inspirations of ambition, of hope, of health, of standing among his brethren of the earth, and what remains as an incentive to mental improvement? What husbandman incurs the toil of seed time and culture, except with a view to the subsequent enjoyment of a golden harvest?
(D. Brown 37)

Banneker was endowed by nature with all those excellent qualifications which are necessary previous to the accomplishment of a great man. His memory was large and tenacious, yet, by a curious felicity, chiefly susceptible of the finest impressions it received from the best authors he read, which he always preserved in their primitive strength and amiable order. He had a quickness of apprehension and a vivacity of understanding which easily took in and surmounted the most subtile and knotty parts of mathematics and metaphysics.

He was endowed by Nature with all those excellent and necessary qualifications which are previous to the accomplishment of a great man. His memory was large and tenacious, yet by a curious felicity chiefly susceptible of the finest impressions it received from the best authors he read, which it always preserved in their primitive strength and amiable order. He had a quickness of apprehension, and vivacity of understanding, which easily took in and surmounted the most subtile and knotty parts of mathematics and metaphysics.

(Johnson 2:114)

He possessed in a large degree that genius which constitutes a man of letters; that quality without which judgment is cold and knowledge is inert; that energy which collects, combines, amplifies, and animates.

Of genius, that power which constitutes a poet; that quality without which judgment is cold, and knowledge is inert; that energy which collects, combines, amplifies, and animates;—the superiority must, with some hesitation, be allowed to Dryden.

(Johnson 2:252)

He knew every branch of history, both natural and civil; he had read all the original historians of England, France, and Germany, and was a great antiquarian. Criticism, metaphysics, morals, politics, voyages and travels, were all studied and well digested by him. With such a fund of knowledge his conversation was equally interesting, instructive, and entertaining.

He knew every branch of history, both natural and civil; had read all the original historians of England, France, and Italy; and was a great antiquarian. Criticism, metaphysics, morals, politics, made a principal part of his study; voyages and travels of all sorts were his favourite amusements. . . . With such a fund of knowledge, his conversation must have been equally instructing and entertaining.

(Johnson 2:299)

Banneker was so favorably appreciated by the first families in Virginia, that in 1803 he was invited by Mr. Jefferson, then President of the United States, to visit him at Monticello, where the statesman had gone for recreation. But he was too infirm to undertake the journey. He died the following year, aged seventy-two.

Like the golden sun that has sunk beneath the western horizon, but still throws upon the world, which he sustained and enlightened in his career, the reflected beams of his departed genius, his name can only perish with his language.

Like the golden sun that has sunk beneath the western horizon, he has sunk into the grave, life's dark and inevitable horizon, but still throws upon the world which he sustained and enlightened in his career, the reflected beams of his departed glory.
(D. Brown 39)

[*Samuel Butler is*] *a man whose name can only perish with his language.*
(Johnson 2:48)

Banneker believed in the divinity of reason, and in the omnipotence of the human understanding with Liberty for its handmaid. The intellect impregnated by science and multiplied by time, it appeared to him, must triumph necessarily over all the resistance of matter.

He believed in the divinity of reason, and in the omnipotence of the human understanding, with liberty as its handmaid. . . . The intellect impregnated by science, and multiplied by time, it appeared to him must triumph necessarily over all the resistance of matter.
(Lamartine 137)

He had faith in liberty, truth, and virtue.

He had faith in liberty, truth, and virtue.
(Lamartine 140)

His remains still rest in the slave state where he lived and died, with no stone to mark the spot or tell that it is the grave of Benjamin Banneker.

He labored incessantly, lived irreproachably, and died in the literary harness, universally esteemed and regretted.

[*He*] *laboured incessantly, lived irreproachably, and died in harness, universally esteemed and regretted.*
(Doran 1:124)

Part of what makes this sequence so impressive is the range of sources that Brown draws from and the number of separate passages that he takes: he lifts three passages from David Paul Brown, a Philadelphian lawyer and abolitionist; three from the literary lion Samuel Johnson; two from Lamartine, a founder of France's Second Republic; and one from Dr. John Doran, a historian of the British stage.[54] One would not think that those disparate, decontextualized fragments could, with so little mortaring, be perceived as the continuous composition of a single author. Neither would one think that passages referring to eight different men—in order, Edmund Smith, John Dryden, Thomas Gray, William Wilberforce, Samuel Butler, Nicolas de Condorcet, Jacques-Pierre Brissot, and Thomas Betterton—could be credibly applied, in so short a space, to one. The fact that the passage can indeed be perceived as a single-author, single-subject eulogy is a testimony to Brown's skill as a compositor. It is also, however, a testimony to a potentially dismaying fact about eulogistic discourse: that in the superlative mode, the differences between descriptions diminish. The more intensely one wants to laud someone, the more likely one is to produce a laudation, a conventional form of praise.

For Brown, however, the interchangeability of verbal characterizations is neither limited to eulogies nor a source of concern. In Cormenin's *Orators of France*, he encountered the following description of the royalist parliamentarian Pierre-Antoine Berryer: "Nature has treated Berryer as a favorite. His stature is not tall, but his handsome and expressive countenance paints and reflects every emotion of his soul. There is a fascination in the soft gaze of his full and finely-cut eyes, his gesture is marvellously beautiful like his delivery."[55] This evidently seemed to Brown like an adequate sketch of the white abolitionist Wendell Phillips, whom he describes, in *Three Years in Europe*, as follows: "Nature has treated him as a favorite. His stature is not tall, but handsome; his expressive countenance paints and reflects every emotion of his soul. His gestures are wonderfully graceful, like his delivery. There is a fascination in the soft gaze of his eyes, which none can but admire."[56] It also evidently seemed to him like a good-enough portrait of Madison Washington, the leader of the slave revolt on the *Creole*, whom he describes, in *The Black Man*, as follows: "Nature had treated him as a favorite. His expressive countenance painted and reflected every emotion of his soul. There was a fascination in the gaze of his finely-cut eyes that no one could withstand" (*C* 504). Later in his fanciful minibiography of Washington, Brown includes the following sentence: "His dignified, calm, and unaffected features announced at a glance that he was endowed with genius, and created to guide his fellow-men" (*C* 504). In addition to sounding very much like Lamartine's description of Pierre Vergniaud, the spokesman of the Girondist party during the French Revolution ("His dignified, calm, and unaffected features announced the conviction of his power"), the description of Washington sounds very much like the description, four chapters later, of Toussaint L'Ouverture ("His dignified, calm, and unaffected features, and broad and well-developed forehead, would cause him to be selected, in any company of men, as one born for a leader" [*C* 524]).[57] It is as if all verbal characterizations are capable of blurring, for Brown, into arbitrary identificatory arabesques. Just as the shape of his name, "William Wells Brown," emerges from and retains a relationship to "flourishes with no meaning," so are the shapes of such descriptive phrases, seen from a sufficient distance, like chalk marks on a fence, resembling one another far more than they resemble any one of their imaginable referents.

It is precisely this kind of nonseriousness about the marks of selfhood that most maddens those who are maddened by plagiarism. "From the lyric poem to the scientific footnote, the printed word is the writer's means of proving and perpetuating his existence," writes Thomas Mallon in the postscript to *Stolen Words: Forays Into the Origins and Ravages of Plagiarism*. "That identity of self and work, and the prospect for continuation, are more precious to him than the promiscuous coin of the realm."[58] He amplifies the point with a telling analogy: "Anyone is relieved to come home and find that the burglar has taken the wallet and left the photo album. When a plagiarist enters the writer's study it's the latter—the stuff of 'sentimental value'—that he's after."[59] The desire not to be plagiarized—the desire that no one should ever be plagiarized—is, for Mallon, the desire to secure the "stuff of 'sentimental value'" on which identity is predicated. To plagiarize is to take the very basis of identity and send it into promiscuous circulation, as if it were nothing more than filthy lucre, the anonymous coin of the realm. Hence the presence of the word "ravages" in the title of Mallon's book, hence his comparisons of plagiarism to rape and murder.[60] Even when what is being plagiarized might seem to be nothing more than, say, a scientific footnote, don't be fooled: it is that without which identity as such cannot exist. Ask not for whom the bell of plagiarism tolls: it tolls for thee.

But words are not sacred icons of selfhood. "As the business of looking things up in the dictionary suggests, all words are stand-ins for other words," Terry Eagleton writes. "All our language is filched and forged, reach-me-down rather than bespoke."[61] In fact, insofar as "we would not call a mark which could happen only once a sign," the capacity of marks to be, as Mallon puts it, "promiscuous," to circulate in other-than-original contexts, is the condition of their ability to signify anything at all. "Language must belong to the Other—to my linguistic community as a whole—before it can belong to me," Eagleton writes. "The self comes to its unique articulation in a medium which is always at some level indifferent to it."[62] There is an intimate link between Brown's awareness of these facts and the empty formality of so many of his fictional and nonfictional descriptions. Instead of struggling against the anonymizing drift of descriptive language, Brown goes with its flow, not in a spirit of resignation but with what strikes me as a strange kind of exuberance. What he loses in authenticity and verisimilitude he gains in lightness and speed.

Take the following description of Frederick Douglass in *Three Years in Europe* (it reappears, slightly modified, in *The American Fugitive in Europe*, *The Black Man*, and *The Rising Son*):

> His vast and well-developed forehead announces the power of his intellect. His voice is full and sonorous. His attitude is dignified, and his gesticulation is full of noble simplicity. He is a man of lofty reason, natural, and without pretension, always master of himself, brilliant in the art of exposing and of abstracting. Few persons can handle a subject with which they are familiar better than Mr. Douglass. There is a kind of eloquence issuing from the depth of the soul, as from a spring, rolling along its copious floods, sweeping all before it, overwhelming by its very force, carrying, upsetting, engulphing its adversaries, and more dazzling and more thundering than the bolt which leaps from crag to crag. This is the eloquence of Frederick Douglass.[63]

Rather than tailoring a description to Douglass—whom he knew very well—Brown dresses him, as he would later dress Banneker, in an assortment of off-the-rack items. He starts with something taken from Cormenin's depiction of Odilon Barrot: "His vast and well-developed forehead announces the power of his intellect. His voice is full and sonorous, and his expression singularly grave. . . . His attitude is dignified without being theatrical, and his gesticulation is full of noble simplicity."[64] He then switches over to Cormenin's depiction of Jacques-Antoine Manuel—"He was a man of lofty reason, natural and without pretension, always master of himself, brilliant and easy in language, skilled in the art of exposing, of abstracting and of concluding"—and, after a transitional sentence of his own, fuses two of Cormenin's descriptions of oratorical styles (one "issuing from the depth of the soul, as from a spring, rolling along its copious floods, sweeping all before it, overwhelming by its very mass, pressing, upsetting, ingulfing its adversaries" and another that is "more dazzling, more thundering than the bolt which leaps from crag to crag") into a single, perfervid evocation of Douglass's declamatory mode.[65] Why? Certainly not because he is incapable of telling us what Douglass looks like, acts like, and sounds like. Perhaps it is because that he felt that only the most ratcheted-up of discourses could do Douglass justice. Perhaps, conversely, it is because he liked the idea of covertly diminishing the specialness of this famously special man. And perhaps it is because he just liked to write like this and did it whenever he could. Because wasn't going to stop playing in any playground. Because loved wildness.

In the June 10, 1853, issue of *Frederick Douglass' Paper*, Douglass reprints a public letter from Brown that had appeared a week earlier in the *Liberator*, with an asterisk next to the following sentence: "Uncle Tom's Cabin has come down upon the dark abodes of slavery like a morning's sunlight, unfolding to view its enormities in a manner which has fastened all eyes upon the 'peculiar institution,' and awakening sympathy in hearts that never before felt for the slave." "His letter is very prettily expressed," Douglass writes, "but he will pardon us if we suspect that his vicinage to Mr. D'Israeli has not been, in all respects, to his advantage. The sentence which we have taken the liberty to mark above, so resembles certain lines which occur in a "Call," published nearly a year ago, by *"the Rochester Ladies' Anti-Slavery Society,"* that we fear friend Brown has, like some other *literary* men, mistaken the beautiful sentiment of another for the creation of his own fancy!"

Douglass then reproduces the sentence in question, which had originally appeared in the August 13, 1852, issue of his newspaper. It reads, "'*Uncle Tom's Cabin*,' by Mrs. Harriet Beecher Stowe, has come down, upon the dark abodes of human bondage, like the morning sunlight, unfolding to view the enormities of slavery, in a manner which has fastened all eyes upon them, and awakened sympathy for the slave in hearts unused to feel."[66]

Eight months earlier, Chancellor of the Exchequer Benjamin Disraeli, a former novelist and future prime minister, had eulogized the duke of Wellington in a speech in which he drew extensively on an earlier funerary oration. "At every moment," Disraeli had declared, a great general

> has to think of the eve and of the morrow—of his flank and of his rear—he has to calculate at the same time the state of the weather and the moral qualities of men. . . . Unquestionably . . . all this may be done in an ordinary manner, by an ordinary man, as every day of our lives we see that ordinary men may be successful Ministers of State, successful authors, and successful speakers; but to do all this with genius is sublime.[67]

As the London *Globe* had gleefully pointed out, in these and several other lines, Disraeli poaches from Adolphe Thiers's 1829 address on the late Marshal Gouvion St. Cyr. The translation of Thiers's address, which had been reprinted in the *Morning Chronicle* in 1848, reads, in part,

> At every moment you must think of the yesterday and the morrow; of your flank and of your rear calculate at the same time on the atmosphere and on the temper of your men. . . . All this, undoubtedly, is compatible with mediocrity, like every other profession; one can also be a middling poet, a middling orator, a middling author; but this done with genius is sublime.[68]

The exposé led, predictably, to a prolonged scandal. "The crime of Mr. Disraeli is not merely the highest literary crime which it is possible to commit, but it is the only literary crime which is never to be forgiven," declared the *Caledonian Mercury*, in one of the calmer of the initial responses.[69] After the *London Times* mounted an elitist defense of Disraeli's appropriativeness—"As for plagiarism, there is not a great orator or poet who has not been a plagiarist, and that on a very extensive scale"—and went on to suggest that journalists should be more supportive of their fellow writers, the scandal intensified.[70] There is a difference between Disraeli's "wholesale plunder" and the "trifling and unconscious borrowings of distinguished writers in general," wrote the *London Morning Chronicle*. "No writer was ever found out in borrowing, to anything like the same extent with Mr. Disraeli, without being branded as a literary thief; and it is monstrous to assert that the republic of letters ever tolerated the irregular and unacknowledged appropriation of words as well as thoughts, of form as well as substance, and of imagery and illustration as well as arguments."[71] To the *London Daily News*, it "smack[ed] of the clannishness of the swell mob" to argue, as the *Times* had, that "because Mr. Disraeli is a literary man, all literary men, for the credit of the profession, ought to wink at any impropriety he may be guilty of."[72] The *Sheffield and Rotherham Independent* agreed: it was "a gross insult" for Disraeli to have to "pass[ed] off as his own the language of another man on an infinitely meaner subject." No "*esprit de corps* among literary men" should keep them from reproving "dishonourable acts" like these.[73]

If Douglass's aim, in his exposé of Brown, was to shock him into stopping by showing how easily he could be caught, to evoke the trial of shame that he might have to endure, and to twist the knife by ironically supplying for him the alibi that the *Times* had supplied for Disraeli—that he was a "*literary*" man—it didn't work. Five months after Douglass's article appeared, Brown published *Clotel*, in which the plagiarism is, for readers conversant with abolitionist discourse, far more obvious than the plagiarism in *Three Years in Europe*. Instead of lifting passages primarily from travel guides and travel narratives, Brown lifts them, in *Clotel*, primarily from antislavery journals and books. Quite often, he plagiarizes from friends and associates; William Lloyd Garrison, who reviewed *Clotel*, probably noticed that Brown reproduces without attribution passages from two of his works—*An Address Delivered Before the Free People of Color* and "Declaration of the National Anti-Slavery Convention"—along with excerpts from several articles that had appeared in the *Liberator*. The abolitionists George Allen (301 words), William Bowditch (583 words), Seth Gates (672 words), Sarah Grimké (621 words), Benjamin Hughes (171 words), Harriet Martineau (24 words), John Gorham Palfrey (48 words), William Weston Patton (510 words), Parker Pillsbury (76 words), Robert Purvis (60 words), John Scoble (43 words), Thaddeus Stevens (599 words), Alvan Stewart (593 words), La Roy Sunderland (187 words), and Theodore Weld (102 words) may have had similar experiences.[74]

Evidently, Brown was unafraid of further exposure. At one point, he even puts into the mouth of an insurrectionary slave a long passage from an article that had appeared in Douglass's former newspaper, *The North Star*.[75] Douglass, however, said no more on the subject, other than to inquire, icily, in his 1863 review of *The Black Man*, "whence has this man this knowledge? He seems to have read and remembered nearly every thing which has been written or said respecting the ability of the negro."[76] And no one else ever brought it up. Brown would get away with it—get to enjoy, in his own peculiar way, this dimension of the experience of writing—for the rest of his career.

That means, of course, that there is no confession for us to turn to, if we continue to be curious to know why he did it. There is, however, a revealing apologia for a fellow plagiarist, the French novelist Alexandre Dumas, in *The Black Man*. "It is well understood that [Dumas] is not the author of all the works under his name, but that young writers gain a living by working out the plots and situations that his fecund brain suggests; when the novel or the play is complete, Dumas gives it a revision, touches up the dialogue, dashes in here and there a spirited scene of his own, and then receives from the publisher an enormous sum," Brown writes. Nevertheless, "such is the vivacity of [Dumas's] descriptions, such the entrain of his narrative, such the boldness of his invention, such the point of his dialogue, and the rapidity of his incidents, so matchless often the felicity and skill of particular passages, that he always inflames the interest of the reader to the end." As a result, in spite of all of the damning revelations of his plagiarisms, "no writer fills a more prominent place in the literature of his country; and none has exercised a more potent influence upon its recent development than this son of the Negro General Dumas" (*C* 544).

Did Brown actually write those words? He did not. Each of the above quotations may be found in an essay by Wilson Armistead in *God's Image in Ebony* (1854)—and perhaps, given Armistead's appropriative tendencies, in some other text as well, a text now buried deeper in the archive of nineteenth-century print culture than our databases can drill. Did Brown enjoy not-writing those words? I think he did. Is it possible for us to enjoy this kind of not-writing about not-writing? I think it is. "You may be angry with him," Brown writes of Dumas, in another passage copied, as far as one can tell, from Armistead, "but you will confess that he is the opposite of tedious" (*C* 544).

CHAPTER

TWO

The Spirit of Capitalization

One day, writes the British ship's captain Nathaniel Uring in his 1726 *Narrative of Voyages and Travels*, Joseph Dudley, the governor of the Massachusetts Bay Colony, encountered "a lusty *Indian* almost naked." Why, Dudley asked the Indian, did he not "work to purchase something to keep him from the Cold?" Upon being asked by the Indian "why *he* did not work," Dudley explained that "he worked with his Head, and had no Occasion to work with his Hands as [Indians] must." After the Indian assured Dudley that he was indeed willing to work, Dudley "asked him to kill him a Calf, for which he would give him a shilling." The Indian promptly killed the calf but then informed Dudley that it would cost him another shilling to have it skinned and dressed. A day later, the Indian sought out Dudley and complained that one of the shillings that he had given him was brass. The governor "readily gave him another," but "soon after the Fellow went back with a Second, which the Governour also changed, but knew the Fellow had put upon him." Seeing him the next day, Dudley

> called to him and told [him] he must carry a Letter presently to *Boston*, which he wrote to the Keeper of *Bridewell*, in order to have the Fellow well lashed; but he apprehending the Consequence, and seeing another *Indian* in the Road, he gave him the Letter, telling him, the Governour said he must carry that Letter presently to *Boston*. The poor Fellow took it innocently, and having delivered the Letter as directed, was whip'd very severely; the Governour soon after seeing the *Indian* again, asked him, if

> he had carried the Letter he sent him with? he answered, No, no *Coponoh*, Head work, pointing to his Head: The Governour was so well pleased with the Fellow's Answer, he forgave him.[1]

The anecdote ends there, but its career in print does not. After reappearing in at least three British periodicals in the 1760s and 1770s, it jumped the Atlantic, and, between 1789 and 1848, was reprinted at least thirty-two times in the United States, in publications ranging from the *Nantucket Inquirer* to the *Portfolio of Entertaining and Instructive Varieties*.[2] In or around 1826, it mutated into a 120-line doggerel poem called "The Indian; or, Self-Interest," in which, halfway through, the Indian morphs into a black man.[3] Around the same time, a new version of the anecdote, featuring Dudley and a pair of black men, began to appear in American newspapers and magazines. By 1832, this substitution had become so common that when Samuel Drake reprinted the original passage from Uring's *Narrative* in the *Collections of the New Hampshire Historical Society*, he felt it necessary to add, in a footnote, that it was probably the forerunner of "a story which is said to have happened in Boston with two negroes, and which has been circulated in almost every newspaper and magazine in the country, in some of which, however, it was hardly cognizable, being but a shadow of it, and as seen at a great distance."[4] The revised version of the anecdote usually took the following form:

> Soon after the settlement of New England, Governor Dudley, taking a walk, met a stout negro begging, and saying he could get no work. The Governor told him to go to his house, and he would give him work. "But," said the negro, "why you no work massa?" "O," said the Governor, "my head works." He, however, turned out an idle, good-for-nothing fellow, and his master found it necessary one day to have him flogged. With this view, he gave him a letter, desiring him to carry it to the keeper of the workhouse. The negro, suspecting its contents, committed it to the care of one of his comrades, who got a sound whipping for his trouble. The Governor having learned this, asked Mungo why he did so? "O, massa," said he, "head work."[5]

Midway through Brown's 1847 *Narrative*, a strikingly similar incident occurs. While waiting on a group of white men in Vicksburg, Mississippi,

Brown writes, he overfilled their wine glasses, and when they raised their glasses to drink, the wine spilled on their clothes. The next day, his master, the slave trader James Walker, gave Brown a note and a dollar and told him to go to the local jail. Suspecting "that all was not right," Brown asked a sailor to read the note and learned that he was to be whipped by the jailor in exchange for the dollar. "While I was meditating on the subject," Brown writes,

> I saw a colored man about my size walk up, and the thought struck me in a moment to send him with my note. I walked up to him, and asked him who he belonged to. He said he was a free man, and had been in the city but a short time. I told him I had a note to go into the jail, and get a trunk to carry to one of the steamboats; but was so busily engaged that I could not do it, although I had a dollar to pay for it. He asked me if I would not give him the job. I handed him the note and the dollar, and off he started for the jail.[6]

Brown concealed himself behind a pile of bricks, hoping "to see how my friend looked when he came out." While stationed there, he overheard one black man tell another that "they are giving a nigger scissors in the jail." When the freeman emerged from the jail, Brown stepped out from behind the brickpile. The freeman immediately accosted him, "complaining bitterly" that he had just "received twenty lashes on his bare back, with the negro-whip" (*C* 29). After denying "any knowledge of what the note contained," Brown paid the freeman for the note the jailor gave him and found someone to read it to him. "As near as I can recollect," he writes, "it was as follows: 'Dear Sir: By your direction, I have given your boy twenty lashes. He is a very saucy boy, and tried to make me believe that he did not belong to you, and I put it on to him well for lying to me.'" Brown then moistened his cheeks and went back to Walker, who "inquired what was the matter. I told him that I had never had such a whipping in my life, and handed him the note." Walker "looked at it and laughed;—'and so you told him that you did not belong to me.' 'Yes, sir,' said I. 'I did not know that there was any harm in that.' He told me I must behave myself, if I did not want to be whipped again." After a brief apology for the "deception I practiced upon this poor fellow," the chapter comes to an end (*C* 29, 30).

The Vicksburg incident, as I will call it, has never been easy for critics to digest. As William Andrews points out, the "manner in which [Brown] tells this story that he claims to be so shameful tempts his implied reader to respond with comic approbation and respect." Instead of "recounting the incident so as to focus on his moral failure," Brown gives "the retelling of that incident . . . the full attention of his imagination and his art"; he "plays out the narrative line leisurely," drawing out scenes "for his own and the reader's delight," as if he "can not, will not, recall it without a measure of pride."[7] Rafia Zafar, the only other critic to perform a full-scale analysis of the scene, likewise observes that "the detail and the relative lack of comment on his behavior *during* the incident (as opposed to the explanations of extenuating circumstances that follow) create severe doubt as to whether or not Brown sincerely repents of his deception. Certainly his whimsical and ironic appellations for the freeman—first 'my friend,' then 'my customer'—swamp his expressions of remorse."[8]

The amoral glee that Andrews and Zafar rightly identify as the dominant feature of the anecdote is ratcheted up even further in the revised version of the incident that appears in Brown's *My Southern Home*. When Pompey, the slave who occupies Brown's original role in the scene, figures out a way to escape his whipping, we are asked to admire his "fertile brain," which has enabled him to be "equal to the occasion" (*C* 760). We then receive not only an extended version of the conversation between Pompey and the freeman but also, thanks to the eavesdropping Pompey, an account of the conversation between the freeman and the jailor. When the freeman is about to be whipped, the narratorial point of view briefly detaches itself from Pompey and enters the jail, enabling us to see the freeman "fastened upon the stretcher, face downwards, his clothing removed, and the strong-armed white negro-whipper standing over him with uplifted whip." Together with Pompey, we hear the "cries and groans of the poor man, as the heavy instrument of torture fell upon his bare back" and perceive, when the freeman reappears on the street, that he is "maddened by the pain from the excoriation of his bleeding back" (*C* 762). Although one might imagine that the greater explicitness of the descriptions would lead to a more elaborate display of compunction, nothing of the kind occurs. Upon being confronted by the freeman, Pompey asks, "What have I done to you?" with "a seriousness that was indeed amusing"; later in their conversation, he asks, "What did you let 'em whip you for?" with "a concealed smile" (*C* 762). In a concluding paragraph, the narrator tells us that "Pompey often spoke of the appearance of 'my fren',' as he called the colored brother, and would enjoy a hearty laugh, saying, 'He was a free man, an' could afford to go to bed, an' lay dar till he got well" (*C* 763). Instead of moralizing on Pompey's laughter, the narrator encourages us to share it; instead of representing the incident as a sign of the warping influence of slavery, he invites us to read it as a sign of "the quick wit of the race" (*C* 760).

In order to avoid a total condemnation of Brown's actions, Andrews and Zafar fall back on one of the most pervasive assumptions in the criticism of early African American writing: that African American writers were not allowed to present themselves as morally compromised beings.[9] After having argued that Brown develops his account of the Vicksburg incident with "the reader's delight" in mind, Andrews reverses field, arguing that "in the self-celebratory moment," Brown "frees himself from the bondage of his white reader's moral approval."[10] Zafar, too, conjures up the specter of an upright, uptight white readership, declaring that Brown's representation of himself as a "not altogether sterling character" is a way of flouting "the hagiographic expectations of his white abolitionist audience." By refusing to pass himself off as an embodiment of "abolitionist-approved, acceptable African American attributes," Zafar argues, Brown "assert[s] his individual agency."[11]

But what if the Vicksburg incident is in fact an expanded version of the Uring anecdote? What if it has no basis in Brown's personal experience? If that is the case—and it would be both an amazing coincidence and a remarkable exception to Brown's usual practices if it were not—then the energies on display in it are generated not by a desire to be true to the facts of his life but by a desire to veer sharply away from those facts.[12] Moreover, if the Vicksburg incident did indeed grow out of a popular comic anecdote, it is unlikely that he inserted it for the sake of antagonizing his white readers. It is far more likely that he inserted it for the sake of *entertaining* those readers, giving them an updated version of a white-authored tale, a tale belonging to the category of "Stuff White People Like." He is more likely, in other words, to have been seeking a pleasure-based relationship with his readers than to have been seeking independence from them.

It is worth reconsidering, with this in mind, the notion that abolitionist audiences were hotbeds of "hagiographic expectations." Those expectations did exist to some degree, as Brown well knew. "Remember what a singular relation you sustain to society," William Lloyd Garrison told a series of black audiences in 1831. "The necessities of the case require not only that you should behave as well as the whites, but better than the whites—and for this reason: if you behave no better than they, (and I do not think the task would be difficult to excel them,) your example will lose a great portion of its influence."[13] ("Remember what a singular relation you sustain to society," Georgiana Carlton tells the slaves she is about to free in *Clotel*. "The necessities of the case require not only that you should behave as well as the whites, but better than the whites; and for this reason: if you behave no better than they, your example will lose a great portion of its influence" [*C* 167].) But if those were the non-negotiable terms of Brown's audiences, how could he have enjoyed over three decades of success as a speaker, writer, and performer? Why were so many of his lectures interrupted by laughter, laughter occasioned, in some cases, by descriptions of occasions on which he had behaved no better than white people? Might the official rewards for being "clean" have been accompanied by unofficial rewards for being interesting—for having a "quick wit," in Brown's words, and for showing signs of a capacity for self-making? Might it have been as important for male slave narrators—and they were almost all male—to show that they were capable of surviving in a brutally competitive social environment as it was to show that they were sensitive to moral considerations? Were the readers of early African American writing more interested in the dramatization of an ability to sustain the paradoxical relationship between scrupulous self-subordination and unscrupulous self-advancement than they were in the presentation of a nonparadoxical, nondramatic, nonmobile goodness?

Rather than attempt to answer those questions here—rather than attempt to provide a full-scale history of the relationship between black abolitionists and their audiences—I will offer, in the spirit of suggestiveness only, an account of how Brown might have answered the above questions if he had been given the chance.[14] He would have said, I think, that the mostly white audiences that he encountered in the United States and England wanted something more than stone-cold sober facts from him. He would have said that they wanted, as Zora Neale Hurston would later put it, "crayon enlargements of life": history aerated by wit, morality effervesced by irony.[15] He would have said that they craved the relief of laughter, and that however much they may have been in the habit of laughing at black people, they seemed to enjoy laughing with them as well. He would have said, finally, that they enjoyed mobility above all else, and that they preferred, accordingly, stricture-escaping subjectivities, however much they might have professed otherwise.[16]

Or so his publications and speeches suggest. By rewriting the ephemera of newspapers into extended humorous sketches—as he did, I am arguing, in the Vicksburg incident, and as he would do throughout his career—and by composing comic narratives of his own, Brown indirectly provides us with a kind of cultural-studies reading of mid-nineteenth-century whiteness.[17] That reading is, in certain respects, distinctly—and perhaps surprisingly—sympathetic. "I love America," he told a British audience in 1849. "I admire her enterprising and industrious people . . . but I hate her hideous institution."[18] What Brown offered up in his lectures, performances, and published works was determined, in large part, by what he thought those enterprising and industrious people would find most interesting and entertaining. He read up, accordingly, on how white Americans entertained and interested one another. He also paid attention, as every good performer does, to the responses of his audiences. By the time of *Clotel*, he had become, in the words of a newspaper reporter who attended one of his lectures, "a travelling repertory of anecdotes," many of which celebrated the unscrupulous seizing of economic and/or comic opportunities.[19] Just as importantly, he had mastered the art of surrounding the stories that he told with a seductive haze of indeterminacy. In a spirit of capitalization, he told tall-seeming tales of capitalization, indicating not only an ability to get ahead—to make something out of nothing by taking swift advantage of opportunities—but an ability to get along: to do, when in confabulating Rome, as the confabulating Romans were doing.

In a review of *The Life of P. T. Barnum, Written by Himself* (1855), Severn Teackle Wallis writes that if Barnum's book were to be buried in a cornerstone and dug up two centuries later, it "would tell a truer and fuller story . . . of the morals and taste of this our country and generation, than all the Bancrofts of after days could contrive, from the most mouldy and respectable records." The story that Barnum's autobiography would tell, Wallis goes on to say, is that there is "sympathy with trick and untruth, among us," that "our sensibilities are not nice," and that "success may render almost any thing tolerable to us." All of "the formal and express memorials we had thought fit to consign to [posterity], as our story," will no doubt insist otherwise, but future generations will "see our features reflected in the objects of our taste. . . . In this country, people rarely buy what they do not want or like, and they do buy Barnum."[20]

But *why* did they buy Barnum? In Neil Harris's well-known analysis of Barnum's attractiveness, the answer is that he appealed to his audience's "operational aesthetic." By "focus[ing] attention on their own structures and operations," Harris argues, Barnum's shows "enabled—or at least invited—audiences and participants to learn how they worked." The public was "grateful for being the subjects of his manipulation," Harris concludes, because he made it possible for them to figure out how he did it.[21] Just as, according to Ian Watt, eighteenth-century British readers sought out fiction in order to gain access to the increasingly inaccessible details of other people's lives—to be "taken behind the scenes, and shown what actually happens in the places we know only by passing them in the street or reading about them in the newspaper"—so, according to Harris, did nineteenth-century American audiences flock to Barnum because he made them feel capable of demystifying an increasingly mysterious cultural environment.[22]

It may be, however, that the "sympathy with trick and untruth" in the nineteenth-century American public ran deeper than that. In an influential revision of Watt's argument, Catherine Gallagher suggests that fictionality, not formal realism, is the crucial feature of the eighteenth-century novel. Readers were less interested in "literal truth" than in "likelihood," Gallagher writes, in part because they lived in a rapidly modernizing world, where "flexible mental states" were increasingly becoming "the sine qua non of . . . subjectivity" and where "no enterprise could prosper without some degree of imaginative play." The novel both responded to and accelerated those developments, rewarding readers who approached it in a "spirit of 'ironic' assent" by increasing their capacity for "cognitive provisionality."[23] Something similar may be said of the cultural function of Barnum. It may be argued, that is, that what he offers his audience is, in the historian James W. Cook's words, not "an egalitarian exercise in cultural sleuthing" but "a more slippery mode of middle-class play—a play whose moral ambiguity and epistemological flexibility were always built into the larger process."[24] What Barnum appeals to is, from this perspective, less an operational aesthetic than what we might call an apparitional aesthetic—a taste for trick and untruth, understood as signifiers of an energetic and unrestrained capacity for invention. In the United States, writes an anonymous reviewer of

Barnum's *Life*, "cuteness"—that is, acuteness—"is held in such great esteem that the fact of being egregiously cajoled and fooled out of our money is lost sight of in admiration for the shrewdness of the man who can do it."[25]

Barnum himself suggests as much. Instead of apologizing for the "clap-trap" in his career as a promoter, he writes, "I cannot doubt that the sort of 'clap-trap' here referred to, is allowable, and that the public like a little of it mixed up with the great realities which I provide."[26] In fact, he observes elsewhere, "the public appears disposed to be amused even when they are conscious of being deceived."[27] It is one of Barnum's most important and profitable insights: that there is, or can be, something sociable about fraudulence, that a surplus of appearance—an over-the-top fictionality—mixes well with "great realities." Hence the barrage of well-worn comic anecdotes with which he begins his autobiography: fifty-two witty sayings and practical jokes in the first six chapters alone. Although there is of course a possibility that some of these anecdotes are drawn from Barnum's own experiences, the effect of reading so many of them in such short order is to make the truthfulness of the opening chapters seem more than a little doubtful.[28] "We have glimmering recollections of certain profusely illuminated comic almanacs in which more veracious relations, strangely similar to those gravely located at Bethel and Danbury [may be found]," writes another one of Barnum's reviewers, the Reverend Thomas M. Eddy. "The trial of the eccentric minister before the consociation is too much like the case of Rev. Zeb. Twitchell, related by the Knickerbocker, a year or two ago, for us to avoid thinking that either Barnum or Old Knick has 'uttered' a literary forgery."[29] It is all, as Eddy puts it later in his review, "baleful and yet fascinating."[30] Even though Barnum does not "consider deception, when for the sake of gain, fun, or cuteness, as any wrong," he nevertheless receives "the *quasi* approval . . . [of] the press" and the delighted patronage of the public.[31] There is something happening here, with respect to the relationship between deception and approval, and Eddy doesn't know what it is. Barnum, however, does.

So does Brown. In the *Narrative*, just before his second escape attempt, he pays twenty-five cents to have his fortune told by a slave named Frank, who has—or so everyone in the area believes—the ability to "penetrate into the mysteries of futurity." "Whether true or not," Brown writes, "he had the *name*, and that is about half of what one needs in this gullible age" (*C* 45). In the ensuing account of the fortune-telling session, Brown does not fully uphold the local belief in Frank's powers, but neither does he fully expose

Frank's claim to those powers as a pretense. When Brown enters Frank's home, Frank divines, unimpressively, that Brown has come to have his fortune told ("how the old man should know what I came for, I could not tell," Brown writes, mock-amazed). Frank goes on to predict that Brown will succeed in escaping from slavery but then foretells that he will encounter many trials along the way, which Brown recognizes, even at the time, as low-hanging fruit ("I thought to myself any fool could tell me that!"). The bottom line of this purely gratuitous episode, for Brown, is that there is no bottom line: Frank's powers can be neither confirmed nor denied. "Whether the old man was a prophet, or the son of a prophet, I cannot say," Brown writes, "but there is one thing certain, many of his predictions were verified" (*C* 46). By communicating, tonally, an enjoyment of the slipperiness of this experience, and by leaving the extent of his own gullibility up in the air, Brown tells us something about his understanding of his audience. He tells us, to return to Wallis's language, that he senses a "sympathy with trick and untruth" among them, a sympathy that is capable, under the right circumstances, of traveling where historians and literary scholars have assumed it could not: into the space of African American narration.

Consider, in this light, the performative interpretation of Brown's *Narrative* that appears in John Passmore Edwards's *Uncle Tom's Companions* (1852), a compendium of "Startling Incidents in the Lives of Celebrated Fugitive Slaves," as Edwards puts it in the subtitle. In his recapitulation of the *Narrative*, Edwards takes an obvious delight in its least principled moments. In his version of Brown's anecdote about appropriating mint julep from the family pitcher during prebreakfast prayers, for example, Edwards adds an explanation ("not being able to have such a luxury openly, he saw no harm in taking a little on the sly"), praise for his aliveness to opportunity ("he had 'an eye to business'"), and a groundless account, inspired by the comic tone of the anecdote, of the mistress's reaction to the breaking of the pitcher ("The old lady, instead of clenching the sonorous supplications of his master with a hearty 'Amen,' gave a hearty shriek and clenched poor Brown").[32] The retelling of the Vicksburg incident is equally animated: Edwards imagines Brown "rejoicing in the skilfulness of his manoeuvre, and congratulating his back on the whipping it had escaped" after tricking the freeman into taking the note, and imagines the freeman looking "wofully chop-fallen" upon emerging from the jail. Most importantly, when the episode is over, instead of reproducing Brown's apology or expressing any disapproval of his own, he writes, "Thus Brown exercised his wits and saved his back. It is not difficult to imagine that one who would try to save his back, would ultimately try to save himself, and that he did so, the sequel will show."[33] Instead of treating the Vicksburg incident as a troubling ethical lapse, Edwards, a British Quaker, treats it as a sign of character, an attractive manifestation of the qualities that will eventually set Brown free.

It is not hard to imagine American readers responding to the Vicksburg incident in the same way. It was, after all, a time-tested tale, and Brown not only reprised it in *My Southern Home* but also retained it in each of his editions of the *Narrative* and referred to it in a footnote to *A Description of William Wells Brown's Original Panoramic Views of the Scenes in the Life of an American Slave* (1850).[34] If he had received any significantly negative feedback about it from his readers, it is unlikely that he would have continued to associate his name with it. It is unlikely, as well, that he would have gone on to represent himself, elsewhere, as a skillful performer of devious maneuvers. In *Three Years in Europe*, for instance, he tells a story of becoming a barber in Monroe, Michigan, deceitfully drawing customers away from a competitor, starting up an uncapitalized bank, and fending off a run on it by instantly exchanging his ultimately worthless banknotes for other forms of cash.[35] The sketch, which the *London Atheneum* described as "thoroughly American," was immediately popular, appearing in the *Cork Examiner*, the *Bristol Mercury*, the *Working Man's Friend and Family Instructor*, the *New York Times*, the *London Despatch*, and *Frederick Douglass' Paper*, and it was subsequently recycled in *Clotel*, *The American Fugitive in Europe* (*C* 271–274), *Biography of an American Bondman* (a memoir attributed to Brown's daughter Josephine but almost certainly written by Brown himself), and *Memoir of William Wells Brown*.[36] Like Frank the fortune teller, Brown has, in this anecdote, only the *name* of barber and banker, but in this gullible and gullibility-loving age, that's all he needs.

Part of what makes all of this fraudulence enjoyable to Brown's audience is its red-white-and-blue style. Whiteness in general may be, as Richard Dyer argues, associated with "enterprise"—"energy, will, ambition, the ability to think and see things through"—but in Brown's day, American whiteness was additionally associated with a quality that is best captured by the word "wit."[37] The barber/banker sketch is "thoroughly American" because it displays, humorously, a zero-stockpile mode of advancement, in which gains are made and tables are turned by means of quick thinking alone. "In a great many folktales," writes Peter Brooks, "the specifically human faculty of ingenuity and trickery, the capacity to use the mind to devise schemes to overcome superior force, becomes a basic dynamic of plot. If the giants of folktale are always stupid, it is because they stand opposed to human wit, which is seen as a capacity for leverage on the world, precisely that which overcomes inert obstacles, sets change in motion, reformulates the real."[38] Superimposed on that dimension of Brown's anecdote, however, is a distinctively modern quality: a location not in the securely imaginary time and space of the folktale but the ambiguous time and space of the fictionality-soaked autobiographical fragment. Did any of this actually happen? Did an African American man set himself up as a barber in 1835 by slandering a white competitor? ("I had to tell all who came in that my neighbor on the opposite side did not keep clean towels, that his razors were dull, and, above all, he had never been to New York to see the fashions. Neither had I." [*C* 271–272]) Did he get away with printing and circulating unbacked paper bills? Maybe. Maybe not. Between those two possibilities, Brown's implied reader slips and slides.

The most obvious precedent for Brown's "transformation of fraudulence from a shameful fact into a point of pride" is the work of the Yankee and Southwestern humorists. In the face of what Karen Halttunen describes as a "middle-class concern—amounting at times to an obsession—about the problem of hypocrisy in a modernizing world," writers like Thomas Bangs Thorpe and Seba Smith cranked out tales whose protagonists embodied, in John Cawelti's words, "a vigorous and amoral image of the mobile society."[39] The archetypal hero of this literature is Captain Simon Suggs, whose "whole ethical system," according to his creator, the Southwestern humorist Johnson Jones Hooper, "lies snugly in his favorite aphorism—'IT IS GOOD TO BE SHIFTY IN A NEW COUNTRY'—which means that it is right and proper that one should live as merrily and as comfortably as possible at the expense of others."[40] In addition to possessing "that tact which enables man to detect the soft spots in his fellow, and to assimilate himself to whatever company he may fall in with," Captain Suggs "has a quick, ready wit, which has extricated him from many an unpleasant predicament, and which makes him whenever he chooses to be so—and that is always—very companionable."[41] Shiftiness is, for Hooper, an amalgam of advantage-creating perceptiveness and self-extricating wit, qualities so appealingly "companionable" that they outweigh—in "A NEW COUNTRY," at least—whatever harm they might cause. It is, of course, hypocritical, but it is also one of the most important of "the arts by which men '*get along*' in the world," and in the cognitively provisional realm of fictionality, a great many people—not only white, not only male, and not only American—delighted in it.[42]

Part of what seems to have made shiftiness so delightful is the quickening of perception and unbinding of thought that tended to accompany it. In the opening scenes of *Some Adventures of Captain Simon Suggs*, as the young Simon is being marched by his father to the mulberry tree where "all formal punishment [was] administered during work hours in the field," his "wits, in view of the anticipated flogging, [are] dashing, springing, bounding, darting about, in hot chase of some expedient suitable to the necessities of the case."[43] The intensity of Simon's desire for an "expedient"—something, anything, that will enable him to evade the kind of beating that a young slave named Bill, his partner in the crime of gambling, has just received—stimulates his "tact," or tactical awareness, making him preternaturally sensitive to the appearance of an escape hatch. That aliveness to opportunity is not, however, turned to any kind of permanent advantage, either in this instance or in any of his subsequent "adventures." His skills are strictly tactical, in Michel de Certeau's sense, returning him, again and again, to his point of origin. "Whatever [a tactic] wins, it does not keep," de Certeau writes. "It must constantly manipulate events in order to turn them into 'opportunities.'"[44] By aestheticizing that ceaseless, nonprogressive manipulation, *Some Adventures of Captain Simon Suggs* converts it into a small-scale psychic resource, a resource from which pleasure, but not progress, may be derived. All that "the Captain ever care[s] for" is the prospect of "making a 'raise,' without fear of *immediate* detection," Hooper writes. "So he isn't taken red-handed, after-claps may go to the devil!"[45]

The spirit of Captain Suggs is what I have already called, with Max Weber's *The Protestant Ethic and the Spirit of Capitalism* in mind, the spirit of capitalization. Capitalism, Weber writes, "is identical with the pursuit of profit, and forever *renewed* profit, by means of continuous, rational, capitalistic enterprise."[46] It is, accordingly, "attuned to a regular market."[47] Whenever a regular market is absent, the dominant economic activity is opportunistic profit seeking, or what Weber calls "capitalistic acquisition." Profit seeking of this kind "has been at home in all types of economic societies which have known trade with the use of money and which have offered it opportunities. . . . Likewise the inner attitude of the adventurer, which laughs at all ethical limitations, has been universal."[48] Far from vanishing with the ascendance of the spirit of capitalism, however, the "inner attitude of the adventurer"—the spirit of capitalization—has flourished just beneath it. "In the course even of modern economic history," Weber writes, nonrationalized, unethical capitalistic acquisition has not been "an occasional case, but rather the rule, with continual interruptions from repeated and increasingly powerful conquests of the capitalistic spirit."[49]

It is tempting to imagine that representations of the spirit of capitalization have a critical edge to them. Terence Whalen, for one, argues that Barnum's enterprises have just such an edge, insofar as they expose, through what Whalen calls "capitalist irony," the "illusory or arbitrary nature of [the] entire economic system."[50] In all likelihood, however, many mid-nineteenth-century Americans approached the fictions of capitalism with the same knowingness, the same "sympathy with trick and untruth," with which they approached Barnum's fictions. In all likelihood, that is, many of them were aware of, and capable of enjoying the exposure of, the gap between the continuous, rational, Protestant spirit of capitalism and the discontinuous, wit-based, ethics-mocking spirit of capitalization. It makes little sense, accordingly, to think of the various ethical irregularities in Brown's autobiographical writings as a means of setting himself apart from his readership, either by asserting the distinctiveness of his marginalized identity or by ironizing the logic of the culture at large. We should think of them, instead, as displays of cultural competence, demonstrations of an ability to shift, with the ease of a native speaker, between what Thomas Chandler Haliburton's fictional Yankee, Sam Slick, describes as the "two languages" of mid-nineteenth-century white Americans: "one for strangers," in which respectability is preserved, and "one for ourselves," in which it is not. "*We speak the English language and the American language*," Slick declares. "*You must larn the American language, if you want to understand the American people.*"[51]

So when Brown advises a fugitive to paint himself white, dress himself as a woman in mourning, and board a steamboat bound for Canada; when he talks a conductor into allowing him to pay for a train ticket by the pound, since he has been forced to ride in a freight car; when he tosses his damp bedsheets out the window of an English hotel room and escapes without paying by threatening to report the hotel's poor housekeeping practices to the *London Times*; when he helps a white abolitionist sell a church pew for ten times the amount of the original offer by arranging to have a black family occupy the pew for a few weeks; when he cures a man of his practice of communing with angels in a cemetery by sending the man's Newfoundland dog into the cemetery with a bedsheet sewn around its neck; when he learns the signal for dumping a bag of flour on him outside a church and then gives the signal—"Let it slide!"—just as some antiabolitionists are exiting the building; or when, as a slave, he takes a few sips of the communion wine that he had been charged with bringing to church and then covers up the theft by filling his mouth with sap and squirting it into the bottle, we should not be too quick to assume that he is acting as a trickster, with all of the West African and black-diasporic connotations that that word has acquired.[52] As Ralph Ellison observes in "Change the Joke and Slip the Yoke," the shape-shifting deceptiveness of African Americans is arguably "more 'Yankee' than anything else," growing out of "an ironic awareness of the joke that always lies between appearance and reality" and "perhaps even an awareness of the joke that society is man's creation, not God's."[53] Ever since their declaration of a not-yet-existent nationality, Ellison writes, white Americans have staged a complex "play upon possibility," a play whose animating principle is that whoever "cannot gain authority from tradition may borrow it with a mask."[54] All the while, however, white Americans have remained "absurdly self-deluded over the true interrelatedness of blackness and whiteness," incapable of seeing that in this "land of masking jokers," the jokers are both black and white, and their most profoundly shared territory is the theater of everyday life.[55] By staging, over and over, his own "play upon possibility," Brown is, in a proto-Ellisonian way, enacting that interrelatedness, modeling a black capacity to be in on the great American joke.

The pleasure that Brown is trying to induce at such moments—the Pleasureville that he is trying to evoke and, together with his readers, temporarily occupy—is, as Freud suggests in *Jokes and Their Relation to the Unconscious*, "a means of undoing [a] renunciation."[56] What has been renounced, in this case, are the "possibilities of enjoyment" that derive from open-ended, companionable, conflict-acknowledging styles of attentiveness in encounters between white and black Americans.[57] The jokes in Brown's lectures and writings do not actually bring those encounters into being; the pleasure that they provide is not the pleasure that comes from "the satisfaction of an instinct (whether lustful or hostile) in the face of an obstacle that stands in its way."[58] All that Brown's jokes offer—all they *can* offer—is what the psychoanalytic theorist Adam Phillips describes as "the pleasure to be got from successfully circumventing the obstacle."[59] If we think about jokes as evasions of obstacles, as opposed to attainments of instinctual satisfactions, there is, as Phillips goes on to observe, "an ironic sense in which the search for obstacles is also the search for pleasure."[60] This is, I think, why Brown makes such frequent use of common racial stereotypes: they give him something to circumvent. At times, that circumvention takes the form of an ironic subversion of the original; at other times, the irony is entirely structural, deriving from the edge-to-edge collocation of racist and antiracist blocks of writing. Either way, the energy of racial stereotypes, the obstacles to an enjoyable interracial sociability, is rerouted into antiracist pleasure.

The best example of that process is Brown's incorporation of comic sketches from American newspapers. Here, for instance, is a filler article that appeared under various titles and in slightly different forms in at least ten different newspapers and magazines between 1844 and 1864:

> A jolly old darkey down South bought himself a new hat, and when it commenced raining he put it under his coat. When asked why he did not keep his hat on his head, he replied, "De hat's mine; bought it wid my own money; head belong to massa—let him take keer of his own property."[61]

And here is the version of the anecdote that appears in *My Southern Home*:

> [Cato] was met on the road by Major Ben. O'Fallon, who was riding on horseback, with a hoisted umbrella to keep the rain off. The Major, seeing the negro trudging along bareheaded and with something under his coat, supposing he had stolen some article which he was attempting to hide, said, "What's that you've got under your coat, boy?"
>
> "Nothin', sir, but my hat," replied the slave, and at the same time drawing forth a second-hand beaver.
>
> "Is it yours?" inquired the Major.
>
> "Yes, sir," was the quick response of the negro.
>
> "Well," continued the Major, "if it is yours, why don't you wear it and save your head from the rain?"

> "Oh!" replied the servant, with a smile of seeming satisfaction, "de head belongs to massa an' de hat belongs to me. Let massa take care of his property, an' I'll take care of mine."
> (*C* 726)

In *My Southern Home*, the hidden-hat anecdote is preceded not only by the narrator's observation that "the genuine wit of the negro is often a marvel to the whites" but by a poem, lifted from another newspaper article, that Cato recites, in public, "to the disadvantage of his master": "De big bee flies high, / De little bee makes de honey, / De black man raise de cotton, / An' de white man gets de money" (*C* 724, 726).[62] It is hard not to conclude, accordingly, that Cato—unlike the "jolly old darkey" of the original anecdote—stole the hat and is using the "head belongs to massa" line to cover up the theft. ("'Is it yours?' inquired the Major. 'Yes, sir,' was the quick response of the negro.") The satisfaction at the end of the original anecdote belongs to white readers who like to laugh at made-up black people's nonsensical behavior and illogical reasoning; the "smile of seeming satisfaction" at the end of Brown's version, the glimmering index of improvisational powers, belongs to Cato.

What Brown wants most, at such moments, is to display to white Americans the presence of a modernity-ready wit and enterprise in black Americans. In *Clotel*, before a fictionalized version of the by-the-pound train-ticket story, Brown's narrator writes, "Slavery is a school in which its victims learn much shrewdness, and William had been an apt scholar" (*C* 156). In the autobiographical version of the sap-for-wine anecdote, which appears in *The Black Man*, Brown attributes the idea of spitting the sap into the bottle—at first he had tried pouring it in, but it had spilled over the neck—to the sharpness of his "inventive faculties"; in the fictionalized version in *My Southern Home*, he attributes it to "the fertile imagination of the race" (*C* 700).[63] And when Ike, an emphatically non-Christian slave in *My Southern Home*, volunteers to offer a prayer and then dresses it up with "some poetry on 'Cock Robin,'" his master's response is to "laugh at his adroitness" and praise him for his "wit" (*C* 695). "The fact is," Brown writes elsewhere, "the world likes to see the exhibition of pluck on the part of an oppressed people" and admires "those who come to the surface by their own genius or energies."[64] However counterintuitive it might seem, in the context of our assumptions that antebellum white readers were filled with "anxieties about the rootlessness and fluidity of one's social identity in a new and highly mobile republic of strangers" and that black writers were forced to be models of rectitude, Brown is, in his exhibitions of the spirit of capitalization, always playing to the crowd.[65]

But did he take it too far? On March 11, 1862, the following advertisement appeared on the front page of the *Poughkeepsie Daily Eagle*:

ATTEND!
FUN AND BENEVOLENCE

> The best Lecture, as some think, of the season, by the request of many leading citizens here, will be repeated by a native of the South, in the Universalist Church, on Wednesday Evening, March 12, '62, presenting the humorous side of slavery on a Southern Plantation. The net proceeds will be given to the "Contrabands." Those wishing to laugh and do good at the same time are invited to attend. Admission 15 cents. Those under 12 years of age 10 cents. Bachelors 10 cents, unless attended by a lady. The doors will be open at 6 ½ o'clock. Lecture begins at 7 ½ o'clock. Tickets at the door.[66]

To all appearances, this lecture was not merely presented to its prospective attendees as a source of fun and mode of benevolence; it was actually *entitled* "Fun and Benevolence." Two days later, the *Poughkeepsie Daily Eagle* reported that "the lecture of W. Wells Brown, last evening, at the Universalist Church, on 'Fun and Benevolence,' was well attended and highly applauded by those present, who went home apparently well satisfied with their evening's entertainment."[67] Even if this were not the case, however, even if the lecture were officially entitled, say, "Life at the South" (as several of Brown's other lectures from this period were), the foregrounding of fun—the concentration on "the humorous side of slavery on a Southern Plantation"—is startling. Why, in March 1862, would one of the country's two most famous black abolitionists put on a performance like this?

Part of the answer is supplied by the *Liberator*'s subsequent article on Brown's tour of upstate New York. "He has done a good work in some towns hitherto beyond the reach of the anti-slavery lecturer," reports the writer of the article. "Poughkeepsie, for instance, has always been considered a place where little or no impression could be made in favor of our cause."[68] Long before his arrival in Poughkeepsie, Brown had been of the belief that in order to do "good work" in towns "beyond the reach of the anti-slavery lecturer," one had to go beyond the reach of the typical antislavery lecture. In November 1857, when he was alternating between giving conventional abolitionist lectures and staging one-man performances of his first play, *Experience; or, How to Give a Northern Man a Backbone*, Brown had told a fellow abolitionist that "there are some places where [the play] would take better than a lecture. People will pay to hear the Drama that would not give a cent in an anti-slavery meeting. We had meetings in Hartford last Sunday, and after three speeches, took up *Ninety Five Cents*. On Wednesday Evening I read the Drama in the same place, charged 10 cents at the door, paid $2.00 for the Hall, and had 5.00 over all expenses. Now, this is more than Mrs. Coleman, Mr. Howland and myself have taken up in Collections for the last ten days."[69] A comedy-filled lecture—a lecture that probably resembled both *The Escape* and the early chapters of *My Southern Home*—probably seemed to Brown like the best way of getting an antislavery message to "take" in an antiabolitionist town like Poughkeepsie, particularly with the young, sex-segregated men whom the advertisement identifies as his target audience.[70]

But Brown had a longer-term goal in mind as well. In spite of the fact that making fun of black people was the dominant feature of mid-nineteenth-century American mass entertainment, and in spite of the glaringly obvious connection between making fun of black people and making light of slavery, Brown chose, in Poughkeepsie and elsewhere, not to back away from fun but to push it further. And if we think in the long term as well—if we think about Brown not just as an abolitionist but as an anticolonizationist, a participant in a movement that preceded and extended beyond the 1831–1865 heyday of antislavery, a movement whose aim was to bring into being a social world that black and white subjects could share—that choice makes sense.[71] Although fun can be a crude instrument of exclusion and denigration, it can also be a lightly invested mode of sociability, a fiction-friendly form of experience in which a range of different subjects can participate. The distinction between these two kinds of fun is by no means clean—"making fun of" cannot be securely differentiated from "having fun with"—and the psychosocial effects of contempt-based fun can be horrific.

But there is such a thing as fictionality-based fun, a fun that thrives—to return to Gallagher's formulations—on "flexible mental states," "imaginative play," and a "spirit of 'ironic' assent." This is the kind of fun that Brown attempts to model and induce, often by taking an originally contemptuous anecdote and infusing it with a more inclusively comic spirit.

Take, for example, what he did with the following sketch, which appeared in the *Spirit of the Times*—where much of the best-known work of the Southwestern humorists was first published—in 1852:

> Poor old Sambo was very pious; and as he became stricken in years, and looked upon the world and its surroundings as vanity and vexation of spirit, he flattered himself into the belief that he was willing and anxious to die—unnatural, certainly; but we have the word of a philosopher, that "Imagination breedeth strange fantasies." So he used to sit in his log-hut, after his day's "task" was over, alone, with a tallow-candle flickering upon the ground-floor; and so he used to work himself into his favorite belief. First he sung a hymn, and edified himself with the anticipation that he should
>
> "Walk down the golden street
> With silver slippers on his feet"
>
> and then rocking himself backward and forward, his eyes closed, and his mouth open, he would ejaculate "and repeat:" "Wheneber de angel ob de Lord shall call, poor old Sambo is ready to go!" Now this became commonly known among the younger darkies upon the plantation, who had a grudge against old Sam because he was "a terror to evil-doers." Accordingly, one night a negro wag crept to the door of the hut and waited for old Sam to begin. First came the hymn, and at length, with a sigh and a groan, he began to sway his body, and out it came—"Wheneber de angel ob de Lord shall call, poor old Sambo is ready to go." "Tap, tap, tap!" upon the door.—"Who dar?" shouted Sam, turning his eyes until the whites alone were visible.—"De angel ob de Lord!"—"What do *he* want?" gasped Sambo.—"He come for old Sambo!" was the dreaded reply.—"Phugh!" out went the candle at one puff: "Dar ain't no Sambo here: he's gone dead mor'n tree weeks!" "E'yah! e'yah! e'yah!" shouted a chorus from without.[72]

And here is Brown's version, which appeared in *Miralda* and *Clotelle*:

Uncle Tony . . . took great pride, when he thought that any of the whites were within hearing, to dwell, in his prayer, on his own goodness and the unfitness of others to die. Often was he heard to say, "O Lord, thou knowest that the white folks are not Christians, but the black people are God's own children." But if Tony thought that his old mistress was within the sound of his voice, he launched out into deeper water.

It was, therefore, on a sweet night, when the bright stars were looking out with a joyous sheen, that Mark and two of the other boys passed the greenhouse, and heard Uncle Tony in his devotions.

"Let's have a little fun," said the mischievous Marcus to his young companions. "I will make Uncle Tony believe that I am old mistress, and he'll give us an extra touch in his prayer." Mark immediately commenced talking in a strain of voice resembling, as well as he could, Mrs. Miller, and at once Tony was heard to say in a loud voice, "O Lord, thou knowest that the white people are not fit to die; but, as for old Tony, whenever the angel of the Lord comes, he's ready." At that moment, Mark tapped lightly on the door.

"Who's dar?" thundered old Tony. Mark made no reply. The old man commenced and went through with the same remarks addressed to the Lord, when Mark again knocked at the door. "Who dat dar?" asked Uncle Tony, with a somewhat agitated countenance and trembling voice. Still Mark would not reply. Again Tony took up the thread of his discourse, and said, "O Lord, thou knowest as well as I do that dese white folks are not prepared to die, but here is old Tony, when de angel of de Lord comes, he's ready to go to heaven." Mark once more knocked on the door.

"Who dat dar?" thundered Tony at the top of his voice.

"De angel of de Lord," replied Mark, in a somewhat suppressed and sepulchral voice.

"What de angel of de Lord want here?" inquired Tony, as if much frightened.

"He's come for poor old Tony, to take him out of the world," replied Mark, in the same strange voice.

"Dat nigger ain't here; he die tree weeks ago," responded Tony, in a still more agitated and frightened tone. Mark and his companions made the welkin ring with their shouts at the old man's answer. Uncle Tony hearing them, and finding that he had been imposed upon, opened his door, came out with stick in hand, and said, "Is dat you, Mr. Mark?

you imp, if I can get to you I'll larn you how to come here wid your nonsense."[73]

The difference between the two versions is enormous. It is not just that "poor old Sambo" turns into Uncle Tony, who likes to tell God and anyone who may be listening—especially his mistress—that white folks are hell-bound, or that the nameless "negro wag" becomes the gifted performer Mark, or that Uncle Tony is given the opportunity to rebuke Mark and his companions, or that various racist details, like the reference to the whites of Sambo's eyes, are dropped. It is that Brown takes his time with the details, luxuriating in the experience of storytelling, and that his characters, too, like to overdo things—or, more exactly, overdo themselves. Uncle Tony dwells "on his own goodness and the unfitness of others to die" whenever white people are around and "[launches] out into deeper water" when his mistress is nearby. For the sake of "fun," Mark imitates his mistress's voice, so that Uncle Tony will "give us an extra touch in his prayer," and goes through two cycles of knock-and-response ("again, "still," "again," "once more") before sepulchrally impersonating the angel of the Lord. Both Uncle Tony and Mark are aficionados of the "extra touch," when it comes to self-presentation, which makes the final sequence—Uncle Tony attempting to impose upon the angel of the Lord and then discovering that he himself has been imposed upon by Mark—not an exposure of a humiliating characterological reality, as it is in the original, but a climactic intensification of an apparitional aesthetic, an aesthetic that is shared by Uncle Tony, Mark, the narrator, and maybe even the "bright stars," which look out, the narrator tells us, in language lifted from *The Odd Fellows' Offering* (1854), "with a joyous sheen."[74]

Is it utopian to imagine that an anecdote like this—an anecdote that Brown may very well have used in his Poughkeepsie lecture as an example of "the humorous side of slavery on a Southern Plantation"—might help to transform the conditions of interracial sociability? Absolutely. As Dyer argues, all entertainment is essentially utopian, insofar as it "offers the image of 'something better' to escape into, or something we want deeply that our day-to-day lives don't provide. . . . Entertainment does not, however, present models of utopian worlds. . . . Rather, the utopianism is contained in the feelings it embodies. It presents, head-on as it were, what utopia would feel like rather than how it would be organized."[75] What the literary and theatrical arts are capable of contributing to our lives is the feel of a future world—a sense of how the light might look, how the food might taste, or how we might experience our coexistence in the wake of a transformation to come. "It is with fiction as with religion," Melville observes in *The Confidence-Man*. "It should present another world, and yet one to which we feel the tie."[76] Art's political potential is necessarily utopian in this sense, necessarily a matter of its power to find us where we are and draw us elsewhere, in the direction of a world that can only be known, at present, through desire—a world in which people "dress as nobody exactly dresses, talk as nobody exactly talks, act as nobody exactly acts."[77]

It is worth thinking, in this context, about the following account of Brown's 1860 speech at the anniversary gathering of the American Anti-Slavery Society, a speech in which he convulses the audience, again and again, by talking about his white relatives:

> When referring to the subject of colonization, [Brown] declared that the colored race would not leave this country and go to Africa, or South America, or to New Mexico. (*Applause.*) They had, through the agency of the slaveholders, too much Anglo-Saxon blood in them. He met the other day a friend who had run away about the time he did, and they had a long talk about their white relations at the South. (*Laughter.*) They talked about his cousin William, Minister Plenipotentiary to the Court of Spain [Hon. William Preston.]—(*Roars of laughter.*) That gentleman married his other cousin Fanny. (*Renewed laughter.*) The Wickliffe family were his cousins. (*More laughter.*) Bob died a few months since, said to have been worth about five million dollars. (*Renewed merriment.*) His cousin, Charles A. Wickliffe, was Postmaster under John Tyler. (*Laughter.*) Perhaps they didn't know who John Tyler was, but certainly they would know his cousin Charles. (*Continued laughter.*) He did not look upon these white relations of his with such pleasure as they might think; still they were his relations. (*Laughter.*) Sometimes they found themselves related to those about whom they did not care much. (*Great laughter.*) If they wanted him to leave his white relations, he wouldn't; and he wanted to stay and defend his colored friends, and labor for their emancipation. (*Applause.*)[78]

The first laugh comes when Brown shifts from a declaration of anticolonizationist sentiments to a description of a conversation with a fellow fugitive slave about their white relatives. The laughter increases when Brown gets down to cases: his cousin the diplomat; his cousin's wife, who is also his cousin; his patrician Wickliffe cousins; his cousin Bob, the millionaire; his cousin Charles, the postmaster under Tyler. The laughter rises one last time when Brown lets the audience in on his feelings about those relatives, feelings that he generalizes, philosophically, into a fact of life: "Sometimes they found themselves related to those about whom they did not care much." A quick, applause-inducing segue follows, and the anticolonizationist argument resumes.

It is no coincidence that these riffs on the racial complexity of the American family come in the midst of an attack on the projects of the American Colonization Society. At the heart of colonizationism is the belief that white and black people cannot share a society and a culture. At the heart of Brown's work is the insistence that they can—that, in fact, they already do. Because being free, for Brown, means being free to participate as fully as possible in American society and culture, he tries, here as elsewhere, to evoke an atmosphere in which white and black people can not only recognize one another's rights but take a pleasurable interest in one another's qualities. After surprising his audience into laughter by casually mentioning a conversation about white family members, he apparently decides to see how many times he can get them to laugh by referring to his "relations." (Nine, it turns out.) Every time he gets them to laugh, the psychic obstacle—the stereotype that prevents them from perceiving the fact of relatedness—is circumvented, with a swift, liberating burst. The exposure of the past, present, and future reality of interracial relations occurs in a mode that is itself highly relational, capable of joining very different people in an enjoyable physiological and psychic experience. Antiracism, still so often stereotyped and resisted as "joyless reformism," is, as Brown shows, capable of providing windfalls of psychic pleasure.[79] Although the world that is brought into view by that pleasure—or, more exactly, by the desire to repeat that pleasure—has not yet been brought into existence, we are closer to it now than Brown and his audience were in 1860, at least in part because Brown and other "black culture-nauts" were willing to take the first, risky steps in its direction.[80]

"So anxious are we to see energy, foresight, and perseverance manifested among us," writes the anonymous author of "A Word to Our People" in the September 1859 issue of the *Anglo-African Magazine*, "that we would even hail as welcome, picking and stealing energy, robbing and cheating energy, anything energy—but let us have force."[81] "Anything energy" may be, in the end, the best description of what Brown hopes to project and communicate to his audiences. "A young man once asked Carlyle, what was the secret of success," Brown writes in *The American Fugitive in Europe*.

> His reply was, "Energy: whatever you undertake, do it with all your might." Had it not been for the possession of energy, I might now have been working as a servant for some brainless fellow who might be able to command my labour with his money, or I might have been yet toiling in chains and slavery. But thanks to energy, not only for my being today in a land of freedom, but also for my dear girls being in one of the best Seminaries in France.
>
> (*C* 342)

Energy of this kind, energy considered apart from any definite source or aim, is an index, for Brown, of virtuality, a capacity to be or do otherwise. As the mark of the potentialized self, without fixed properties, "anything energy" swims against the cultural stream of stereotypes, the seemingly endless images and descriptions of depotentialized others, stuck with their inherited traits. It is the spirit of "nobody exactly," the spirit of fictionality, the spirit of capitalization. It is not inherently beneficent; it can underwrite exploitation just as easily as it can undermine authority. It is, however, the presiding spirit of modern times, Brown's as well as our own; it may even be, as the feminist philosopher Elizabeth Grosz suggests, the spirit of life itself: a "joyous excess or superfluousness of inner force."[82] By channeling his energies into the production of extra touches, trick and untruth, a surplus of appearance—by choosing to become, like Barnum, a "caterer of amusements"—Brown makes himself vulnerable to a wide range of moral, socioeconomic, cultural, and aesthetic critiques.[83] He also, however, makes available to us a generative awareness of our "versionality," our "ruthless capacity for self and/or other reinvention."[84] Maybe, he suggests, we don't always have to "*feel right*," in Stowe's famous phrase, to make the world a better place.[85] Maybe, sometimes, we just have to be willing to let ourselves feel good.

CHAPTER

THREE

The Aesthetic of Attractions

The reporter for the *New York Herald* who entered the Minerva Rooms on an unusually cold and rainy afternoon in May 1849 encountered a "gloomy and melancholy looking spectacle":

> Seated on benches, one rising above another, were about one hundred individuals, of both sexes, and of all ages, colors, and classes of society, talking in a low voice about abolition, Texas, New Mexico, John C. Calhoun, John Quincy Adams, Daniel Webster, and a variety of other persons and matters connected remotely or intimately with slavery or the abolition of slavery in this hemisphere. The gloom which prevailed out of doors, in consequence of the dismal weather, seemed to have followed those composing the assemblage; and unlike the rain which poured from their umbrellas, and meandered in miniature rivulets from every comer, it seemed to have unfavorably connected itself with everyone present.[1]

Ordinarily, the spectacles in the Minerva Rooms, a recently opened venue on the corner of Broadway and Grand Street, were of a different type. In the previous three years, this "humble place of amusement" had hosted, among other things, minstrel shows, song-and-dance performances by albino children, concerts by blind people, the exhibition of the Grand Panorama of Taylor's Campaigns in Mexico, and the display of a miniature replica of Manhattan and Brooklyn.[2] On this occasion, however, it was the location of the annual meeting of the American Anti-Slavery Society, a meeting that was, for now, mostly focused on nominations, elections, reports, and complaints about the lack of heat. At one point, at the urging of Lucretia Mott, Wendell Phillips left the stage in search of someone who might be able to "make a fire for the comfort of the audience." Eventually, "it got so dark that our reporter could not see, and his fingers so benumbed that he could not write," and he "was compelled, in self defence, to adjourn."[3]

That evening, the reporter returned. The room "was, if anything, cooler and more unpleasant than it was in the afternoon." A diffuse, low-energy discussion of a variety of topics was underway. Suddenly, the reporter writes, the conversation was "interrupted by a hemming and coughing emanating from one end of the room, a tolerably good indication that somebody was going to sing. In a moment or two the indications ceased, and our friend Brown . . . gave vent to his inspirations, and entertained the company with [a] song."[4] To the tune of "Auld Lang Syne," William Wells Brown sang the following verses, which he appears to have composed:

Fling out the Anti-Slavery flag
On every swelling breeze;
And let its folds wave o'er the land,
And o'er the raging seas,
Till all beneath the standard sheet,
With new allegiance bow;
And pledge themselves to onward bear
The emblem of their vow.

Fling out the Anti-Slavery flag,
And let it onward wave
Till it shall float o'er every clime,
And liberate the slave;
Till, like a meteor flashing far,
It bursts with glorious light,
And with its Heaven-born rays dispels
The gloom of sorrow's night.

Fling out the Anti-Slavery flag,
And let it not be furled,
Till like a planet of the skies,

It sweeps around the world.
And when each poor degraded slave,
Is gathered near and far;
O, fix it on the azure arch,
As hope's eternal star.

Fling out the Anti-Slavery flag,
Forever let it be
The emblem to a holy cause,
The banner of the free.
And never from its guardian height,
Let it by man be driven,
But let it float forever there,
Beneath the smiles of heaven.

That seemed to get things going. Parker Pillsbury, "one of the big guns of the cause," gave a blistering speech on "the church system of the present day," in the midst of which he verbally wrangled with audience members who were offended by his assertion that Trinity Church, on the corner of Broadway and Wall Street, would be "a fine ruin before two hundred years."[5] Lucy Stone, described by a contemporary as "a little meek-looking Quakerish body, with the sweetest, modest manners and yet as unshrinking and self-possessed as a loaded cannon," assailed the church with only slightly less vehemence for its toleration of slavery.[6] And then Brown stood up again. Here is part of the reporter's account of the speech he gave:

> He said he appeared before them . . . not only as a refugee slave, but also as the son of a slave-holder. Indeed it has been asserted, that he is related to the present President of the United States, but however that may be, or however related he may be to the slaveholders, by the tenderest ties of blood, he would not on that account refrain from saying what he experienced of the horrors of slavery. The gashes which he bears on his back have made too great an impression on him to allow his doing so. He then said he would read a few choice gems from the St. Louis *Republican*.
>
> VOICE—Have you got the paper?
>
> No, but it is edited by a Mr. Charles, whom I knew very well, for I worked for him, and he whipped me like smoke. (Laughter.) The impressions

> which he made on my back, have made an impression of him on my memory. Much has been said against the church, but if it did not aid, and abet, and promote slavery, no attack would be made upon it. The abolitionists are called infidels, but give him the infidelity of the abolitionists, which knocks the fetters from the slave, in preference to the Christianity of the church, which fastens them on his limbs. (Applause.) Go to the South—see Theological Institutes selling slaves, and breeding slaves, for the purpose of raising funds wherewith to make ministers. When I lived down South, and my master—and here let me give you a description of my old master, for he made an impression on me which I would like to make upon you—he was a whining, praying, complaining, psalm-singing man, who ordered me, every evening at nine o'clock, to go down to the "niggers," and call them to prayers. (Laughter.) Every night he called them in, and the influence which the master had, in putting them all asleep, by prayer, was remarkable. He possessed a magnetic power, which [La Roy] Sunderland could not touch. (Laughter.) Well, Saturday was always fixed for reading the Bible, and at every verse he would tell the niggers to ask him the meaning of any passage which they did not understand. He was extremely proud of being asked; for he was proud of being thought an expounder of the Bible. Well, he never asked him the explanation of any passage but once, and then he applied to him to know the meaning of that passage of scripture "Whatever he would that others would do unto you, you do to them?" "Why," said he, "Where did you hear that? I never read it to you." (Laughter.) "I got it in the city," I replied. "Just like the City," said he; "You can never send a servant to the city, but he is spoiled." (Renewed laughter.) "Now, mind you, Sambo," said he, "I'll explain this to you, but never ask me such a question again." (Roars of laughter.)

After "continu[ing] in this strain for some minutes longer," Brown sang another song, "The Fugitive Slave to the Christian," and sat down to "loud cheering."[7]

Most antislavery speeches did not overlap quite so obviously with prevailing modes of popular entertainment. In general, as the historian W. Caleb McDaniel has observed, abolitionists preferred "sane and decent" public events, in which the speeches were earnest and the audiences were, relatively speaking, quiet.[8] At a time when American spectatorship was mostly a loud, rowdy affair, speeches that promoted cascading laughter broke down the distinctions between abolitionist meetings and other kinds of public events, including the kinds that were usually held at the Minerva Rooms. For abolitionists who saw decorum as a crucial element of their strategy, a way of fending off the association of antislavery with radical excess, any blurring of the line between moral suasion and theatrical exhibition was, to say the least, counterproductive.

But Brown saw things differently. In the above instance, he seems to have tailored his speech to the audience in front of him, an audience that contained, as Pillsbury observed during his speech that evening, an unusually large number of young men from the ranks of "those who earned their daily bread by the sweat of their brow."[9] After warming them up with joking banter and the germ of a tall tale about his relationship to President Zachary Taylor—in *The Black Man*, he would declare himself to be a descendent of Daniel Boone—Brown shifts to a more standard mode, announcing that he will read some documents of slavery's barbarism. Challenged on the authenticity of what he is about to read, he chooses not to get into a confrontation, as Pillsbury had; instead, he simply changes the subject. Then, in the midst of a denunciation of the church's support of slavery, he abruptly shifts modes again: "When I lived down South, and my master—and here let me give you a description of my old master, for he made an impression on me which I would like to make upon you." The anecdote that he goes on to tell is nominally related to the subject of Christianity and slaveholding, but it is told primarily, if not entirely, for the sake of the pleasure that he intends it to provide. Earlier in the day, Pillsbury had speculated, after visually canvassing the audience, that a "great many present have no doubt attended . . . for amusement's sake, as they would a theatrical exhibition."[10] That evening, Brown evidently reached the same conclusion, and decided, mid-speech, to give the people what they seemed to want.[11]

Two weeks later, the abolitionist Samuel May Jr., who had attended the New York meeting, expressed his misgivings about Brown's methods in a letter to the British abolitionist John Bishop Estlin. "He is a very good fellow, of very fair abilities, and has been quite true to the cause," May wrote. "But he likes to make popular and taking speeches, and keeps a careful eye on his benefit. The Anti-Slavery cause has been everything to him, in point of elevating and educating him; and giving him a respectable position, etc. He owes much to it and he ought to be true to it."[12] In 1851, after William and Ellen Craft had joined Brown on the lecture circuit in

England, Estlin gave voice to similar qualms. "We have been endeavouring to improve the tone of Brown and Crafts Exhibition[,] altering their too *showman like* hand bills," he wrote to May. "Some of their hand-bills have been headed 'Arrival of 3 Fugitive Slaves from America'!!! as if 3 monkeys had been imported, and their public appearance has been too often of the *exhibitive* kind. Neither B. nor, of course Craft, was quite *up* to the sort of position they ought to take."[13] In the most general sense, what May and Estlin are reacting against is the presence of the spirit of capitalization, a spirit that is, as far as they are concerned, incompatible with the cause. More specifically, however, they are reacting against the way in which that aliveness to opportunity leads, in the context of public performance, to showman-like behavior. To make "popular and taking speeches," one has to keep a careful eye not only on one's own benefit but also on the faces of the listeners. To pull in a large number of listeners, moreover, one has to present oneself in "*exhibitive*" ways. Adjusting oneself to the varying composition and changing temper of one's audiences is not, for May, being true to the cause; advertising yourself in exclamatory, come-one-come-all ways is not, for Estlin, being "*up*" to the demands of respectability.

In the previous chapter, I argued that fun, in Brown's work, is a pluralization of fictionality, a shared experience of imaginative flexibility. Having fun is, or can be, a way of actively experiencing our relatedness not on the basis of an a priori philosophical or theological conviction but on the basis of an apparitional aesthetic, a taste for states of being in which, as Wallace Stevens puts it, "you yourself were never quite yourself / And did not want nor have to be."[14] What I will argue in this chapter is that this apparitional aesthetic is inseparable, in Brown's case, from what Tom Gunning, referring primarily but not exclusively to early cinema, calls "the aesthetic of attractions."[15] In the Minerva Rooms lecture, Brown does not just capitalize on opportunities for fun; he shifts between performative modes in a way that both corresponds to a wide range of mid-nineteenth-century cultural practices and anticipates future developments. Everywhere in his work, in fact, the dominant structural aesthetic is attractional, typified by, in Gunning's words, a

> drive towards display, rather than creation of a fictional world; a tendency towards punctual temporality, rather than extended development; a lack of interest in character "psychology" or the development of motivation;

> and a direct, often marked, address to the spectator at the expense of the creation of a diegetic coherence . . . along with [an] ability to be attention-grabbing (usually by being exotic, unusual, unexpected, novel).[16]

If we go looking in Brown's works for a coherent fictional world, credibly motivated characters, and extended narrative development, we are doomed to disappointment. But if we go looking, instead, for the exhibitive, and if we think about the showman-like presentation of "noncontinuous suites of tableaux" as the manifestation of a broadly shared and historically significant aesthetic, we will be capable not only of appreciating Brown's works on their own terms but of understanding more clearly why plagiarism appealed to him.[17] By studding his pages with fragments of secondhand writing and doing next to nothing to smooth the transitions between that writing and his own, he generated works that are bound neither to a singular voice nor to a sustained feeling, works that do not give rise to a fully realized, finished imaginative world. Out of the bric-a-brac of the past and the opportunities of the present, he generated works that keep faith, instead, with everything "ephemeral, fugitive, contingent upon the occasion": the view from a train window, a walk down a city street, a night at the theater, a day in a bazaar, the exhibition of a panorama, the rapidly scanned faces of an expectant crowd.[18]

Clotel is a "catalogue of excesses": "exploding steamboats, persevering packs of dogs, violated bodies, insurrections, conflagrations, pestilences."[19] *The Escape* "operates through a piling-up method," successively representing, in distorted form, "the already distorted qualities of the characters or types through which slavery was represented: the wicked mistress, the lascivious master, the ignorant field hands, the duplicitous house servant, the tragic mulatta, the heroic slave, the heartless and uncouth slave trader."[20] *My Southern Home* is a "loosely organized succession" of "high jinx played by slaves on masters, minstrel scenes of slaves vying with one another for status, outlandish displays of racist preaching, high stakes riverboat gambling, traditional African dancing in New Orleans' Congo Square, corn husking by night, Emancipation Day observed in a South Carolina slave cabin."[21]

The list—both of Brown's narrative elements and of Brown's critics' descriptions of those elements—could go on. For something other than a neutral or negative aesthetic response to this aspect of Brown's work, however, we have to go back to the nineteenth century. "On Monday evening a large audience assembled to hear Mr. Brown recite his Anti-Slavery Drama, 'Experience or how to give a Northern Man Backbone,'" writes a reporter for the *Anti-Slavery Bugle* in February 1857. "It is truly an amusing performance—happily conceived and successfully executed. The audience testified of their enjoyment by frequent and hearty applause. The continually shifting and changing scenes—thrilling incidents—wit and humor and the animation of the speaker relieve the mind of all monotony."[22] A reporter for the *Vergennes* (Vt.) *Citizen* similarly observes that once Brown "warms up with the theme" of a lecture, "you lose sight of the speaker, and flashes of wit and sparkling gems of thought, scattered with rapidity and force, convince you that no ordinary man is swaying the feelings of a deeply interested and breathless auditory."[23] The helter-skelter feel of Brown's work—the shifting and changing scenes, the scatterings of wit and thought—is, for these respondents, desirable, a means of "reliev[ing] the mind of all monotony."[24] In place of an autobiographical subject and a conventional narrative form, Brown offers his audiences an array of special effects, not because he was incapable of doing anything else but because, as he knew very well, that's the way they liked it.

It was the way they liked it all century long, in fact, on both sides of the Atlantic and in both theatrical and quasi-theatrical venues. In the theater, the historian Robert Lewis writes, a

> typical evening's bill consisted of a play, usually abridged, and a comic after-piece, with orchestral music. . . . The melodramas that were a third of all plays performed at mid-century contained the most diverse elements. They were often vehicles for startling special effects, when stage managers conjured up sensational fires, waterfalls, volcanoes, or shipwrecks, or introduced horses, dogs, even an elephant. Entr'acte entertainment before and after the play included ventriloquists, magicians, jugglers, acrobats, dancers, minstrels, comedians, and singers of every description.[25]

"The theatre survives for other purposes than the representation of the drama," declares the author of an 1854 *Putnam's Monthly* article on "Places of Public Amusement." "Tableaux, burlesques, thrilling melo-dramas, ballets, spectacles, horses, dwarfs, giants, rope-dancers, any thing that is monstrous and wonderful, form now the great attractions of the theaters, and any thing is considered as 'legitimate' by the public, which affords amusement, and as proper, by the manager, which fills his house." Even the lecture room, the writer goes on to say, "has now become a kind of compromise between the theatre and the Church; it is a neutral ground, upon which all parties and conditions may, and do meet, and the peripatetic star lecturer occupies nearly the same position which Roscius did in the early days of the stage."[26] It is not just that mid-nineteenth-century audiences had a taste for the apparitional, for the kind of ramped-up fictionality that I discussed in the last chapter. It is that they had a taste for the *serially* apparitional, for non-narrative exhibitions of the "monstrous and wonderful," for a multiplicity and variety of "shows."

In the lecture room, where one couldn't exactly bring in a waterfall or an elephant, that aesthetic often gave rise to a high-speed sampling of rhetorical modes. Here, for instance, is the poet/journalist George Washington Bungay's account of an 1847 lecture in Boston's Tremont Temple by the temperance activist Philip S. White:

> There is a resurrection now among the bowed heads; he has just made a thrilling appeal, which moved the audience like a shock from an electric battery. Now he relates a tale of pity, which is drawing tears from eyes "unused to weep." Now he surprises his attentive hearers with an unanticipated stroke of humor, which makes them laugh until they shake the tear-drops from their cheeks. . . . He throws light on the question by the coruscations of his attic wit; drives home a truth by solid argument, and clinches it by a quotation from Scripture; convulses the auditory by using a ludicrous comparison; convinces them by presenting sober-faced statistics; entertains them by relating an appropriate anecdote, and fires their indignation against the traffic, while the rumdealers present shake in their shoes.[27]

Shock, sentiment, humor, wit, argument, allusions, nonsense, statistics, anecdotes, and anathemas: who could ask for anything more? Not Bungay, who declares that White's "sparkling satire, keen wit, eloquent declamation, happy comparisons, classical allusions, rib-cracking fun, and heart-melting pathos, render him one of the most efficient public speakers in America."[28] Like the reviewers of Brown's performances, Bungay positively desires these kinds of whipsawings, which simultaneously create an impression of novelty and return, anaphorically, to the slot into which everything in the speech is inserted, the slot marked "and now for something completely different."

Brown, who would incorporate much of the above passage into *The Rising Son*, responded to the presence of that desire in several different ways.[29] In relatively informal settings, like the Minerva Rooms, and in front of largely male, working-class audiences, he tended to sing, detour into comic anecdotes, and punctuate his arguments with documentary evidence. On more formal occasions, he tended to shift, in addition, into sentimental, literary, and declamatory modes. In May 1862, for example, at an American Anti-Slavery Society gathering in New York City's Church of the Puritans, he begins by referring to the surprise that some white Americans had felt when slaves ran across lines to the Union Army. "Why should you have supposed for a moment," he asks, "that, because a man's color differs a little from yours, he is better contented to remain a slave than you would be, or that he has no inclination, no wish, to escape from the thraldom that holds him so tight? What is it that does not wish to be free?"[30] He then quotes from "Give Me Freedom," a poem that had appeared, among other places, in Samuel Brooke's *Slavery and the Slave-Holder's Religion*:

> Go, let a cage with grates of gold,
> And pearly roof, the eagle hold;
> Let dainty viands be its fare,
> And give the captive tenderest care;
> But say, in luxury's limits pent,
> Find you the king of birds content?
> No; oft he'll sound the startling shriek,
> And dash the cage with angry beak:
> Precarious freedom's far more dear
> Than all the prison's pampering cheer.[31]

To intensify the effect of the poem, he injects a slightly altered version of Brooke's commentary on it:

> As with the eagle, so with man. He loves to look upon the bright day and the stormy night; to gaze upon the broad free ocean, its eternal surging tides, its mountain billows and its foam-crested waves; to tread the steep

> mountain side; to sail upon the placid river; to wander along the gurgling stream; to trace the sunny slope, the beautiful landscape, the majestic forest, the flowery meadow; to listen to the howling of the winds and the music of the birds. These are the aspirations of man, without regard to country, clime, or color. (Loud applause.)
> (*C* 948)[32]

Effect created, applause received, the attraction vanishes, to be replaced by the original topic of the speech: "What shall we do with the slave of the South?" After a thumping itemization of what the American slave has done for the world—"He has cleared up the swamps of the South, and has put the soil under cultivation; he has built up her towns and cities and villages; he has enriched the North and Europe with his cotton and sugar and rice"—Brown rises to a crowd-pleasing formulation: "The slave has shown himself better fitted to take care of himself than the slaveholder. (Renewed applause.)" The applause seems to inspire him to rise further: "He is the bone and sinew of the South; he is the producer, while the master is nothing but a consumer, and a very poor consumer at that. (Laughter)" (*C* 948). Shortly thereafter, he repeats the process. First, a climactic rhetorical formulation: "I do not expect the slave of the South to jump into equality; all I claim for him is, that he may be allowed to jump into liberty, and let him make equality for himself. (Loud applause.)" Then, a comic amplification: "I have got some white neighbors around me; they are not very intellectual; they don't associate with my family (laughter and applause); but whenever they shall improve themselves, and bring themselves up by their own intellectual and moral worth, I shall not object to their coming into my society. (Renewed merriment)" (*C* 949). Finally, after insisting that "the time has come" for emancipation, Brown offers up a stanza of a poem and sits back down, to "loud and prolonged applause" (*C* 952).

Modal transitions of this kind may be found just about everywhere in Brown's published work. In *Clotel*, most obviously, Brown repeatedly switches from plain-spoken, informational language into high-cultural declamations, sentimental apostrophes, comic dialogues, or finely detailed descriptions and then, as if nothing has happened, switches back. On many occasions, these switches occur at the juncture between plagiarized and original writing, as in the following passage, in which the plagiarized sections—extracted from Garrison's *Address Delivered Before the Free*

People of Color and James Montgomery's *Gleanings from Pious Authors*—are italicized:

> Mrs. Carlton was urged by her friends to send the emancipated negroes to Africa. . . . Some thought they should be sent away because the blacks are vicious; others because they would be missionaries to their brethren in Africa. "But," said she, "*if we send away the negroes because they are profligate and vicious, what sort of missionaries will they make? Why not send away the vicious among the whites for the same reason, and the same purpose?*"
>
> Death is a leveller, and neither age, sex, wealth, nor usefulness can avert when he is permitted to strike. *The most beautiful flowers soon fade, and droop, and die; this is also the case with man; his days are uncertain as the passing breeze. This hour he glows in the blush of health and vigour, but the next he may be counted with the number no more known on earth.*[33]
>
> (*C* 168)

Here is another example, decked out with plagiarized passages from Theodore Weld's *Slavery as It Is* and a newspaper article about the Dismal Swamp:

> "The kindness meted out to blacks would be unkindness if given to whites. We would think so, should we not?" "Yes," replied [Carlton]. "If we would not consider the best treatment which a slave receives good enough for us, we should not think he ought to be grateful for it. Everybody knows that slavery in its best and mildest form is wrong. *Whoever denies this, his lips libel his heart. Try him! Clank the chains in his ears, and tell him they are for him; give him an hour to prepare his wife and children for a life of slavery; bid him make haste, and get ready their necks for the yoke, and their wrists for the coffle chains; then look at his pale lips and trembling knees, and you have nature's testimony against slavery.*"
>
> "Let's take a walk," said Carlton, as if to turn the conversation. The moon was just appearing through the tops of the trees, and the animals and insects in an adjoining wood kept up a continued din of music. *The*

> *croaking of bull-frogs, buzzing of insects, cooing of turtle-doves, and the sound from a thousand musical instruments, pitched on as many different keys, made the welkin ring.*[34]
> (*C* 137)

In each of these cases, Brown uses the plagiarized passages not only to change up the discursive mode but also to slow down the forward movement of the narrative. The sentences that I have italicized protrude from *Clotel*'s discursive plane, calling attention to their difference from the sentences around them while contributing little or nothing to the development of character or plot. That suspension of narrative progress is even more obvious, and even more puzzling to many contemporary readers, in a series of plagiarized inserts that are too long to reproduce here, including the bloodhound hunt in chapter 3, the pugnacious speech by Henry Morton in chapter 20, and the contrasting of the Pilgrims and the Jamestown colonists in chapter 21. By filling *Clotel* with passages like these, passages that break up the narrative in flamboyantly exhibitionist ways, Brown works against what Gunning calls "the tradition of contemplative subjectivity."[35] Brown doesn't jettison narrative entirely, of course, but he does offer, by means of his "periodic doses of non-narrative spectacle"—the analogues of gags in slapstick and song-and-dance numbers in musicals—another "configuration of spectatorial involvement," another way of being present as a reader.[36]

Nowhere is that interruptive dimension of *Clotel* more fully on display than in chapter 22, "A Ride in a Stage-Coach." If we exclude the opening and concluding paragraphs, retain the set-ups, and merely note the insertion points of the "gags" and "numbers," the chapter, which occupies twelve of the first edition's 245 pages (*C* 171–177), reads as follows:

> A ride in a stage-coach, over an American road, is unpleasant under the most favourable circumstances. But now that it was winter, and the roads unusually bad, the journey was still more dreary. However, there were eight passengers in the coach, and I need scarcely say that such a number of genuine Americans could not be together without whiling away the time somewhat pleasantly. Besides Clotel, there was an elderly gentleman with his two daughters—one apparently under twenty years, the other a

shade above. The pale, spectacled face of another slim, tall man, with a white neckerchief, pointed him out as a minister. The rough featured, dark countenance of a stout looking man, with a white hat on one side of his head, told that he was from the sunny South. There was nothing remarkable about the other two, who might pass for ordinary American gentlemen.

(gag)[37]

After a hearty laugh in which all joined, the subject of Temperance became the theme for discussion. In this the spectacled gent. was at home. He soon showed that he was a New Englander, and went the whole length of the "Maine Law." The minister was about having it all his own way, when the Southerner, in the white hat, took the opposite side of the question. "I don't bet a red cent on these teetotlars," said he, and at the same time looking round to see if he had the approbation of the rest of the company. "Why?" asked the minister. "Because they are a set who are afraid to spend a cent. They are a bad lot, the whole on 'em." It was evident that the white hat gent. was an uneducated man. The minister commenced in full earnest, and gave an interesting account of the progress of temperance in Connecticut, the state from which he came, proving, that a great portion of the prosperity of the state was attributable to the disuse of intoxicating drinks. Every one thought the white hat had got the worst of the argument, and that he was settled for the remainder of the night. But not he; he took fresh courage and began again.

(number)[38]

This narrative, given by the white hat man, was received with unbounded applause by all except the pale gent. in spectacles, who showed, by the way in which he was running his fingers between his cravat and throat, that he did not intend to "give it up so." The white hat gent. was now the lion of the company.

"Oh, you did not get hold of the right kind of teetotallers," said the minister. "I can give you a tale worth a dozen of yours," continued he.

(number)[39]

> "But you talk too fast," replied the white hat man. "You don't give a feller a chance to say nothin'." "I heard you," continued the minister, "and now you hear me out."
>
> (number)[40]
>
> This turned the joke upon the advocate of strong drink, and he began to put his wits to work for arguments. "You are from Connecticut, are you?" asked the Southerner. "Yes, and we are an orderly, pious, peaceable people. Our holy religion is respected, and we do more for the cause of Christ than the whole Southern States put together." "I don't doubt it," said the white hat gent.
>
> (number)[41]
>
> This last speech of the rough featured man again put him in the ascendant, and the spectacled gent. once more ran his fingers between his cravat and throat. "You live in Tennessee, I think," said the minister. "Yes," replied the Southerner, "I used to live in Orleans, but now I claim to be a Tennessean." "You people of New Orleans are the most ungodly set in the United States," said the minister.
>
> (number)[42]

None of these interchanges involve the main characters—Clotel, who is disguised as a white man, is being flirted with, all this time, by the teenaged sisters—and none of it affects the plot. At no point, moreover, is there a reference to race or slavery. It is, as Hurston writes of the porch talk in *Their Eyes Were Watching God*, "a contest in hyperbole and carried on for no other reason."[43] Without any accumulation of narrative or thematic tension, there is no progression toward climax, no crystallization of meaning, no reward for close reading. There is only a ride in the company of evanescent caricatures, diversified by attractions—several of them imported from elsewhere—and ending with the phrase, "the coach again resumed its journey" (*C* 179).[44]

As I indicated earlier in this chapter, Brown's critics don't much like—or, at least, don't often confess to liking—these kinds of nonteleological structures. They do, however, tend to believe that they have a subversive political significance. According to John Ernest, Brown is a "cultural editor" who "draw[s] from the materials of the culture and . . . rearrang[es] those materials in a revealing demonstration of cultural contradictoriness and tension"; according to M. Giuliana Fabi, Brown's refusal to "impose any fictional order or sense of progression" on his materials "oblig[es] the reader to experience the incoherence and displacement that [he] sees as central to slave life"; according to Eve Allegra Raimon, the "complex assortment of seemingly disparate textual elements" in *Clotel* contributes to a "proto-postmodern" critique of "established social categories."[45] At the heart of all such arguments is the assumption that form follows conviction, that Brown's compositional practices are aligned with his political commitments. But political radicals are not necessarily formal radicals, and the implications of the forms they choose do not necessarily correspond with the aims of the movements to which they belong. In "A Ride in a Stage-Coach," for instance, Brown is not exposing "national disjunction and dramatiz[ing] the fractures in the American mythic narrative."[46] He is, instead, converting stark antagonisms into structurally equivalent occasions for striking effects. Instead of showing a Northerner and a Southerner in bitter conflict, he shows them "whiling away the time somewhat pleasantly," taking up roles for the sake of taking up roles, which is, he tells us, what all "genuine Americans" in stagecoaches do (*C* 171).

That is not to say, of course, that Brown never actually denounces slavery and racism. It is simply to say that this is not all that he does—or, more precisely, that the attractional structure of his work affects those denunciations in ways that we have not yet recognized. Attractions have, in Gunning's words, "one basic temporality, that of the alternation of presence/absence which is embodied in the act of display. In this intense form of the present tense the attraction is displayed with the immediacy of a 'Here it is! Look at it.' "[47] An attraction is, accordingly, experienced

> as a temporal irruption rather than a temporal development. While every attraction would have a temporal unfolding of its own and some (a complex acrobatic act, for instance, or an action with a clear trajectory, such as an onrushing train) might cause viewers to develop expectations while watching them, these temporal developments would be secondary to the sudden appearance and then disappearance of the view itself.[48]

If we locate Brown's works in the context of what Gunning describes as "the illusionistic arts of the nineteenth century"—if we think about the nineteenth century as "a period of intense development in visual entertainments . . . in which realism was valued largely for its uncanny effects"—then a book like *Clotel* appears before us less as a vehicle for abolitionist discourse than as a vehicle for attractions, abolitionist and otherwise.[49] Abolitionist attractions—such as the chapter-length excerpts from Lydia Maria Child's "The Quadroons" and the uncredited samplings of speeches by Garrison, Sarah Grimké, and Thaddeus Stevens—and nonabolitionist attractions—such as the hit-and-run sentimentalism of the passages lifted from "The Mother," "A Peep Into an Italian Interior," and Helen de Kroyft's *A Place in Thy Memory*—occupy the same narrative slot. "*Any* lecture of mine," Mark Twain writes in an 1871 letter, "ought to be a running narrative-plank, with square holes in it, six inches apart, all the length of it, and then in my mental shop I ought to have plugs (half marked 'serious' and the others marked 'humorous') to select from and jam into their holes, according to the temper of the audiences."[50] All that needs to be added to Twain's comment to make it applicable to Brown is that there is really only one hole, that it can be made to appear at any point, and that there are more than two types of plugs out there.

The politics of the antislavery discourse in *Clotel* are, accordingly, not as clear-cut as one might imagine. Again and again, the narrator and characters like Georgiana Carlton and Henry Morton say, often in other people's words, abolitionist things. But because they say those things in the midst of a herky-jerky, variety-show-style narrative, their mini-speeches tend to function less as symbols, in Charles Sanders Peirce's terminology, than as indices—less as transparent communications of convictions than as "sayings," effect-oriented flourishes, that draw our attention to the illusionistic arts that have produced them. Here are the opening sentences of two of these oratorical bursts, drawn, respectively, from speeches by James McDowell and Alvan Stewart:

> "Yes, yes," answered Georgiana: "you may place the slave where you please; you may dry up to your utmost the fountains of his feelings, the springs of his thought; you may yoke him to your labour, as an ox which liveth only to work, and worketh only to live; you may put him under any process which, without destroying his value as a slave, will debase and

> crush him as a rational being; you may do this, and *the idea that he was born to be free will survive it all.*"
> (*C* 139; emphasis in original)

> On the last day of November, 1620, on the confines of the Grand Bank of Newfoundland, lo! we behold one little solitary tempest-tost and weatherbeaten ship; it is all that can be seen on the length and breadth of the vast intervening solitudes, from the melancholy wilds of Labrador and New England's iron-bound shores, to the western coasts of Ireland and the rock-defended Hebrides, but one lonely ship greets the eye of angels or of men, on this great thoroughfare of nations in our age.
> (*C* 165)

By means of set-pieces like these—set-pieces that refer, campily, to their own status as set-pieces—Brown solicits, in Gunning's words, his audience's "awareness of (and delight in) [his] illusionistic capabilities."[51] However impeccably abolitionist his statements may be, the way in which he makes them—or remakes them—owes less to the protocols of antislavery discourse than to the manifestations, all around him, of the aesthetic of attractions.

Clotel is, in this sense, part of what Walter Benjamin describes as the "phantasmagoria" of modern life.[52] Among its relatives are the arcades of Paris, which Brown saw during his visit to the city in 1849; the Crystal Palace, to which he devoted two chapters in *Three Years in Europe*; and the panoramas and magic lantern shows that he both saw and displayed.[53] The essential feature of all such cultural phenomena is, as Wolfgang Schivelbusch observes, montage, which enables one to perceive "in immediate succession objects and pieces of scenery that in their original spatiality belonged to separate realms."[54] The items for sale in the glassed-over arcades, the industrial products on display in the glassed-in Crystal Palace, and the images in moving panoramas all acquire, by means of this technique, a quintessentially modern desirability, a desirability inseparable from the light-bathed representational spaces in which they have been arrayed.[55] Although mid-nineteenth-century writers could not draw on the seductiveness of color, glass, and light, they could—and did—seize on literary or rhetorical means of creating attractions and modernity-specific modes of juxtaposing and displaying them. The rapid modal swerving of Fanny Fern's *Ruth Hall*; the "hurry-graphs" of her brother, Nathaniel Parker

Willis; the startlingly elliptical sentences of Elizabeth Stoddard's *The Morgesons*; the show-stopping insanity of the "Governor Pyncheon" chapter in Hawthorne's *The House of the Seven Gables*; the "intellectual chowder," as Evert Duyckinck called it, of *Moby-Dick*—all of it participated, along with *Clotel*, in the mid-nineteenth-century expansion of consumerist space and the emergence of cinematic time.[56]

On the one hand, then, the now-you-see-it-now-you-don't structure of *Clotel* at least partially derealizes many of its abolitionist statements. On the other hand, by "commencing with the consideration of an *effect*," as Poe puts it in "The Philosophy of Composition," Brown infuses those statements with the vital, volatile spirit of modernity.[57] Abolitionists always ran the risk, Robert Fanuzzi reminds us, of seeming "irrelevant, out-of-step, and incongruous with the freewheeling, fractious public sphere of Jacksonian political culture."[58] By projecting the "articles and tokens of abolitionist publicity" into a looser, lighter "medium of sociality," Brown is trying to make antislavery both a thing of the present and a resource for the future.[59] He is not travestying those articles and tokens; he is flinging them out, like flags, so that they might acquire new life. Antislavery flags were, as Brown knew, mostly inert; they tended to be affixed to the walls at meetings and bazaars, where their content—they typically bore slogans, such as "No Union with Slaveholders," or biblical verses—could be silently, cognitively consumed.[60] To fling out an antislavery flag is to give an indexical flourish to an icon of a cause, to signify the presence of an originating force, just as the movement of a weathervane signifies the presence of a breeze or the rising of smoke signifies the presence of fire. In the Minerva Rooms, at a moment of desultoriness, Brown sang about the way in which a certain kind of energy can make antislavery messages *move*: "on every swelling breeze," the imagined flag flaps; "o'er the raging seas," it "onward wave[s]"; and at the moment of universal emancipation, "like a meteor flashing far, / It bursts with glorious light." In *Clotel*, he tells and retells antislavery stories, makes and remakes antislavery arguments, in the same spirit, so that those stories and arguments will move in us in the same swift, bursting way, so that abolitionism will feel, at least for the moment, like modernity's child.

Maybe too much so. Modernity is, it should go without saying, a destructive as well as a creative force. To insert abolitionism and black American identity into the representational spaces of modernity is to transform them into commodities, distanced, necessarily, from the ideologies, cultures, and selves they represent. Circulating in the company of other commodities, competing for the gaze of consumerist subjects, Brown's images of abolitionism and blackness are luminous, certainly, but also potentially redundant or trivial: stars among stars in a vast sky. How, under circumstances like these, is it possible to retain the distinctiveness of abolitionism and blackness?

One response to that problem is to refuse any engagement with modernity, to identify oneself and interact with others in defiantly pre- or anti-modern ways. Another response, the one that Brown obviously chooses, is to explode into hypermodernity, to shine as brightly as it is possible to shine. Shining in that way, making oneself and one's convictions attractive, is predicated, for Brown, on distinctiveness. "It may be said of us, that we have used very strong language," he says in an August 1854 speech in Manchester, England. "Why, sir, has not the time come for strong language? . . . People want something strong,—they are willing to hear it; then I say, why not give it them?" (*C* 891). In *My Southern Home,* he writes, approvingly, that although newspaper accounts of "the separation of families" by the internal slave trade "never wanted readers," they "were not unfrequently made stronger by the fact that many of the slaves were as white as those who offered them for sale" (*C* 754–755). Most tellingly, he ends his career in print with the following anecdote, which brings *My Southern Home* to a close:

> "Don't call me a negro; I'm an American," said a black to me a few days since.
>
> "Why not?" I asked.
>
> "Well, sir, I was born in this country, and I don't want to be called out of my name."
>
> Just then, an Irish-American came up, and shook hands with me. He had been a neighbor of mine in Cambridge. When the young man was gone, I inquired of the black man what countryman he thought the man was.
>
> "Oh!" replied he, "he's an Irishman."
>
> "What makes you think so?" I inquired.
>
> "Why, his brogue is enough to tell it."
>
> "Then," said I, "why is not your color enough to tell that you're a negro?"

> "Arh!" said he, "that's a horse of another color," and left me with a "Ha, ha, ha!"
>
> Black men, don't be ashamed to show your colors, and to own them. (*C* 850)

In the final analysis, blackness is, for Brown, both a brogue, a rich inflection of a common tongue, and a flag whose colors can and should be rallied around. Understood in those terms, it is capable of being an object of enjoyment without being, for that reason, an object of contempt.

We are again in utopian territory. Any effort to present an alternative to the racism of nineteenth-century Anglo-American culture is obviously at risk of being overwhelmed by what the critic Stephen Best describes as "a sea of representations of a temporally arrested blackness."[61] As far as Brown is concerned, however, all that one can do, in the face of that reality, is, as the ghost of Baby Suggs says to Denver in Toni Morrison's *Beloved*, "know it, and go on out the yard."[62] By engaging in what the historian Kennell Jackson calls "black cultural traffic," Brown accepts the risks of circulating in a space in which black people are distorted and demeaned.[63] He does so because he recognizes, in addition to those risks, an opportunity, one that depends on a relentless introduction of novelty and an equally relentless evocation of mobility. Like the "cut" in African-American music—"an abrupt, seemingly unmotivated break . . . and a willed return to a prior series"—the irruption of an attraction skips us "back to another beginning."[64] Like the cinematic cut, moreover, that irruption creates the possibility of montage, the extension of an event into an expansive, internally differentiated space. In shot after shot, chapter after chapter, book after book, Brown separates himself from the identification of blackness with "infrahumanity," as Paul Gilroy calls it, while maintaining an ironic distance from the prospect of "superhumanity."[65] He is, insistently, not any one thing; he is an unfinishable series of things made possible by a potential that everyone shares.

He is, perhaps, Joseph Jenkins. "While strolling through Cheapside one morning," Brown writes in *The American Fugitive in Europe*, he sees, "for the fiftieth time," a "good-looking man, neither black nor white, engaged in distributing bills to the thousands who throng that part of the city of London." Brown stands "for some moments watching and admiring his energy in distributing his papers" (*C* 382). Several days later, Brown sees "the same individual in Chelsea, sweeping a crossing; here, too, he was equally as energetic as when I met him in the city." Later still, "while going through Kensington," Brown hears "rather a sweet, musical voice singing a familiar psalm, and on looking round," discovers that it is "the Cheapside bill-distributor and Chelsea crossing-sweeper," now "selling religious tracts" (*C* 382). A week passes. Brown attends a performance of *Othello* in a saloon on the City Road. When the actor playing Othello comes on stage, it is—"would you think it?"—the same man, appearing under the name of "*Selim, an African prince*" (*C* 383, 382). Over a year later, Brown goes into a chapel in London in which a "colored brother" is delivering a temperance sermon. When the minister takes off his glasses, Brown recognizes him as "the bill-distributor of Cheapside, the crossing-sweeper of Chelsea, the tract-seller and psalm-singer of Kensington, and the Othello of the Eagle Saloon. I could scarcely keep from laughing outright when I discovered this to be the man that I had seen in so many characters" (*C* 384). After the sermon, Brown introduces himself to the man, Joseph Jenkins, and learns that he is not only "a native of Africa"—an excerpt from *Incidents Connected with the Life of Selim Aga, a Native of Central Africa* is offered up as a veritable account of his early years—but the "leader of a band" that plays "for balls and parties, and three times a week at the Holborn Casino." He is, Brown concludes, "the greatest genius that I had met in Europe" (*C* 386).

The spirit of this probably spurious sketch, which Brown reuses in *The Black Man*, is profoundly at odds with what the critic Bernard Bell describes as "the primary unifying principle in the Afro-American novel": "the quest for dignity as a free people of African ancestry and the fulfillment of individual potential by merging a divided, alienated self into a truer and better unified, literate self."[66] There is no "quest for dignity" here, just a manifestation of an already-present energy and adaptability. There is, more importantly, no surmounting of "a divided, alienated self." Division and alienation are working out just fine for Jenkins, or Selim, or whoever—if anyone—he may be. He is, to borrow a phrase that Melville applies to Benjamin Franklin, a "Jack of all trades, master of each and mastered by none."[67] Instead of fulfilling his potential, Jenkins reactivates it; instead of unifying himself, he diversifies his options. Just as Brown himself was a temperance activist, an abolitionist, an orator, a raconteur, a singer, a panorama showman, a novelist, an essayist, a playwright, an actor, a biographer, a historian, a memoirist, and a medical practitioner, so is Jenkins a dazzlingly flexible being, an appealingly masterless man. "Society [is] suspicious of all *inelasticity* of character, of mind and even of body," Henri Bergson writes in *Laughter*, "because it is the possible sign of a slumbering activity as well as of an activity with separatist tendencies."[68] What Brown's readers are invited to see in the "neither black nor white" figure of Jenkins is, flatteringly, their own elasticity, their own capacity to play with and profit from everything that they might become. The space into which we are ushered by this sketch is, like so many of the other spaces in which Brown creates his effects, a "space in which you could find out what you *might* want . . . not your real, deep, authentic desires but your inclinations, your whims, your half-chances . . . that whole repertoire of experiments that you are."[69]

"In the earliest Lumiere exhibitions," Gunning writes, "the films were initially presented as frozen unmoving images, projections of still photographs. Then, flaunting a mastery of visual showmanship, the projector began cranking and the image moved. Or as [Maxim] Gorky described it, 'suddenly a strange flicker passes through the screen and the picture stirs to life.'" The attractiveness of the early cinematic attraction is concentrated, according to Gunning, in that "strange flicker," that "astonishing moment of movement."[70] Much of the attractiveness of Brown's literary and oratorical performances has a similar source. Every time that he makes one of his modal or stylistic cuts, something new stirs to life within "an ever homogenizing textual field."[71] The perception of that newness is intensified, for the white members of his original audiences, by the knowledge that an ex-slave produced it; just as part of early cinema's "Here it is!" is the apparatus itself, so is part of Brown's "Here it is!" the novelty of black authorship or showmanship. "Mr. Wm. Wells Brown read last evening his anti-slavery drama," writes a correspondent to the *Liberator* in June 1856. "Do you know how capital a hit it is? Our people were fairly taken off their feet with delight."[72] For the people of Groveland, Massachusetts, on that evening, and for every other actual or virtual audience that he addressed, Brown staged "astonishing moment[s] of movement," distinctively black and abolitionist versions of Gorky's "strange flicker." By presenting his audiences with attractions, he attracted them to the present, to the moment of display, its mobility and delightfulness. By saying, over and over, "Here it is!", he was saying, on the lower frequencies, to everyone capable of hearing it, "Here we are."

CHAPTER

FOUR

The Beautiful Slave Girl

On April 29, 1847, the *New York Evangelist* published the following item under the heading "An Auction":

> While traveling at the south, a short time since, one day, as I was passing through a noted city, my attention was arrested by a concourse of people upon the public square.
>
> Soon I saw two men coming through the crowd attended by a female. They entered the ring around the stand. The sequel showed them to be an auctioneer, the unfortunate merchant, and the more unfortunate young lady, for slave she could not be. The auctioneer stepped upon the stand and ordered her to follow. She dropped her head upon her heaving bosom, but she moved not. Neither did she weep—her emotions were too deep for tears. The merchant stood near me. I attentively watched his countenance. 'Twas that of a father for the loss of an only daughter. Daughter he had not; but I understand that he intended to adopt her, who, instead of being now free, was doomed to perpetual slavery. He appeared to have a humane heart. With tears in his eyes he said, "Helen, you must obey—I can protect you no longer." I could bear no more—my heart struggled to free itself from the human form. I turned my eyes upwards—the flag lay listlessly by the pole, for not a breeze had leave to stir. I thought I could almost see the spirits of the liberty martyrs, whose blood had once stained that soil, and hear them sigh over the now desecrated spot.

> I turned to look for the doomed. She stood upon the auction stand. In stature she was of the middle size; slim and delicately built. Her skin was lighter than many a Northern brunette, and her features were round, with thin lips. Indeed, many thought no black blood coursed in her veins. Now despair sat on her countenance. O! I shall never forget that look. "Good heavens!" ejaculated one of the two fathers, as he beheld the features of Helen, "is that beautiful lady to be sold?"
>
> Then fell upon my ear the auctioneer's cry—"How much is said for this beautiful healthy slave girl—a real albino—a fancy girl for any gentleman? (!) How much? How much? Who bids?" "Five hundred dollars," "eight hundred," "one thousand," were soon bid by different purchasers. The last was made by the friends of the merchant, as they wished to assist him to retain her. At first no one seemed disposed to raise the bid. The crier then read from a paper in his hand, "She is intelligent, well informed, easy to communicate, a first rate instructress." "Who raises the bid?" This had the desired effect. "Twelve hundred"—"fourteen"—"sixteen," quickly followed. He read again—"She is a devoted Christian, sustains the best of morals, and is perfectly trusty." This raised the bids to two thousand dollars, at which she was struck off to the gentleman in favor of whom was the prosecution. Here closed one of the darkest scenes in the book of time.
>
> This was a Southern auction—an auction at which the bones, muscles, sinews, blood and nerves of a young lady of nineteen, sold for one thousand dollars; her improved intellect, for six hundred more; and her Christianity—the person of Christ in his follower, for four hundred more.[1]

When this article came to Brown's attention, he was in the midst of composing *A Narrative of the Life of William W. Brown*, which would be published in July 1847. In his account of his final conversation with his mother, he incorporates, as I noted in chapter 1, two parts of the article's second paragraph. Later that year, in a lecture before the Female Anti-Slavery Society of Salem, he told his audience, "I have with me an account of a Slave recently sold upon the auction-stand," and went on to offer an abbreviated version of its depiction of the woman's sale.[2] Five years later, he returned to the article again, this time for the purposes of fiction. "A True Story of Slave Life," which was published in the December 1852 issue of the *Anti-Slavery Advocate*, opens with the following paragraph:

> In October of 1844, amongst a number of slaves who were exposed for sale at a slave auction in Richmond, Virginia, was a woman of middle size, slim, and delicately built. Her skin was lighter than many a northern brunette's and her features were oval, with thin lips; indeed, many thought no African blood coursed through her veins. The day was as fine as one could wish to behold. The auctioneer's flag hung listless by the pole, and not a breeze had leave to stir.[3]

In this mashing together of lines from the third and second paragraphs of "An Auction," very little is changed. The auction itself, however, is radically transformed:

> "Who bids for this nice young woman? How much, gentlemen? Real albino, fit for a fancy girl for any one. She enjoys good health, and is an excellent house servant. How much do you say?" "Five hundred dollars." "Only five hundred for such a girl as this? Gentlemen she is worth double that sum. I am sure if you knew the superior qualities of the girl, you would give more. Here, gentlemen, I hold in my hand a paper certifying that she has a good moral character—" "Seven hundred." "Ah, gentlemen, that is something like. This paper also states that she is very intelligent." "Eight hundred." "She is a devoted Christian and perfectly trustworthy." "Nine hundred," "Nine-fifty," exclaimed a second, "Ten hundred," said a third, and the woman was struck off to the last bidder for one thousand dollars.[4]

In the article, the dialogue is broken up by—and subordinated to—the voice of the narrator; here, it is vivid, rapid, and uninterrupted. In the article, the auctioneer pumps the bids up twice, through references to intelligence and Christianity; here, he pumps them up three times, throwing in a reference to moral character. Finally, in the article, other than characterizing the slave woman as a "real albino" and reading two commendatory sentences to the crowd, the auctioneer contributes nothing out of the ordinary to the event. Here, he spreads out, verbally buttonholing the buyers ("How much, gentlemen?"), feigning surprise ("Only five hundred for such a girl as this?"), and rewarding them with praise ("Ah, gentlemen, that is something like"). Our attention is drawn away from the "fancy girl" and toward the means by which her desirability is ratcheted up: the simulation of a personal relationship between buyer and seller, a fraternal and "gentlemanly" bond.

A year later, in *Clotel*, Brown returns to the scene. This time, however, while retaining the emphasis on the auctioneer that he had introduced in "A True Story of Slave Life," he expands the narrative in a significantly different direction. In his description of Clotel on the auction block, Brown lingers over the details of her physical appearance: "There she stood, with a complexion as white as most of those who were waiting with a wish to become her purchasers; her features as finely defined as any of her sex of pure Anglo-Saxon; her long black wavy hair done up in the neatest manner; her form tall and graceful, and her whole appearance indicating one superior to her position" (*C* 67). Then, after the auctioneer's patter, carried over from "A True Story of Slave Life," has escalated the bids—"Nine hundred." "Nine fifty." "Ten." "Eleven." "Twelve hundred."—Brown interrupts the action:

> Here the sale came to a dead stand. The auctioneer stopped, looked around, and began in a rough manner to relate some anecdotes relative to the sale of slaves, which, he said, had come under his own observation. At this juncture the scene was indeed strange. Laughing, joking, swearing, smoking, spitting, and talking kept up a continual hum and noise amongst the crowd; while the slave-girl stood with tears in her eyes, at one time looking towards her mother and sister, and at another towards the young man whom she hoped would become her purchaser.
>
> Abruptly, the auctioneer returns to the business at hand: "The chastity of this girl is pure; she has never been from under her mother's care; she is a virtuous creature." The bids resume their climb and Clotel is "struck" for fifteen hundred dollars.
>
> (*C* 67–68)

The break in the bidding accomplishes at least two things. First, by dramatizing the auctioneer's reestablishment of a rough camaraderie with the men in the crowd, it emphasizes the theatricality of the auction as a whole. As when Brown interrupts his speech in the Minerva Rooms with crowd-pleasing anecdotes, the auctioneer uses the tricks of the showman to keep the audience in the game, temporarily diminishing the aura with which he is invested so that he can, at the right moment, reinitiate the drama of the sale. Second, by tracking the movement of Clotel's gaze, Brown's narrator intensifies the sense of in-betweenness with which she has already been invested. Suspended between seller and buyer, split between "white" prestige and "black" debasement, and hovering, emotionally, between family and suitor, she stands, on the neither-here-nor-there space of the auction block, as the embodiment of a radical intermediacy. In this peculiarly directionless narrative space, the contradiction that suspends her identity in all of the above ways—the contradiction of slavery in a republic—is thrown into the sharpest possible relief.

But there is something else happening here, something other than sociopolitical critique lurking in the spatial, temporal, racial, cultural, economic, and maturational space that Clotel occupies in this scene and that we imaginatively occupy with her. It is not taken up in the ensuing paragraph, which emphasizes the finality of the event ("This was a Southern auction, at which the bones, muscles, sinews, blood, and nerves of a young lady of sixteen were sold for five hundred dollars; her moral character for two hundred; her improved intellect for one hundred; her Christianity for three hundred; and her chastity and virtue for four hundred dollars more" [*C* 68]). It fades with the revelation that Clotel has been purchased not by a stranger, as is the case in "An Auction" and "A True Story of Slave Life," but by her lover, Horatio Green. It is, moreover, present only *in potentia*, only to the degree that the reader extends himself or herself affectively into the scene. Still, it is there. It is, in brief, the desire to delay, to pause the action, to linger over the details, to attend to the hubbub: "laughing, joking, swearing, smoking, spitting, and talking." At this juncture—one of Brown's favorite phrases—it is possible for the reader to be struck, to some indeterminate degree, by the fluid, uncertain temporality of the present participle. In response, and to an equally indeterminate degree, it is possible for the reader to sustain that temporality, to participate, imaginatively, in holding onto the time before it is too late, before Clotel is exchanged for cash, taken away, and raped.

Slavery and rape are virtually synonymous for Brown.[5] When he says, in his lecture to the Female Anti-Slavery Society of Salem, "Slavery has never been represented; Slavery never can be represented" (*C* 856), he means that the conventions of polite Anglo-American culture make it impossible for anyone to depict, with a reasonable degree of accuracy, the sexual violence that defines the American South. "It can scarcely be expected," he says in an 1856 lecture,

> that those of us who understand the workings of slavery in the Southern States will bring before you the wrongs of the slave as we could wish. Lan-

> guage will not allow us; and if we had the language, the fastidiousness of the people would not permit our portraying them. . . . Those of us who have lived in slavery could tell you privately what we cannot tell you publicly of the degradation in the domestic circle of the master.
>
> (*C* 910)

Slavery in America is condensable into rape not only because rape is a crucial historical element of it but because the logics of slavery and rape are, as Brown makes clear, so much alike. "What is a Slave?" he asks elsewhere in his lecture to the Female Anti-Slavery Society. "A Slave is one that is in the power of an owner." What is a slave owner? One who has paid for "power ad infinitum over another" (*C* 856). And what is the purest distillation of that power, as indicated by the relative prices of various types of slaves? The power to buy and rape "fancy girls."[6]

This is of course not to say that light-skinned female slaves were the only ones on whom rape-power was exercised. Rape-power was everywhere in slavery, and it is unlikely that very many slaves escaped some form of contact with it, whether in their own experiences or in the experiences of kin and friends. It is simply to say that in light-skinned female slaves, the history and theory of slavery as rape-power were most clearly visible.[7] The "change in color" in the American slave population "is attributable solely to the unlimited power which the slave owner exercises over his victim," Brown writes in *Three Years in Europe*. "There seem to be no limits to the system of amalgamation carried on between master and slave. . . . On a plantation employing fifty slaves, it is not uncommon to see one third of them mulattoes, and some of these nearly white."[8] It is a testimony not so much to the attractiveness of "nearly white" women as to the attractiveness of the image of slave-power/rape-power in its most distilled and heightened form that their prices were so high—in today's dollars, the final bid in "An Auction" is almost fifty thousand dollars and that the reason for those prices was so well known. ("For what purpose such high sums were given all those who were acquainted with the iniquities of American Slavery will readily suspect," Brown writes in *A Description of William Wells Brown's Original Panoramic Views*.)[9] Why did slavery have such widespread support? Not because white people did not know about such things, Brown suggested to the Female Anti-Slavery Society, but at least in part because they did.[10] "Slavery has become popular," he said, "because it has power" (*C* 861). What were slave owners doing with power granted to them by the nation? Participating in, or indirectly profiting from, "a market in interracial sex."[11] And everyone who knew anything about the workings of slavery knew it.

Brown's light-skinned slaves and ex-slaves are often read as, in Alice Walker's words, a concession to "the capacities of the audience at hand," a concession for which black people "pay dearly—in anger, hurt, envy, and misunderstanding—to this day."[12] But if we read his near-white characters as replications of white fetish objects deployed for the sake of gaining white readers, we miss, as Ann duCille observes, his critique of the positioning of "sexualized white-skinned slave women" as "the objects of the white male gaze."[13] We also miss, as I will be arguing here, a subtler counterpoint to slavery's fetishizations, one that involves not moving beyond fetishism—which no one can ever completely or consistently do—but fetishizing differently. Why, critics have wondered, does Brown spend so much time talking about the appearance of light-skinned slave women? Maybe it is because the nearly otherworldly beauty that was conventionally attributed to such women is, for Brown, a sign of that which is in excess of power's self-affirming grasp. By inducing fascination—a purposeless, digressive, ultimately perverse lingering—beauty of that kind has the capacity to obstruct the finalization of power's image of itself. That obstruction is, obviously, temporary. It is also *temporal*, intrinsically opposed to the spatializations, the mappings and emplacements, on which power depends. By emphasizing the beauty of the beautiful slave girl and by placing her, so often, in transitional spaces, Brown draws us toward, perhaps even into, a special kind of time: the time before it is too late. In a fetishistic state of suspension, triggered by "a frozen, arrested, two-dimensional image," one dangles, for an uncertain but finite period, at "the last point at which it was still possible to believe. . . ."[14]

The first horn lifts its arm over the dew-lit grass
and in the slave quarters there is a rustling—
children are bundled into aprons, cornbread

and water gourds grabbed, a salt pork breakfast taken.
I watch them driven into the vague before-dawn
while their mistress sleeps like an ivory toothpick

and Massa dreams of asses, rum and slave-funk.
I cannot fall asleep again. At the second horn,
the whip curls across the backs of the laggards—

sometimes my sister's voice, unmistaken, among them.
"Oh! pray," she cries. "Oh! pray!" Those days
I lie on my cot, shivering in the early heat,

and as the fields unfold to whiteness,
and they spill like bees among the fat flowers,
I weep. It is not yet daylight.
—Rita Dove

The preceding poem, Rita Dove's "The House Slave," is inspired, as readers of Brown undoubtedly know, by the first chapter of the *Narrative of William W. Brown*. More specifically, it is inspired by the first edition's version of the chapter, which provides Dove with her resonant final line. Here are the final sentences of that chapter:

> During the time that Mr. Cook was overseer, I was a house servant—a situation preferable to that of a field hand, as I was better fed, better clothed, and not obliged to rise at the ringing of the bell, but about half an hour after. I have often laid and heard the crack of the whip, and the screams of the slave. My mother was a field hand, and one morning was ten or fifteen minutes behind the others in getting into the field. As soon as she reached the spot where they were at work, the overseer commenced whipping her. She cried, "Oh! pray—Oh! pray—Oh! pray"—these are generally the words of slaves, when imploring mercy at the hands of their oppressors. I heard her voice, and knew it, and jumped out of my bunk, and went to the door. Though the field was some distance from the house, I could hear every crack of the whip, and every groan and cry of my poor mother. I remained at the door, not daring to venture any farther. The cold chills ran over me, and I wept aloud. After giving her ten lashes, the sound of the whip ceased, and I returned to my bed, and found no consolation but in my tears. It was not yet daylight.
> (C 10)

The effect of that last sentence is profoundly intensified by the white space extending beneath it. Although it is not yet daylight, it is already too late. His mother has been whipped ten times. He has heard it from the house, the location of the power to whip. In a few minutes he will have to get back out of bed and serve the people in whose interests his mother was just whipped. Time opens barrenly, pointlessly in front of him, "unfold[ing] to whiteness," like the cotton fields in Dove's poem. The whole day, the whole next day, and the whole of every day to come, evacuated in advance of any place for his desire, any meaning for his love.

The first edition's version of the chapter lends itself to this kind of extrapolation. But in the second edition, published in 1848, and in all of the editions that followed, the imaginative extension of that traumatic moment is pointedly foreclosed. Instead of suspending the sentence "It was not yet daylight" over white space, inviting the reader to fill out its significance, Brown cuts the sentence and tacks on a banalizing synopsis: "Experience has taught me that nothing can be more heart-rending than for one to see a dear and beloved mother or sister tortured, and to hear their cries, and not be able to render them assistance. But such is the position which an American slave occupies."[15] Then he just keeps going, moving on, without even a paragraph break, to a story about a resistant slave, a story that had occupied a separate chapter in the 1847 version. It is as if he is fending off the possibility of a lyrical reading, the possibility of an affective occupation of the episode.

In order to understand why he might want to do this, it may be helpful to turn to two other descriptions of the whipping of female slaves in early African American literature. The first is from Frederick Douglass's *My Bondage and My Freedom* (1855); the second is from Solomon Northrup's *Twelve Years a Slave* (1853).

> My sleeping place was on the floor of a little, rough closet, which opened into the kitchen; and through the cracks in its unplaned boards, I could distinctly see and hear what was going on, without being seen by old master. Esther's wrists were firmly tied, and the twisted rope was fastened to a strong staple in a heavy wooden joist above, near the fire-place. Here she stood, on a bench, her arms tightly drawn over her breast. Her back and shoulders were bare to the waist. Behind her stood old master, with cowskin in hand, preparing his barbarous work with all manner of harsh,

> coarse, and tantalizing epithets. The screams of his victim were most piercing. He was cruelly deliberate, and protracted the torture, as one who was delighted with the scene. Again and again he drew the hateful whip through his hand, adjusting it with a view of dealing the most pain-giving blow. Poor Esther had never yet been severely whipped, and her shoulders were plump and tender. Each blow, vigorously laid on, brought screams as well as blood. "*Have mercy; Oh! have mercy*" she cried; "*I won't do so no more*;" but her piercing cries seemed only to increase his fury. . . . After laying on some thirty or forty stripes, old master untied his suffering victim, and let her get down. She could scarcely stand, when untied.[16]

> When the stakes were driven down, [Epps] ordered [Patsey] to be stripped of every article of dress. Ropes were then brought, and the naked girl was laid upon her face, her wrists and feet each tied firmly to a stake. Stepping to the piazza, he took down a heavy whip, and placing it in my hands, commanded me to lash her. . . .
>
> "Oh, mercy, massa!—oh! Have mercy, *do*. Oh, God! Pity me," Patsey exclaimed continually, struggling fruitlessly, and the flesh quivering at every stroke.
>
> When I had struck her as many as thirty times, I stopped, and turned round towards Epps, hoping he was satisfied; but with bitter oaths and threats, he ordered me to continue. I inflicted ten or fifteen blows more. By this time her back was covered with long welts, intersecting each other like net-work. . . . My heart revolted at the inhuman scene, and risking the consequences, I absolutely refused to raise the whip. He then seized it himself, and applied it with ten-fold greater force than I had. The painful cries and shrieks of the tortured Patsey, mingling with the loud and angry curses of Epps, loaded the air. She was terribly lacerated—I may say, without exaggeration, literally flayed. The lash was wet with blood, which flowed down her sides and dropped upon the ground. At length she ceased struggling. Her head sank listlessly on the ground. Her screams and supplications gradually decreased and died away into a low moan. She no longer writhed and shrank beneath the lash when it bit out small pieces of her flesh.[17]

Douglass and Northrup bring us visually, as well as aurally, into the scene of the assault. They emphasize the nakedness, partial or entire, of the women. They specify with terrible precision the way in which the women are fixed in place. They close in on intimate details: Esther's soft, rounded shoulders, the pieces of flesh flying off Patsey's back. They convey the slow passage of time.

They fetishize, in other words, the torture itself. They do so, undoubtedly, for a reason: to make white readers sense the horror of the kinds of violations to which slaves are exposed. As several of Douglass's critics have pointed out, however, the high-definition visualization of a woman's flogging screens something else out, as fetishes invariably do.[18] What is being conjured up but held at bay by each of these prolonged scenes of sexualized torture is a shadow scene in which a man occupies the woman's position. Although each of the descriptions adverts to that possibility—the "fate of Esther might be mine next," Douglass writes, and Epps threatens Northrup with "a severer flogging" if he refuses to obey his orders—it is, for the time, a possibility only, eclipsed by the sensory immediacy of the woman's physical and psychological suffering. The scenes invoke, by these means, an equation of whipping and womanhood—invoke, that is, a psychic logic in which a whipped woman is revealed *as* a woman, whereas a whipped man is only temporarily, counterfactually feminized. A whipped woman is, in this logic, nothing more than "the sign and condition of another's freedom," an abjectness that must be brought to light and held still so that men can be imaginatively withheld from view.[19]

Brown wants nothing to do with that logic. The description of his mother's whipping in the 1847 *Narrative* is as close as he comes to a participation in the repetition of the sexualized scene of torture, and even that restrained participation seems to have been too much for him: too melodramatic, too indicative of helplessness, too conducive to reverie. In the 1849 and 1850 editions of the *Narrative*, he sticks with the emotionally defused format of the 1848 edition. In *Biography of an American Bondman*, nominally the work of his daughter Josephine, he condenses the scene into four sentences:

> When only about ten years old, the tender feelings of the young slave were much hurt at hearing the cries and screams of his mother, and seeing the driver flogging her with his negro-whip. As he heard the loud, sharp crack of the lash, and the groans of her who was near and dear to him, William felt a cold chill run through his veins. He wept bitterly, but could render

> no assistance. What could be more heart-rending than to see a dear and beloved one abused without being able to give her the slightest aid?[20]

And in *Memoir of William Wells Brown*, the last version of his autobiography, he deletes the scene entirely. Nowhere else in his massive body of writing does he present an extended dramatization of a woman being whipped.[21] Even in the most sensational of his works, the panorama that he exhibited in England, he passes quickly, in his descriptive commentary, over two images of women being whipped. In View Second, he writes, "On the right of you, you see a woman who will not go on, and a slave in the act of taking away her young child. She has been separated from it, and they are now whipping her to make her proceed without it." And in View Ninth, he writes, "In the distance you observe a woman being whipped at the whipping-post, near which are the scales for weighing the cotton." With the exception of a quatrain from a John Greenleaf Whittier poem in View Second—"What, ho! our countrymen in chains! / The whip on Woman's shrinking flesh! / Our soil yet reddening with the stains / Caught from her scourging, warm and fresh!"—that's all the elaboration that he provides.[22]

What he elaborates on in its place, as I have already indicated, is the image of the beautiful slave girl. That iconic figure, which he appropriates from the work of white writers, first appears in his work in chapter 4 of the *Narrative*. Immediately after a scene in which Brown and his sister Elizabeth weep together at the thought of being separated, we cut to a scene on board the steamboat *Enterprize*, where Brown is serving as a waiter. As a gang of slaves comes on deck in Hannibal, Missouri, one of them attracts the attention of the passengers and crew:

> It was a beautiful girl, apparently about twenty years of age, perfectly white, with straight light hair and blue eyes. But it was not the whiteness of her skin that created such a sensation among those who gazed upon her—it was her almost unparalleled beauty. She had been on the boat but a short time, before the attention of all the passengers, including the ladies, had been called to her, and the common topic of conversation was about the beautiful slave-girl. She was not in chains. The man who claimed this article of human merchandize was a Mr. Walker,—a well known slave-trader, residing in St. Louis. There was a general anxiety among the passengers and crew to learn the history of the girl. Her master kept close

> by her side, and it would have been considered impudent for any of the passengers to have spoken to her, and the crew were not allowed to have any conversation with them. When we reached St. Louis, the slaves were removed to a boat bound for New Orleans, and the history of the beautiful slave-girl remained a mystery.
> (*C* 18)

Versions of this mute, ephemeral figure crop up again and again in Brown's work. In an April 1855 letter to the *National Anti-Slavery Standard*, Brown writes that while on a lecture tour in Ohio, he

> had an hour's conversation with a party of [four fugitives] . . . who were seeking freedom on the other side of *Jordan*. One of them was a woman nearly white, with a fine infant in her arms, much whiter than herself. . . . This fugitive in the land of her birth was one of the finest looking women that I have thus far seen in the West. She had an expressive and intellectual forehead, and a countenance full of dignity and heroic bearing. Her dark golden locks rolled back from her almost snow-white brow, and floated over her swelling bosom. The tears that stood in her mild blue eyes, showed that she was brooding over her wrongs, and that thoughts too deep for utterance filled her bleeding heart. The child, I have said, was whiter than its mother; indeed, one would not suppose from its appearance that a drop of African blood coursed through its blue veins. My heart grew softer as I gazed upon the mother, while she pressed soft kisses on its sad smiling lips, while the small dimpled hands of this innocent creature were slily hid in the warm bosom on which it nestled.[23]

In *Clotelle*, he merges the 1847 passage and the 1855 passage to produce the following scene:

> Among the numerous passengers who came on board [the steamboat] was another slave-trader, with nine human chattels which he was conveying to the Southern market. The passengers, both ladies and gentlemen, were startled at seeing among the new lot of slaves a woman so white as not to be distinguishable from the other white women on board. She had in her arms a child so white that no one would suppose a drop of African blood flowed through its blue veins.

> No one could behold that mother with her helpless babe, without feeling that God would punish the oppressor. There she sat, with an expressive and intellectual forehead, and a countenance full of dignity and heroism, her dark golden locks rolled back from her almost snow-white forehead and floating over her swelling bosom. The tears that stood in her mild blue eyes showed that she was brooding over sorrows and wrongs that filled her bleeding heart.
>
> The hearts of the passers-by grew softer, while gazing upon that young mother as she pressed sweet kisses on the sad, smiling lips of the infant that lay in her lap. The small, dimpled hands of the innocent creature were slyly hid in the warm bosom on which the little one nestled.[24]

Why is this scenario so appealing to Brown? For one thing, as in the case of "An Auction" and its derivatives, it is set in a transitional space: on a steamboat heading south or on the Underground Railroad heading north. For another, again as in the auction scenes, it simultaneously evokes and screens out a scene of rape. Although the scene from the *Narrative* implies that the "beautiful slave-girl" is the concubine of the slave-trader Walker, that implication is blurred by the emphasis in the conclusion of the paragraph on "mystery." In the latter two scenes, rape is more strongly implied—"The blood of some proud Southerner, no doubt, flowed through the veins of that child," Brown writes—but the soft-focus sentimentalism of the scene makes it possible to imagine that an inner purity, externalized in the infant, has carried the woman through the ordeal.[25] To prolong and intensify that evocation of maternal sanctity, Brown mixes in some lines from a poem, Amelia Welby's "Lines Written on Seeing an Infant Sleeping on Its Mother's Bosom," in which we are told that the infant's "small dimpled hands were slyly hid / In the warm bosom that it nestled on," that the mother "prest / Soft kisses o'er its red and smiling lips," and that the speaker's "heart grew softer as [she] gazed upon / That youthful mother."[26] What Brown wants, clearly, is for us to dwell on the image of the young mother, to invest that image with pathos—and then, when she disappears, as she almost immediately does, to go no further. He takes a thinly specified figure ("a woman"), adds some unremarkable descriptions of her features ("expressive and intellectual forehead," "swelling bosom," "mild blue eyes"), lyrically encourages our attentiveness to her, then cuts away, leaving us with something more than a face in a crowd, certainly, but less—much less—than a character.

He leaves us, that is, with a fetish object, an object whose primary function is to serve, in Laura Mulvey's words, "as a mask, covering over and disavowing the traumatic sight of absence, especially if the 'absence' sets off associations with the wounded, bleeding body."[27] By focusing our attention on the frozen, emblematic image of the slave woman in transit, Brown puts "a phantasmatic topography" in the place of a wounded and wounding absence.[28] Fetishistic substitutions of this kind are usually thought to close off several things at once: the fetish object's relationship to the real world, the fetishist's relationship to other people, and the possibility, for fetish object and fetishist alike, of change. As Mulvey points out, however, the repetition and elaboration of the fetishistic subject-object relationship almost inevitably opens things up. That opening-up takes two basic forms. In the first, the awareness of the foreclosed reality is increased: "the more the fetish exhibits itself, the more the presence of a traumatic past is signified."[29] In the second, the awareness of the transformability of the fetish object is increased: an "investment in visual excess and displacement of signifiers produces a very strong texture," intensifying "aesthetic pleasure and formal excitement" and "mov[ing] signification considerably further away from the problem of reference."[30]

Most contemporary theorists of fetishism, Mulvey included, try to widen the first of those openings. "My interest here is to argue that the real world exists within its representations," Mulvey writes in her introduction to *Fetishism and Curiosity*. "Just as simulacra seem to be poised to take over the world, it is all the more important to attempt to decipher them."[31] Most critics of Brown simultaneously share that strategy and identify him with it. Martha Schoolman, to take only one example, argues that Brown "keep[s] firmly in view the structural relationship between the pleasures of cosmopolitan circulation and the racial, economic, and political asymmetries that often make it possible," thereby bearing witness "to the results of external events that can be forgotten or misremembered, but never undone."[32] One of the most frequently cited examples of Brown's employment of this strategy is the protest that he staged in response to the exhibition of Hiram Powers's *The Greek Slave* in the Crystal Palace. In a public letter that appeared in the *Liberator* and elsewhere in 1851, the abolitionist William Farmer reports that "Wm. Wells Brown took 'Punch's Virginia Slave'"—a satirical image of a black slave woman in the same pose and state of undress as the white slave woman in Powers's popular statue—"and deposited it within the enclosure by the 'Greek Slave,' saying audibly, 'As an American fugitive slave, I place this "Virginia Slave" by the side of the "Greek Slave," as its most fitting companion.' "[33] As Michael Chaney points out, Brown thereby "turns the statue's signifying context around—from a staging area of romantic escapism to a political space in which national culture, identity, and white hegemony are contested through counter-representation and juxtaposition."[34] By saying, in effect, "Look upon this picture, and on this"—a passage from *Hamlet* that he liked to quote—Brown makes it clear that the statue's elision of African American slavery is, as Toni Morrison has argued with respect to the hyperwhite conclusion of Poe's *Narrative of Arthur Gordon Pym*, an effort to "evade and simultaneously register the cul de sac, the estrangement, the non sequitur that is entailed in racial difference."[35]

On other occasions, however, Brown simply advances the carousel, projecting picture after picture after picture. When he uses a slightly misquoted version of the line from *Hamlet* as the epigraph to the Joseph Jenkins sketch and *The Escape*, for instance, what he means to evoke is not a hypotactical reorganization of the relationship between reality and unreality but a paratactical gliding from one unreality to the next. Instead of contrasting the actual with the apparent, he escorts us, in each case, through arcades of apparitions, past brightly lit displays of stereotypes and roles. He generates, in the process, a "very strong texture" of illusoriness, a peculiarly absorbing substitute for the texture of reality. The same may be said of his phantasmatic descriptions of the beautiful slave girl. By progressively embellishing the accounts of her appearances on the auction block and the steamboat deck, he draws her away from the traumatic reality that she signifies. Just as, in baroque German tragedies, the emphasis is "not on the *plot*. . . but the *play*," so, in Brown's various stagings of the figure of the beautiful slave girl, is the emphasis not on the world of slavery, the world from which she comes or toward which she goes, but on a mercifully nowhere-tending chain of signifiers.[36] Theatricalization of this kind "cannot simply overcome time and mortality," writes the critic Samuel Weber, "but it can temporarily arrest, interrupt, or suspend their progress."[37]

One of the best examples of this sort of theatrical suspension is Brown's appropriation of "Pauline," a newspaper article about "a young and beautiful girl" who "attracted the admiration of her master" and "became the victim of his lust." After being accused by her mistress of striking her, Pauline was "tried, and found guilty, and condemned to die." During the trial, it was discovered that Pauline was pregnant, and she was returned to the prison cell until her child was born. The author of the article pauses the action at this point in order to evoke the obscenity of that experience:

> There, for many weary months, uncheered by the voice of kindness, alone, hopeless, desolate, she waited for the advent of the new and quickening life within her, which was to be the signal of her own miserable death. And the bells there called to mass and prayer-meeting, and Methodists sang, and Baptists immersed, and Presbyterians sprinkled, and young mothers smiled through tears upon their new-born children; and maidens and matrons of that great city sat in their cool verandahs, and talked of love, and household joys, and domestic happiness; while all that dreary time the poor slave girl lay on the scanty straw of her dungeon, waiting—with what agony the great and pitying God of the white and black only knows—for the birth of the child of her adulterous master.[38]

On several occasions, Brown repeats the melancholic opening clauses of this passage—in every version of *Clotel*, he describes Clotel in jail as being "uncheered by the voice of kindness, alone, hopeless, desolate" (*C* 188)—but the section of the passage toward which he is most powerfully drawn is the denomination-by-denomination listing of Sabbath rituals. In "A Narrative of American Slavery," a section of *Three Years in Europe* that he would reuse in *Clotel*, Mary tells her long-lost lover George that on a Sunday in New Orleans,

> the bells called the people to the different places of worship. Methodists sang, and Baptists immersed, and Presbyterians sprinkled, and Episcopalians read their prayers, while the ministers of the various sects preached that Christ died for all; yet there were some twenty-five or thirty of us poor creatures confined in the '*Negro Pen*' awaiting the close of the Holy Sabbath, and the dawn of another day, to be again taken into the market, there to be examined like so many beasts of burden.
> (*C* 209)[39]

He also recycles the passage, in exactly the same form, in "A True Story of Slave Life."[40]

In *Miralda*, however, he opens up the passage in ways that take it, in Mulvey's words, "considerably further away from the problem of reference." "The bells of thirty churches were calling the people to the different places of worship," he writes.

> Crowds were seen wending their way to the houses of God; one followed by a negro boy carrying his master's Bible; another followed by her maid-servant holding the mistress' fan; a third supporting an umbrella over his master's head to shield him from the burning sun. Baptists immersed, Presbyterians sprinkled, Methodists shouted, and Episcopalians read their prayers, while ministers of the various sects preached that Christ died for all.[41]

He throws himself even further into the description of the next day's sale:

> The clock on the calaboose had just struck nine on Monday morning, when hundreds of persons were seen threading the gates and doors of the negro-pen. It was the same gang that had the day previous been stepping to the tune and keeping time with the musical church bells. Their Bibles were not with them, their prayer-books were left at home, and even their long and solemn faces had been laid aside for the week. They had come to the man-market to make their purchases. Methodists were in search of their brethren. Baptists were looking for those that had been immersed, while Presbyterians were willing to buy fellow-Christians, whether sprinkled or not. The crowd was soon gazing at and feasting their eyes upon the lovely features of Miralda.
>
> "She is handsomer," muttered one to himself, "than the lady that sat in the pew next to me yesterday."
>
> "I would that my daughter was half so pretty," thinks a second.
>
> Groups are seen talking in every part of the vast building, and the topic on 'Change, is the "beautiful quadroon."[42]

It is as if Brown has now played this scene so often—*Miralda* is the fourth of the seven works in which some version of it appears—that he can't play it seriously any more. The reference to the immersion of Baptists and the sprinkling of Presbyterians, in particular, seems to have become a kind of private joke. In addition to appearing twice in this chapter, it shows up in the updated version of the auction scene; after someone bids eight hundred dollars, the auctioneer says, "she was first sprinkled, then immersed, and is now warranted to be a devoted Christian, and perfectly trustworthy," which raises the bidding to nine hundred dollars.[43] What was once a part of a journalistic account of a tragedy has become, eight years after its first deployment, a resource for comic digressions.

It would be easy to judge Brown harshly for this. Here, too, however, we need to think about what he does say in relation to what he doesn't say. In the original article, this is what immediately follows the section that Brown repeatedly uses:

> Horrible! Was ever what George Sand justly terms "the great martyrdom of maternity"—that fearful trial which love alone converts into joy unspeakable—endured under such conditions? What was her substitute for the kind voices and gentle soothings of affection? The harsh grating of her prison lock,—the mockings and taunts of unfeeling and brutal keepers! What, with the poor Pauline, took the place of the hopes and joyful anticipations which support and solace the white mother, and make her couch of torture happy with sweet dreams? The prospect of seeing the child of her sorrow, of feeling its lips upon her bosom, of hearing its feeble cry—alone, unvisited of its unnatural father; and then in a few days—just when the mother's affections are strongest, and the first smile of her infant compensates for the pangs of the past—the scaffold and the hangman! Think of the last terrible scene,—the tearing of the infant from her arms, the death-march to the gallows, the rope around her delicate neck, and her long and dreadful struggles, (for, attenuated and worn by physical suffering and mental sorrow, her slight frame had not sufficient weight left to produce the dislocation of her neck on the falling of the drop,) swinging there alive for nearly half an hour—a spectacle for fiends in the shape of humanity![44]

By fixating on the description of the woman in the cell, Brown is choosing to retain, in Freud's words, "the last impression before the uncanny and traumatic one. . . . the last moment in which the woman could still be regarded as phallic."[45] He is choosing, that is, not to participate, as the author of "Pauline" does, in the production of a climactic "spectacle for fiends." In *Clotel*,

Clotel escapes from jail, eludes her pursuers for a time, and finally, rather than submit to recapture, disappears into the Potomac. The focus, throughout, is on self-directed, self-preservative actions, not, as in "Pauline," on a ghastly suffering and death. In *Miralda*, Miralda is transferred from the jail to the auction block, where she is purchased by a wealthy man who takes her out of the country, marries her, emancipates her, and dies. Like the slavery-to-riches tale from which it derives—the story of Delia in *Narratives of the Sufferings of Lewis and Milton Clarke* (1846)—it is, in Gilles Deleuze's words, a "protest of the ideal against the real."[46] By delaying the onset of slave-power/rape-power for his female characters and/or imagining outcomes for them that are, at the very least, consistent with dignity, Brown fetishistically "suspends belief in and neutralizes the given in such a way that a new horizon opens up beyond the given and in place of it."[47]

Crucially, however, the more Brown fetishizes, the more obvious the artificiality of his idealization becomes. To keep holding off a catastrophe that he cannot help calling up, he keeps going back to certain agonizing but prolongable scenarios. With each repetition, those scenarios drift further in the direction of mannerism and comedy. Instead of halting that drift—instead of protecting those representations from the consequences of their own artifice by drawing them back toward "the given"—Brown simply allows it to happen. Even when he does not actively embrace the comic potential of that repetition, he does little or nothing to make the old material seem responsive to the new compositional moment or at home in its new textual environment. In *Clotel*, the plagiarized description of Clotel's escape and suicide takes up most of a chapter and is followed by polemical ruminations on the fictional event and a long Grace Greenwood poem on the historical event. In *Memoir of William Wells Brown*, however, the same description is presented, during an account of Brown's experiences on the river, as something that he once saw a slave woman do in Vicksburg, and immediately after its dramatic final lines—"and then, with a single bound, she vaulted over the railings of the bridge, and sunk for ever beneath the waves of the river"—he just picks up where he left off. ("While employed on this steamboat, I laid the plan by which I gained my freedom.")[48] In *My Southern Home*, the transition out of the escape-and-suicide description is even more startlingly nonchalant. "In the meantime," Brown writes, "Mr. and Mrs. Savage were becoming more and more interested in the child, Lola, whom they had adopted, and who was fast developing into an intellectual and beautiful girl, whose bright, sparkling hazel eyes, snow-white teeth and alabaster complexion caused her to be admired by all" (*C* 750). It is not that nothing has happened; it is that a block of text that he has already reproduced five times has made an appearance—has appeared *as* an appearance, something that we are not meant to decompose into a temporal stream of arbitrary and vacillating signifiers but to behold as an incorruptible totality. We have been addressed less as readers than as viewers—in five of its appearances the passage is accompanied by an engraving—and asked to respond less as critics in search of fresh food for thought than as fetishists in search of unfresh representations, decreasingly potent but increasingly bearable emblems of the unsayable.

In exchange for the power to stimulate us into an excruciating awareness of the realities of slavery, Brown acquires, as a result of his attraction to an atmosphere of simulation, a capacity to intensify our awareness of the kinds of relationships to the world that artifice enables us to have. "The fixation on the fetish is generally viewed as a pathological repetition compulsion, bound up in the return to the thing which gives satisfaction and cutting the fetishist off from relation to others," writes the critic E. L. McCallum. But if we "view fetishism's repetition less as fixation and more as iterability"—the potential for restatement on which meaning depends—it is possible to conceive of fetishism in an entirely different way.[49] "Strictly speaking," McCallum observes, "iterability marks the inevitable failure of an utterance to conform to the speaker's intentions, the always-open possibility that an utterance will be repeated in some drastically different context that will rewrite its original meaning." If one is capable of acknowledging the implications of iterability, fetishism is, or can be, a "form of mastery . . . that is grounded in an ambivalent sense of knowing better, knowing that one's mastery is limited."[50] This is exactly the kind of mastery that Brown's beautiful-slave-girl fetishism makes it possible for us to have. Fetishism is clearly a problem if its principal characteristic is an "investment in fixity and stasis." It is not nearly as much of a problem, maybe not even a problem at all, if its principal characteristic is an "investment in ambivalence."[51]

Five times in Brown's works—in *Three Years in Europe*, *Clotel*, *Miralda*, and both editions of *Clotelle*—an ex-slave woman reunites with her lover in a room whose "walls were hung with fine specimens from the hands of the great Italian masters, and one by a German artist, representing a beautiful monkish legend connected with the 'Holy Catharine,' an illustrious lady of Alexandria" (*C* 206).[52] The painting to which Brown refers is Heinrich Mucke's *The Translation of St. Catherine of Alexandria*, which Brown saw in an issue of *People's and Howitt's Journal*, where it was accompanied by the following commentary:

> The noble engraving which we to-day present to our readers, is the embodiment, by the German artist Mucke, of a beautiful monkish legend connected with "the Holy Catherine," an illustrious lady of Alexandria, who suffered martyrdom under the Emperor Maximin, about A.D. 307. She was to have perished by the wheel, but it is related that upon the first turn of this terrible engine, the cords with which she was bound were broken asunder by the invincible power of an angel, and so she was delivered from that death. According to the chronicle, her body was afterwards translated by angels to the Great Monastery at the top of Mount Sinai in Arabia, where it remains to this day, in a fair tomb of marble.[53]

Is there anything to this "beautiful monkish legend"? No and yes:

> The true meaning of this translation most probably is, that [Catherine's body] was carried by the monks of Sinai to their monastery, that they might devoutly enrich their dwelling with such a treasure, it being well known that the name of an angelical habit was often used for a monastic habit, and that monks, on account of their purity and functions, were called angels. The painter has, however, adopted the more literal and beautiful reading of the legend—for art has always a glorious faith, believing that which is most pure, and least entangled with material associations.[54]

Most probably, she wasn't delivered from that death, the writer acknowledges. Most probably, she was broken on the wheel. This is, for the writer, precisely why we should cherish the depiction of another outcome, even if—maybe especially if—it focuses on the in-between state of "translation," in which Catherine, eyes closed, cradled by angels, rides through the air. Below her, if we choose to look there, is "a rainy and sorrowful-looking sea." Where we are invited to look, however, is not only at Catherine herself but also at the angel who bears the "gleaming sword of martyrdom" in her honor, the angel who "tenderly supports her feet," and the angel whose face, "full of compassion and love, is turned towards the wan features of Catherine."[55] Being invested in ambivalence means learning neither to scoff at such things nor to believe in their reality. It means risking the desire for their reality, tenderly supporting their possibility, entangling ourselves with their fanciful disentanglement from "material associations," coming to know, more and more intimately, their fancifulness, and hovering, for as long as possible, in that state.[56]

Into the room in which the painting of St. Catherine hangs comes "a lady—a beautiful brunette—dressed in black, with long curls of a chestnut color hanging down on her cheeks. Her eyes were of a dark hazel, and her whole appearance indicated that she was a native of a southern clime" (*C* 206). She is Mary/Miralda/Clotelle; her lover, who is waiting in the room, is George/Jerome. Ten years earlier, she had changed places with him in a jail cell, enabling him to escape to Canada. She was then "sold to a negro trader, and taken to the New Orleans market." That was the last that he had heard of her. When she enters the room, he rises to his feet, then sinks back onto the sofa. To no one in particular, he says, "It is her." "After this," Brown writes, "all was dark and dreamy: how long he remained in this condition it was for another to tell." When George/Jerome regains consciousness, Mary/Miralda/Clotelle is gone. Her father-in-law, however, is sitting beside him on the sofa, holding a bottle of smelling salts. "Wait a while," the father-in-law says, "and I will tell you all" (*C* 207). Ten minutes pass. George/Jerome rises and adjusts his clothes. Soon, all will be revealed; soon, the promise of the chapter's title—"The Happy Meeting"—will be fulfilled. But not yet. All is dreamy. St. Catherine sails through the air.

CHAPTER

FIVE

The Sound of Fame

It is like what we imagine knowledge to be:
dark, salt, clear, moving, utterly free,
drawn from the cold hard mouth
of the world, derived from the rocky breast
forever, flowing and drawn, and since
our knowledge is historical, flowing, and flown.

—ELIZABETH BISHOP

When Brown performed his second play, *The Escape*, he appeared before his audiences, as he had in the performances of its predecessor, *Experience; or, How to Give a Northern Man a Backbone*, by himself. He was, however, not entirely alone. In act 1, scene 3, when the respectable, mixed-race lovers Glen and Melinda converse, the voice of Samuel Moises Schmucker becomes a part of the performance. The following lines, which Brown gives to Melinda, are taken almost verbatim from Schmucker's novel *The Yankee Slave-Driver*:

> It was a glorious moonlight night in autumn. The wide and fruitful face of nature was silent and buried in repose. The tall trees on the borders of Muddy Creek waved their leafy branches in the breeze, which was wafted from afar, refreshing over hill and vale, over the rippling water, and the waving corn and wheat fields. The starry sky was studded over with a few light, flitting clouds, while the moon, as if rejoicing to witness the meeting of two hearts that should be cemented by the purest love, sailed triumphantly along among the shifting vapors.[1]

Later on, other authors impalpably share the stage. When Brown-as-Glen says, "My heart pants and my soul is moved whenever I hear her voice" and "Oh, heavy curse, to have thoughts, reason, taste, judgment, conscience and passions like another man, and not have equal liberty to use them" (*C* 444), for instance, he is reprising lines from Giovanni Pacini's *Saffo*—or, more exactly, the English translation of its libretto—and James Sheridan Knowles's *Love*.[2] And when, in the character of the aptly named Mr. White, Brown word-paints the transformation of "a mind, a living soul, with the germs of faculties which infinity cannot exhaust, as it first beams upon you in its glad morning of existence, quivering with life and joy, exulting in the glorious sense of its developing energies, beautiful, and brave, and generous, and joyous, and free" into "a dead soul entombed in a living frame" (*C* 453), it is the orotundity of Edwin Whipple, the author of *Lectures on Subjects Connected with Literature and Life*, that is swelling the scene.[3] ("This is not a meeting house," says Brown-as-barkeeper, indignantly, when Brown-as-White is done [*C* 453].) All alone on the lecture platform, taking on the voices of slaveholders and abolitionists, black people and white people, men and women, and doing so, at times, in language borrowed from elsewhere, Brown is peculiarly, almost unnervingly, estranged from what we ordinarily think of as selfhood.

There are times, however, when Brown must have spoken in propria persona. At the beginning of act 5, scene 5, for instance, he must have uttered the words, "FERRYMAN, *fastening his small boat. Ferryman,* [*advancing, takes out his watch*]" (*C* 463). If he had not, his brand-new character's ensuing line—"I swan, if it ain't one o'clock"—would have made no sense, insofar as the last scene had ended with a group of people around a breakfast table. He must have uttered those words, moreover, in a voice that at least resembled his usual speaking voice, so as to indicate that they did not come from anywhere or anyone in the world of the play. But this world-engendering voice, invested with privilege, utters nothing oracular, stylish, or self-identifying in *The Escape*. All that it speaks of is stage business: entrances, exits, gestures, and tableaux. "*He goes to the mirror, and discovers that his coat is torn—weeps.*" "*He gets angry, and rushes about the room frantic.*" "*Rolls up his sleeves.*" "*Weeps*" (*C* 422–423).

"Where in the World Is William Wells Brown?" asks Ann duCille in the title of one of the best critical essays on Brown.[4] In *The Escape*, one conceivable answer to that question is that he is distributed among the thirty-seven characters that speak in the play. To one degree or another, he is, presumably, inside the characters of Glen, Melinda, Dr. Gaines, Mrs. Gaines, Cato, Hannah, Mr. White, etc. But how deeply can one person be inside thirty-seven characters in an 18,000-word play? How invested can an actor be in lines like "Come, sit thee down, and have some breakfast," "Tank you, madam, I'll do dat," "This is pleasant for thee to meet one of thy friends," and "Yes sir, it is" (*C* 462), especially if he has to deliver them in rapid succession in a series of different voices?

Another conceivable answer to duCille's question, the one that I will pursue here, is that Brown is located not within but between the speeches of the characters in *The Escape*—and, extending beyond *The Escape*, in the interstices of his work as a whole. If we imagine being in the audience for one of the play's public readings and hearing Brown speak the stage directions aloud, if we imagine associating the playwright's voice not with the characters but with the performative statements that conjure them up and move them around, it is possible to imagine Brown in ways that take us beyond our conventional understandings of authorship. In his performances of *The Escape*, Brown is not a medium between the audience and the diegesis; he is, as I have already indicated, a relay point within the diegesis. In the real time of the performance, he is what makes a character "appear," what makes that character "move" and "speak," what stills and silences that character so that another character might move and speak, what shifts scenes, what advances time, and what brings the revels to an end. When one overemphasizes characterological or authorial expressivity, when one treats art as an intimate revelation of, or complex perspective on, certain forms of individuality, one loses sight of these humble but inescapable functions. By speaking the stage directions—"the most abject part of the traditional drama"—in something like his own voice, Brown not only makes those functions visible but actively identifies himself with them.[5] Like a marionetteer who can be seen, strings in hands, above his marionettes, Brown presents himself, unabashedly, as the means by which the show goes on.

But how in the world are we supposed to read William Wells Brown if he—"he"—is less an identifiable subject than a manipulator of identity effects, less a point of origin than a space in which already-existing elements are redistributed? As duCille pointed out back in 1993, when only a few of Brown's plagiarisms had been identified, his "highly appropriative style makes . . . a formalist reading difficult. *Clotel* has many linguistically powerful passages—wonderfully lyrical moments that sing above the pain and 'propaganda' as welcome poems—but we do not always know whom to credit for such moments."[6] Formalists are not the only kinds of critics who have found themselves at a loss. "If Brown's citational practices dismay readers in search of originality," Lara Langer Cohen writes, "they equally fail to comport with more gratifying models of citation like signifyin(g), mimicry, or performativity, for while sometimes Brown transfigures his sources ironically, more often he copies them faithfully."[7] What can we do, as critics, when we cannot safely attribute to the author in question either aesthetic power or politically subversive intent? What can we do when our most gratifying modes of analysis are not applicable? We can, Cohen suggests, go back to the drawing board; we can develop ways of "theorizing modes of textual production that exceed origination to encompass reading, maneuvering, and rearranging."[8] We can read the Brown that we have, not the Brown that we would be most comfortable having.

The success of any such effort will depend, I think, on a willingness to think differently about fame. Why do professors teach some writers and not others? What would be read and taught if, tomorrow, not only the names of authors but our memory of their names disappeared from their publications? What would happen if—setting aside for now the prospect of an apocalyptic obliteration of names—we cared less about the identities attached to texts? Perhaps we would start to grasp, and take pleasure in grasping, the irony of putting a name to a text, segregating a text from a context, differentiating between an event and the ordinary passage of time. Perhaps we would start to think of the distinctions that make selves and histories possible—distinctions that we cannot help but make—as sources of fun, avenues to sociability. And perhaps we would start to catch, in the voices of now-scare-quoted "authors," the strangely seductive sound of language anonymously spoken. Like the water in Elizabeth Bishop's "At the Fishhouses," language is, ultimately, inhuman: "cold dark deep and absolutely clear," an "element bearable to no mortal."[9] When it is spoken as closely as possible to its absoluteness, however, language is, as it were, human degree zero, human without being individual, human without being capable of grounding aesthetic and social distinctions. What can we read for in Brown if we cannot read for badges of distinctiveness? Language put in motion, the inertia of the synchronic overcome, again and again, by the energy of the diachronic: water drawn, continually, from "the cold hard mouth / of the world," water "derived from the rocky breast / forever," water "flowing and drawn," and, "since / our knowledge is historical," since it is drawn by mortals, water "flowing, and flown."

"Fame is the recompense not of the living, but of the dead," William Hazlitt writes in the opening paragraph of "On the Living Poets" (1818).

> The temple of fame stands upon the grave: the flame that burns upon its altars is kindled from the ashes of great men. Fame itself is immortal, but it is not begot till the breath of genius is extinguished. For fame is not popularity, the shout of the multitude, the idle buzz of fashion, the venal puff, the soothing flattery of favour or of friendship; but it is the spirit of a man surviving himself in the minds and thoughts of other men, undying and imperishable. It is the power which the intellect exercises over the intellect, and the lasting homage which is paid to it, as such, independently of time and circumstances, purified from partiality and evil-speaking. Fame is the sound which the stream of high thoughts, carried down to future ages, makes as it flows—deep, distant, murmuring evermore like the waters of the mighty ocean.[10]

Two conceptions of fame are at work in this passage, as Benjamin B. Thatcher, the American editor of *The Poetical Works of Mrs. Felicia Hemans* (1835), noticed. "It has been said by a fine writer," Thatcher writes in his introduction,

> that fame is the recompense not of the living, but of the dead,—its temple standing over the grave, and the flame of its altar kindled from the ashes of the great. There is truth in the thought, as well as beauty in the expression of it. . . . But is it alone, on the other hand, the spirit of a man *surviving himself*, as Hazlitt describes it, in the minds and thoughts of other men? Or, as he splendidly represents it again, is it only "the sound which the stream of high thoughts, carried down to *future ages*, makes as it flows—deep, distant, murmuring evermore like the waters of the mighty ocean?" This is fame, indeed. No reputation can be called *such*, that will not endure that test.[11]

Recognizing that, in the words of the critic Andrew Bennett, a masculinist "appeal to a posthumous reception is central to the project of Romantic poetics," Thatcher extracts from Hazlitt—"the first great fame theorist of the modern age"—an alternative to the privileging of putatively immortal poets, an alternative that makes it possible for Hemans, who was popular in her lifetime, to be valued.[12] Fame is "the influence of mind upon mind, independently of every personal consideration," Thatcher writes. What Hemans's mind most powerfully communicates to her reader's mind, according to Thatcher, is an awareness of the abidingness of "nature"—the only thing "strange enough, and strong enough" for the purposes of poetry—and the dignity of the overlooked: all those "of whom fame speaks not, with her clarion voice, / In regal halls."[13] Understood in these terms, her poetry may be said to perform a paradoxical "assertion of self-effacement . . . one which gains its prominence, its renown or name, from a desire for oblivion," a "desire to survive as identity-less, effaced, invisible, forgotten, obliterated, anonymous—in other words, a desire for survival which amounts to non-survival."[14]

Sometime before 1860, Brown read Thatcher's preface. In both *Miralda* and *Clotelle*, his narrator interrupts a description of Geneva to offer the following reflections:

> Fame is generally the recompense, not of the living, but of the dead,—not always do they reap and gather in the harvest who sow the seed; the flame of its altar is too often kindled from the ashes of the great. A distinguished critic has beautifully said, "The sound which the stream of high thought, carried down to future ages, makes, as it flows—deep, distant, murmuring ever more, like the waters of the mighty ocean." No reputation can be called great, that will not endure this test.[15]

Intentionally or not, Brown evokes, even more forcefully than Thatcher, a deindividuated conception of fame. Because the sentence that is supposed to provide the test of greatness is missing its original subject and verb—"Fame is"—the test of greatness in *Miralda* and *Clotelle* is a statement that states nothing, a sentence whose sense ultimately disappears into the "waters of the mighty ocean," a fragment that would look, if broken at its punctuation marks, like this:

> The sound which the stream of high thought,
> carried down to future ages,
> makes,
> as it flows—
> deep,
> distant,
> murmuring ever more,
> like the waters of the mighty ocean.

No reputation can be called great, apparently, if it cannot endure the test of such shapely, senseless sayings. No writing can last if it does not "include a certain resistance to thinking, a particular kind of (non-)thinking which in its beguiling subtleties, its blank reserves, its vacant musings, its baffling recreance, disturbs the hard-won discriminations of philosophy."[16]

I am, of course, overreading a probable error. Yet the sentences that Brown took from "literary" writers—both those whose names have survived (Hazlitt, Irving, Johnson, Martineau, Willis, Simms) and those whose names have been mostly or nearly entirely forgotten (Grace Aguilar, Dinah Marie Muloch Craik, Agnes Strickland, William Macdowall Tartt)—are, for the most part, sentences of this kind. Here, for instance, are three of the sentences in Aguilar's *Home Scenes and Heart Studies* (1852) that Brown found appealing enough to transfer, with modifications and truncations, to *Miralda*:

> It was evening in Venice—the queen of the Adriatic, her marble palaces and princely halls, her stately bridges and her dreary prisons, lay sleeping in gorgeous beauty, flushed by the glowing splendor of the setting sun, lingering as loath to fade away and be lost in the more sombre hues of twilight, which, rising from the east, was softly and balmily stealing over the expanse of heaven, bearing silence, and repose, and quiet loveliness on her meekly pensive brow.[17]

> The stars still smiled at their own sparkling rays gleaming up from the gushing water; the pensive moon still touched the glossy leaves with her diamond pencil, still lingered on the verdant mount, leaving rich shadows on the luxuriant vales; the sun still sent forth his bright beams, to revive and cherish the glistening flowers, to whisper of his unfailing love;

> still did he bid them drink up the dewdrops, which, trembling beneath his earnest gaze, yet sprung up from their homes at his first call, eager to lose themselves in him.[18]

> Night fell; the lovely southern night, with its silvery moonshine on the gleaming waters, its glistening stars, appearing suspended in the upper air as globes of liquid light, with its fresh, soft breezes, bearing such sweet scents from the odoriferous shores, that a poet might have fancied angelic spirits were abroad, making the atmosphere luminous with their pure presence, and every breeze fragrant with their luscious breath.[19]

What Brown seems to have been most attracted to in these sentences is their deep, distant, ever-murmuring rhythm. "We ought to say a feeling of *and*, a feeling of *if*, a feeling of *but*, and a feeling of *by*, quite as readily as we say a feeling of *blue* or a feeling of *cold*," William James writes in *Principles of Psychology*. "Yet we do not: so inveterate has our habit become of recognizing the existence of the substantive parts alone, that language almost refuses to lend itself to any other use."[20] Like the fragmentary sentence from Hazlitt, the sentences from Aguilar have what we might call, following James, a feeling of ",". The last sentence, for instance, specifies ("Night"), respecifies ("the lovely southern night"), modifies ("with its silvery moonshine on the gleaming waters"), appends ("its glistening stars"), modifies the appendage ("appearing suspended in the upper air as globes of liquid light"), and remodifies, driftingly, with multiple commas, the original specification ("with its fresh, soft breezes, bearing such sweet scents from the odoriferous shores, that a poet might have fancied angelic spirits were abroad, making the atmosphere luminous with their pure presence, and every breeze fragrant with their luscious breath"). We are meant to sense, in these sentences, the lingering of impalpable presences: light, certainly, and odor, but also narratorial attention and, beneath or beyond that attention, the rules of grammar. Without those rules, Aguilar could not generate the syntactical structures that make it possible for her to convey both the ongoing presence of the narrator and the ongoing presence of light in the world. The sentences may be said, accordingly, to bring us closer to certain nonhuman entities on the far horizon of subjectivity—language as such, light as such—and to do so, crucially, in pleasurably syncopated ways.

A comparable feeling of "," seems to have attracted Brown to many of the sentences that he lifted from the travel writing of Nathaniel Parker Willis. Among the nine passages from Willis that Brown uses in *The American Fugitive in Europe* are a description of a Turkish valley—"it winds away into the hills toward Belgrade, its long and even hollow, thridded by a lively stream, and carpeted by a broad belt of unbroken green sward swelling up to the enclosing hills, with a grass so verdant and silken that it seems the very floor of faery"—a description of the ruins of a Roman bath—"one labyrinth of gigantic arches and ruined halls, the ivy growing and clinging wherever it can fasten its root, and the whole as fine a picture of decay as imagination could create"—and a description of the landscape along the Susquehanna, "where the lawns were made, the terraces defined and levelled, the groves tastefully clumped, the ancient trees ready with their broad shadows, the approaches to the water laid out, the banks sloped, and, in everything, the labor of art seemingly all anticipated by Nature."[21] The first passage becomes, in Brown's hands, a description of the interior of Tintern Abbey—"we found ourselves standing on a floor of unbroken green grass, swelling back to the old walls, and looking so verdant and silken that it seemed the very floor of fancy" (*C* 306)—the second becomes a description of Melrose Abbey—"one labyrinth of gigantic arches and dilapidated halls, the ivy growing and clinging wherever it can fasten its roots, and the whole as fine a picture of decay as imagination could create" (*C* 318)—and the third becomes a description of the Scottish countryside, "where the lawns were made, the terraces defined and levelled, the groves tastefully clumped, the ancient trees, though small when compared to our great forest oaks, were beautifully sprinkled here and there, and in everything the labor of art seemed to have been anticipated by Nature" (*C* 314). Displaced from their original frames of reference, the descriptions serve less to convey sights than to perpetuate sounds. By exploiting Willis's exploitation of the iterability of apposite clauses, Brown enables his sentences to remain open for, in Hawthorne's words, "another, and another, and, after all, another moment."[22]

Brown's interest in the structure, as opposed to the content, of other writers' sentences is most fully on display in his appropriations of anaphoras. In *The American Fugitive in Europe*, immediately after turning a description of British laborers in an 1851 essay entitled "Popular Enlightenment" into a description of American slaves, he replaces the contents of one of that essay's anaphoric runs with contents of his own. The original sequence—

> *It is not enough*, however, to enter the gorgeous transept of a Crystal Palace, and look eastward and westward, in overawed admiration of the magnificence of the structure, and the profuse splendor of the industrial products spread around. *It is not enough* to extol the genius, or skill, or artistic refinement, written on the piled-up manufactures of the mightiest nations of the globe. *It is not enough* to wander in mute, or in loud-tongued adoration through such a labyrinth of human emulation evoked from the toils of human industry.

—gives rise to the following sequence:

> *It is not enough* that the people of my country should point to their Declaration of Independence which declares that "all men are created equal." *It is not enough* that they should laud to the skies a constitution containing boasting declarations in favour of freedom. *It is not enough* that they should extol the genius of Washington, the patriotism of Henry, or the enthusiasm of Otis.
>
> (*C* 294; emphasis added)

In "An Appeal to the People of Great Britain and the World" (1851), he does the same thing with some lines from Isaac Scribner's *Review of the Rev. U. C. Burnap's Sermon on Bible Servitude*. The reiterative openings of Scribner's overheated sentences—

> *By the everlasting cries and shrieks of the slave* whose howlings rise like the Revelator's perpetual smoke of torment, I denounce it. *By their blood*, whose voice, like Abel's, cries to heaven for vengeance, as it runs from lacerated veins in southern forests until their swamps and everglades are paved with bleached skull-bones, I denounce it. *By that spirit of liberty and equality* that was born in this Commonwealth, rocked in, the cradle of liberty, and baptized in the blood of my fathers, I denounce it. *By that still nobler, higher and holier spirit of him who was born in a stable*—rocked by the winds of heaven in a manger, and on Calvary's hill was baptized in the blood of the Son of God, I denounce it.

—are converted into a toned-down but still emphatic series of invocations and pleas:

> *By the cries of the slave*, which come from the fields and swamps of the far South, we ask you to do this! *By that spirit of liberty and equality* which you all admire, we would ask you to do this. *And by that still nobler, higher, and holier spirit of our beloved Saviour*, we would ask you to stamp upon the head of the slaveholder, with a brand deeper than that which marks the victim of his wrongs, the infamy of theft, adultery, man-stealing, piracy, and murder, and, by the force of public opinion, compel him to "unloose the heavy burden, and let the oppressed go free."
> (*C* 880)

Taking advantage of the fact that "subject-predicate linkages . . . [are] 'loosened' in anaphora, insofar as its rhythmic pattern tends to emphasize the spectacular variation and proliferation of predications over the bond or logical connection between any individual predicate and its subject," Brown plagiarizes his source text's anaphoric subjects, strips them of their original predicates, and affixes predicates of his own.[23] He does not do it because he wants to say something original; there is nothing very special about the predicates that he inserts into the openings. He does it because he wants to interrupt the ordinary rhythms of his prose with the forceful, attractional rhythms of anaphoric declamations, to make use of the use that another writer has made of the generativity of a syntactical form.

He does it, in other words, for the sake of the openings. Instead of attending, as a reader, to character-revealing details or plot-developing events or a masterfully idiosyncratic style, Brown attends, in cases like these, to something essentially asubjective: "the point from which words begin to become their appearance, and the *elemental depth* upon which this appearance is opened while at the same time it closes."[24] Why does Brown plagiarize, in *Clotel* and its three revisions, an anonymous newspaper description of two white robbers being chased by bloodhounds? Because he likes the way that time is held open in it: the way that the beginning of the hunt is broken down into a succession of individual acts that take us on a "zigzag course" through a swamp; the way that the appearance of an independent clause—"they pursue"—is delayed by a parade of introductory dependent clauses ("Here, in this common highway—the thoroughfare for the whole country around—through mud and through mire, meeting wagons and teams, and different solitary wayfarers, and, what above all is most astonishing, actually running through a gang of negroes, their favourite game, who were working on the road") (*C* 77); and the way that the writer quick-shifts, once the end is near, through a series of fragmentary descriptions ("Nearer and nearer the whimpering pack presses on; the delusion begins to dispel; all at once the truth flashes upon them like a glare of light; their hair stands on end; 'tis Tabor with his dogs") (*C* 78).[25] The same may be said of his deployments of a magazine description of a Jewish burial ground—"This was a most singular spot, remote, undefended, spreading over the summit of a cliff that rose abruptly to a great height above the sea; but so grand in its situation, in the desolate sublimity which reigned around, in the reverential murmur of the waves that washed its base, that it was one of our favorite resorts"—and a newspaper description of a tenement fire: "Broad sheets of fire would envelope and entwine the frail buildings in their burning folds, threatening the whole with inevitable and speedy conflagration, and then a change of wind would turn the impending danger aside, and lift the smoky pall again, as if to show that the work of destruction was not yet accomplished."[26] Even before Brown excised those sentences from their original locations, they were, in essence, simulacra of literariness, writings that Writing wrote. When he transferred them to the pages of *Clotel*, it was not with the aim of elevating his literary stature; it was with the aim of bringing into *Clotel* the sound of an impersonal Fame, the sound of famousness, the sound of writing that is capable of perpetuating itself in the absence of any apparent purpose.

By means of such sentences, Brown provides us with the uncanny experience of a time in which the past—or, more exactly, a feeling of pastness—floats like a precipitate in a solution. Such sentences can be, as he well knows, a form of cultural capital. After being hired as a clerk in a British "manufacturing house," Jerome, the hero of *Clotelle*, "turn[s] his attention to literature," reading "Johnson's 'Lives of the Poets,' the writings of Dryden, Addison, Pope, Clarendon, and other authors of celebrity." He gains, as a result, "a great advantage over the other clerks, and cause[s] his employers to respect him far more than any other in their establishment."[27] For socially aspirational readers like Jerome, "the writings of . . . authors of celebrity" are, in part, a means of identifying with the category of the upwardly mobile middle-class worker. By enabling such readers to associate themselves with that imaginary community, celebrity writings offer, as John Guillory argues, a peculiar form of narcissistic pleasure: not the pleasure of "an individual's recognition of his or her individuality" but the pleasure of an "identification with a social body expressed or embodied in the common possession of writer and reader, a common language."[28] That is, however, not all that they offer. In addition to being a form of cultural capital, writings with a Hazlittian sound of fame in them are, as I have been suggesting, writings that are capable of bringing us closer to the always-vanishing point at which structure is superseded and history begins. In addition to offering the narcissistic pleasure of an identification with a social body, they offer the narcissistic pleasure of an identification with potentiality as such, with a body of pure virtuality.

In Brown's critical statements on literature—most of which are, unsurprisingly, derived from other people's critical statements on literature—that impersonally narcissistic dimension of literary experience looms large. The greatness of Shakespeare, he writes in a passage taken from a speech on the legacy of Thomas Hood, is indicated not only by the fact that "it would not be difficult to find in most modern works traces of [his] influence" but by the fact that no one "can tell how much of the national character is due to the operation of [his] works" (*C* 389).[29] The greatness of Pope, he writes in a passage based on Lord Carlisle's *Two Lectures on the Poetry of Pope* (1851), is indicated by the fact that "many have quoted [his] lines without knowing that they were Pope's" (*C* 365).[30] Just as literary influence is, in its broadest sweep, unrecognizable, so is literary creativity, in the final analysis, nonindividual. Genius—"that energy which collects, combines, amplifies, and animates" (*C* 491)—comes "unbidden and unsought: as the wind awakes the chords of the Aeolian harp, so the spirit breathes upon the soul, and brings to life all the melody of its being" (*C* 591). Genius is that which "arrange[s] and harmonize[s]" the "individual forms of beauty" (*C* 586); it is an "alembic" in which "manners and modes of thought" are "etherealised and refined" (*C* 843). Or so Brown—transcribing from, in order, Samuel Johnson's *Lives of the Poets* (1781), an 1851 essay on John Clare, an 1853 article on "Poetry and the Drama," and David Macbeth Moir's *Sketches of the Poetical Literature of the Past Half-Century* (1851)—suggests.[31] Finally, in language taken from Robert Vaughan's 1846 review of Philip James Bailey's

Festus, Brown argues that the effect of genius's unbidden, collecting, arranging, refining, amplifying energy is to animate the reader's equally impersonal potentiality. Poetry, Brown copies/writes, "ennobles the sentiments, enlarges the affections, kindles the imagination, and gives to us the enjoyment of a life in the past, and in the future, as well as in the present. . . . Under its light and warmth we wake from our torpidity and coldness to a sense of our capabilities" (*C* 326).[32] "The mind left to itself from infancy, without culture, remains blank," he copies/writes elsewhere (*C* 476).[33] In each of us, however, the "same *high capacious powers* of mind lie folded up" (*C* 354).[34] When literary experience is at its most intense, impersonal genius impersonally unfolds impersonal capacities. In the space of literature, a space in which "relations, configurations, forces are affirmed through sound, figure, rhythmic mobility," a space in which words are "not obliged to serve to designate anything or give voice to anyone," one is merely and profoundly put in motion, not as a fully organized individual but as an unworldly assemblage of possibilities.[35]

"To write is to make oneself the echo of what cannot cease speaking," Maurice Blanchot writes. By becoming that echo, one "make[s] *perceptible* . . . the giant murmuring upon which language opens."[36] To read Brown not in spite of but by way of his plagiaristic extravaganzas is to allow oneself to rise and fall on that giant murmuring, that deep, distant, oceanic oscillation, in which each word "says," before any sense can be made of it, simply that it is here, and that it is here because the structure of language has made it possible for it to be here. It is, moreover, to experience that movement, that sliding of elements, not only as a stimulus to one's unfolding but as the basis of sociability. As Leo Bersani and Ulysse Dutoit argue, "repeatable being—being that continuously fails to be unique—creates a hospitable world of correspondences." Once relations are "no longer blocked by difference," no longer deprived of circulatory vitality by a culture of self-sameness, they can "multiply as networks of similitudes."[37] Brown's writing, the relation of Brown's writing to other people's writing, the relation of Brown's writing to the structure of language, the relation of Brown's writing to its readers—all of it fails to be unique; all of it multiplies as networks of similitudes. All of it signals the presence of a world in which we "do not appear primarily as individuals," a world in which we appear, instead, as a "*way of being-moved*," ceaselessly emerging from and returning to that which "can never be reduced to the property or product of an individual."[38]

Near the end of *The Escape*, Cato, a fugitive slave, appears on a street in the North. "I wonder ef dis is me?" he asks. "By golly, I is free as a frog. But maybe I is mistaken; maybe dis ain't me" (*C* 457). For a moment, it seems as if Cato is going to experience the same kind of existential vertigo that Brown had experienced after gaining his freedom; in the *Narrative*, after entering the home of Wells Brown, the Ohioan Quaker from whom he would take his middle and last names, Brown declares that "the fact that I was a freeman—could walk, talk, eat and sleep as a man, and no one to stand over me with the blood-clotted cowhide—all this made me feel that I was not myself" (*C* 51). But Cato is not nearly as concerned with having a unitary self. "Cato, is that you?" he asks himself. "Yes, seer," he answers himself. "Well," some version of himself concludes, "now it is me, an' I am a free man" (*C* 457). Instead of representing free subjectivity as a state so remote from slavery that escaped slaves cannot at first know who they really are, Brown transforms that starry idealization—an idealization to which he had contributed in the *Narrative*—into the set-up for a punch line. With two syllables—"Yes, seer"—Brown punctures the pretentiousness of civic republicanism and romantic individualism, turning Cato's version of the ontological question that torments Melville's Byronic titan—"Is Ahab, Ahab?"—into an easy-to-answer question about naming.[39] Does Cato answer to the name Cato? Of course. Does he take that name seriously? Does he identify his being with it? Of course not. "Now, what shall I call myself?" Cato asks. "I'm now in a suspectable part of de country, an' I muss have a suspectable name. Ah! I'll call myself Alexander Washington Napoleon Pompey Caesar. Dar, now, dat's a good long, suspectable name, and every body will suspect me" (*C* 457). If you have to have a name, you might as well have a long one, one that testifies not to the depth of your essence but to the breadth of your versionality. Why not? It's just a name. And in this world, even the most respectable name is suspectable. Play the game, but don't believe in it. That much you owe yourself.

In an essay on Byron in *The Spirit of the Age*, Hazlitt writes that unlike Walter Scott, Byron

> holds no communion with his kind; but stands alone, without mate or fellow.—
>
> "As if a man were author of himself,

> and owned no other kin."
>
> He is like a solitary peak, all access to which is cut off not more by elevation than distance. . . . He exists not by sympathy, but by antipathy. . . . [He] chiefly thinks how he shall display his own power, or vent his spleen, or astonish the reader either by starting new subjects and trains of speculation, or by expressing old ones in a more striking and emphatic manner than they have been expressed before. He cares little what it is he says, so that he can say it differently from others. . . . He is often monotonous, extravagant, offensive. . . . [He] does not exhibit a new view of nature, or raise insignificant objects into importance by the romantic associations with which he surrounds them; but generally (at least) takes commonplace thoughts and events, and endeavours to express them in stronger and statelier language than others.[40]

In *The American Fugitive in Europe*, Brown reproduces much of Hazlitt's analysis of Byron in the following critique of Thomas Carlyle:

> As a writer, Mr. Carlyle is often monotonous and extravagant. He does not exhibit a new view of nature, or raise insignificant objects into importance, but generally takes commonplace thoughts and events, and tries to express them in stronger and statelier language than others. He holds no communion with his kind, but stands alone without mate or fellow. He is like a solitary peak, all access to which is cut off. He exists not by sympathy but by antipathy. Mr. Carlyle seems chiefly to try how he shall display his own powers, and astonish mankind, by starting new trains of speculation or by expressing old ones so as not to be understood. He cares little what he says, so as he can say it differently from others.
>
> (*C* 335–336)

Much of what Brown means to accomplish as a writer can be inferred from this passage. He means to be multitonal, to cast overlooked objects in a new light, to exist by sympathy, to communicate clearly—to be, in short, relational, versatile, inclusive, and responsive. He means to be a writer who, like Hazlitt's Scott, "casts his descriptions in the mould of nature, ever-varying, never tiresome, always interesting and always instructive, instead of casting them constantly in the mould of his own individual impressions"; a writer who "takes away that tightness at the breast which arises from thinking or wishing to think that there is nothing in the world out of a man's self"; a writer who "emancipat[es] the mind from petty, narrow, and bigoted prejudices"; and, strange as it may seem, a writer who plagiarizes faithfully.[41] Unlike Hazlitt's Byron, who offers nothing but a monotonously "original" self-aggrandizement, Brown shares the stage with others, in what appears to have been a conscious choice to be, like Hazlitt's Scott, an essentially "*dramatic* writer."[42]

"In America," Brown writes toward the end of *My Southern Home*, "the negro stands alone as a race. He is without mate or fellow in the great family of man" (*C* 847). More than anything else, Brown longed, throughout his career, for spaces in which it might be possible to be with mates and fellows, in which each of us might do something other than stand alone. The best way of creating and bringing others into such spaces, he believed, was by capitalizing on the contemporary attraction to self-ironizing extravaganzas of self-making. By composing, with an unscrupulous artfulness, scenario after scenario in which the obstacle of a fixed, segregatory individuality is circumvented, he hoped to reanimate, in Adam Phillips's words, "our longing not to be too strange to each other, or to ourselves, not to be too determinedly unique."[43] Hope, unlike optimism, is vulnerable to disappointment, and Brown was undoubtedly disappointed many times. He kept going back, however, to the kinds of spaces that maximized, for him, the prospect of an irony-laced interracial sociability, spaces in which one never has to do anything more than pretend that one is the author of oneself, in which one can overhear, in even the most artificial-seeming modes of address, the ongoing motion of that which is greater than oneself. Back, say, to Pleasureville. With, in the words of Albert E. Pillsbury, who was a boy in New Hampshire when he first met Brown, "the twinkle of his eye, which always signaled the utterance of a particularly good thing."[44]

APPENDIX A

Plagiarism in Brown's Works

The following list of Brown's plagiarisms—represented by searchable passages—is keyed to the bibliography of sources in Appendix B. Plagiarisms appearing in the list for the first time are indicated by passages of five words or more; plagiarisms that have appeared at least once before (Brown recycled many of his plagiarisms) are indicated by phrases of four or fewer words.

PLAGIARISM IN *NARRATIVE OF WILLIAM W. BROWN* (1847)

Chapter 6

a shudder, a feeling akin to horror shot (Wait 124): 11 words

Chapter 10

She dropped her head upon her heaving bosom ("An Auction"): 38 words

Chapter 11

Dark and revolting as is the picture here drawn (Foster 23): 9 words

ADDITIONAL PLAGIARISM IN *NARRATIVE OF WILLIAM W. BROWN* (1848)

Appendix

You cannot keep the human mind forever locked (Purvis 16): 101 words
The following are mostly abridged selections (Davis 1): 164 words
Reader, you uphold these laws (Davis 4): 127 words
averse to the importation of slaves from the states (Tappan 17): 55 words

ADDITIONAL PLAGIARISM IN *MEMOIR OF WILLIAM WELLS BROWN* (1859)

Home is the chief school of human virtue (Channing 80): 238 words

PLAGIARISM IN *THREE YEARS IN EUROPE*

Letter 2

as a mirror, with a soft mist (Willis, *Pencillings*, 75): 10 words
decorated with a group of figures in alto relievo (G. Wright 173): 31 words
Ireland, the land of genius and degradation (Stanton 125–126): 43 words

Letter 3

energy of her motion, the beauty of her shape (Willis, *Pencillings*, 139): 36 words
rests in calm repose upon its superlative beauty (Fox 1): 31 words
The church itself consists of a vast nave (*Galignani's* 209): 55 words
Behind the Madeleine is a small but well-supplied (*Galignani's* 212): 24 words
The bas-reliefs of the shaft pursue a spiral direction (*Galignani's* 480–81): 76 words

Letter 4

His speeches are a continuous flow of rapid, fervid (Stanton 317): 13 words

Letter 5

a wild boar, the other, a wolf (*A New Guide* 111): 15 words
but its proportions are very elegant (*A New Guide* 134): 12 words
consists of a square pavilion two stories high (*A New Guide* 141): 25 words

Letter 6

formed of the finest red syenite, and covered (*Galignani's* 195): 38 words
which nothing but his dauntless courage warded off (Breckenridge 203): 25 words
the "Genius of Liberty"; in his right hand (*Galignani's* 288): 15 words
the rider on the red horse at the opening (*Galignani's* 303): 22 words
nations conquered by Louis XIV., with colossal statues (Planta 311): 20 words
The Genius of War summons the nation to (*Galignani's* 194): 37 words

Letter 8

It rears its irregular walls and massive towers (Irving, *Sketch-Book*, 110): 36 words

Letter 9

much that has been obscure with respect to Lycia (Clarke n.p.): 17 words
the racing of pens over sheets of paper (Irving, *Sketch-Book*, 155): 36 words
To be appreciated it must be seen, or rather felt (Cox 2:74): 173 words

Letter 10

the lines about his mouth were exquisitely sweet (Dixon 35): 45 words
an enormous face, huge nose, mouth widely grinning ("Street" 51): 213 words
Shakspeare, who wrote of man, to man, and for man (Danforth 275): 38 words
His genius was vast and powerful in its grasp (*Memorials* 154): 47 words

Letter 11

there seemed nothing between her and the earth (Willis, *Inklings*, 1:218): 17 words
screen, of the most gorgeous and florid architecture (*New Guide* 29): 20 words
vastness and beauty impress the observer with awe (*Stranger's* 44–45): 17 words
literature, science, and art—the progressive history ("Untitled" 54): 53 words
Ancestral monuments he has none; written documents ("Popular" 276): 67 words
a sounder taste, a more exact intellect (Cormenin 245): 30 words

Letter 12

as it reposes in the lap of pastoral luxuriance (*History of Kirkstall* 1–2): 85 words
a retired inn or pot-house, and the haunt (*History of Kirkstall* 32): 69 words
around the spot by the deeds of remote ages (Brettell 1): 46 words
trod the sombre walks of the long-banished monks (Carter 25): 66 words
formed by the Byrons, for the use of King Charles (*Home* 50): 23 words
a few polished oak steps into the West Corridor (*Home* 56): 23 words
intended by Lord Byron for himself and his dog (*Home* 58): 37 words
two leaden statues of Pan and a female Satyr (Carter 29): 45 words
After crossing an interesting and picturesque part (Carter 29): 24 words
carried beyond the bounds of reason and propriety (Carter 30): 54 words
become a lasting memento of the noble bard (Carter 30): 55 words
the celebrity of Shakspeare's mulberry, and Pope's willow (Carter 31): 14 words
to the rich tracery of a former age (Carter 25): 19 words
where repose the ashes of the poet, marked only (Carter 35): 31 words
the lapse of years softens the errors of the man (Carter 38): 33 words

Letter 13

The Castle of Chepstow is still a magnificent pile (Willett 20): 17 words
ecclesiastical relic of the olden time (Dix 88): 80 words
so verdant and silken that it seems the very floor (Willis, *Pencillings*, 149): 17 words
In contemplating these ruins more closely (Brettell 75): 80 words
The ruin, generally speaking, is unusually perfect (Willett 57): 25 words
but the roof has long since fallen in (Willett 66): 13 words
the recollection of genius of the highest order (Corry and Evans 273–274): 92 words
The room forms an irregular octagon (*Cursory Observations* 50–51): 83 words
exercised the talents, of a Miller, a Bryant (Corry and Evans 281): 26 words
the sun to shine, the flowers to bloom (Corson 26): 25 words
Above the door are the nearly obliterated remains (Corson 288): 38 words
whether we regard the picturesque disorder (*Black's Picturesque* 18–19): 77 words
its fertile fields, luxuriant woods (*Black's Picturesque* 173): 8 words

Letter 14

present pleasing contrasts, scarcely surpassed (Corson 295–296): 86 words
the groves tastefully clumped, the ancient trees (Willis, *Letters*, 111): 28 words
will live and be beloved for ever (Willis, *Letters*, 97): 12 words
that the enthusiasm of others abated his (Willis, *Rural Letters*, 291): 9 words

Letter 15

carvings of leaves and flowers, wrought in stone (Irving, *Abbotsford*, 11): 22 words
Scene after scene swept through my fancy (Willis, *Pencillings*, 132): 9 words
It is one labyrinth of gigantic arches (Willis, *Pencillings*, 81): 49 words
The ground about was piled up with magnificent (Willis, *Pencillings*, 129): 17 words
same hand that waved its wand of enchantment (Willis, *Pencillings*, 213): 16 words
The floor is of black and white marble (*Black's Picturesque* 121–122): 43 words
There was the broad-skirted blue coat (Willis, *Pencillings*, 213): 15 words
close to where the high altar formerly stood (*Scottish Tourist* 301): 25 words
When I retired for the night, I found it (Irving, *Abbotsford*, 51): 24 words
vie with each other in splendid extravagance (Laing 376): 14 words

Letter 16

it seems as if nature had amused herself (Willis, *Pencillings*, 173): 8 words
The eye lost its powers in gazing (Willis, *Inklings*, 1:211): 8 words

It ennobles the sentiments, enlarges the affections (*Memorials* 165–166): 109 words
This name must be lifted up as a beacon ("Hartley Coleridge" 71–72): 845 words
lawns that extend like sheets of vivid green (Irving, *Sketch-Book*, 1:120): 69 words

Letter 17

air as rousing to the spirits as a blast (Willis, *Pencillings*, 234): 17 words
the stream of industry and toil pulses ("Address" 1): 50 words
so lost in astonishment and absorbed ("Transept" 9): 42 words
Rhodes must hide their diminished heads ("Introduction" 2): 22 words
this amalgamation of rank, this kindly blending ("Introduction" 2): 51 words
does not exhibit a new view of nature (Hazlitt 157): 35 words
He holds no communion with his kind (Hazlitt 150): 35 words
he can say it differently from others (Hazlitt 151–152): 34 words

Letter 18

Here, in the transept, with the glorious sunlight ("Fine Arts" 49): 363 words

Letter 19

which Oxford has not unaptly been styled (Dix 107–108): 63 words
our admiration, but Oxford claims our veneration (Dix 121): 30 words
His profile was more striking than his front face (Dix 119): 46 words
a thoughtful and somewhat sullen brow (Macaulay 2:160): 18 words

Letter 20

Washington was the hero and model patriot (Giles 14): 36 words
the pensive sympathies that pervaded the assembly (Burritt 37): 13 words
By that still nobler, higher and holier spirit (Scribner 22): 22 words
theft, adultery, manstealing, piracy, and murder (Foster 11): 28 words

Letter 21

tender and blameless in his family affections (Cormenin 120): 30 words
How many services never to be forgotten (Cormenin 108): 15 words
When the sturdiest characters gave way (Cormenin 195): 33 words
There is a fascination in the soft gaze (Cormenin 231): 40 words
manners the most affable, temper the most gentle (Cormenin 151): 33 words
nothing offensive in his personalities (Cormenin 234): 27 words
His vast and well-developed forehead announces (Cormenin 200–201): 29 words
man of lofty reason, natural and without pretension (Cormenin 146): 22 words

more dazzling, more thundering than the bolt (Cormenin 255): 13 words
He wears an exterior of remarkable austerity (Cormenin 263): 17 words

Letter 22

his hair soft, straight, fine and white (Jay, *Inquiry*, 129): 25 words
of a beautiful monkish legend connected with ("Translation" 255): 19 words
the fountains of mingled grief and joy stole out ("Mother"): 22 words
the bells there called to mass and prayer-meeting ("Pauline"): 17 words

Letter 23

into a bolder outline and a loftier altitude (Miller 26): 20 words
One of the cardinal truths of religion and freedom ("Ralph"): 35 words

ADDITIONAL PLAGIARISM IN *THE AMERICAN FUGITIVE IN EUROPE* (1855)

Chapter 21

small mean-looking house of wood and plaster (*An Account* 365): 49 words
the parish church, a large and venerable (*An Account* 370): 35 words
In whatever light we view education (Stewart, "Education," 325): 128 words

Chapter 22

The Castle rises from the point of a headland (T. Wright, *History*, 116): 30 words
exquisite effusion of the youthful genius (T. Wright, *History*, 105): 11 words
do homage to the memory of the divine poet (T. Wright, *History*, 108): 18 words
amidst the noise and bustle of civil dissentions (T. Wright, *History*, 110): 16 words
watered by the translucent Wye (Spence 30–32): 83 words
The views around Hereford are very sylvan (Spence 34): 22 words
The destructive exploits of conquerors may dazzle (Bigland 78): 56 words

Chapter 24

A statue of the renowned chief, cut by Thom (*Ayrshire* lii): 43 words
chiselled out of solid blocks of freestone (*Guide* 102): 127 words
vowed love while the woods of Montgomery (Cunningham 3:20): 12 words
a more than Simonides in pathos (Moir 123): 48 words

Chapter 26

intermixture of foibles with virtues (Wakefield 123): 16 words

Chapter 27

how he used to hang over its one arch (Gilfillan, "Lord Byron," 411): 106 words

Chapter 28

To this valley I stretch forth my affections (Aga 11): 80 words
my pride was raised to no small degree (Aga 18): 110 words

Chapter 29

consists of a bronze bust of the poet ("Monument"): 113 words
Hood was not a merely ephemeral writer ("Oration"): 469 words
may that morn have brightened into perfect day ("Late"): 13 words

Chapter 30

There shine the fine open glossy brow (Gilfillan, "Edward Irving," 3): 11 words

PLAGIARISM IN *CLOTEL*

Chapter 1

the foundation of all civilization and culture (Bowditch 56–57): 283 words
at which the bones, muscles, sinews, blood, and nerves ("An Auction"): 41 words
What words can tell the inhumanity, the atrocity (Allen 15–16): 78 words

Chapter 3

here these faithful animals, swimming nearly all the time ("Hunting"): 598 words

Chapter 4

was one far retired from the public roads (Child 115–116): 132 words
she well knew that a union with her proscribed race (Child 117–118): 93 words
The iris of her large, dark eye had the melting (Child 118–119): 36 words
The edicts of society had built up a wall (Child 116): 14 words
love, and surrounded by an outward environment (Child 119–123): 352 words

Chapter 5

looks and manner were expressive of deep (Whittier, "Great," 120): 11 words
breaking the night-silence with the shrieks (Whittier, "Great," 120): 37 words
you will hear the burst of bitter lamentation ("Views"): 23 words

Chapter 6

The once unshorn face of nature now ("Prospects"): 10 words
poplars lift their tapering tops almost to prop (de Kroyft 23): 26 words
We have searched in vain for any authority (Hutson 401–402): 242 words
The Bible furnishes to the slaveholder armour (Thornwell 108): 170 words
Her form was tall and graceful, her features ("Charlotte" 275): 22 words
We must try the character of Slavery (Allen 13): 223 words
True Christian love is of an enlarged (*Gleanings* 50): 20 words
Now, to suit this rule to your particular (Bowditch 41–42): 186 words
Now, eye-servants are such as will work (Bowditch 35): 189 words
Take care that you do not fret or murmur (Bowditch 44–45): 508 words
There is only one circumstance which may appear (Bowditch 47): 307 words
Q. What command has God given to servants (Bowditch 50): 300 words

Chapter 7

Friends and neighbors! you have congregated to see ("Curious"): 159 words
Mr. J. Higgerson attempted to correct a negro man ("Shocking"): 240 words
No community can be prosperous where honest labor (Palfrey 53): 48 words

Chapter 8

Her head grew dizzy, and her heart fainted (Child 123–125): 335 words
too pure to form a selfish league with crime (Child 125–128): 437 words
their barouche rolled along a winding road (Child 128–129): 60 words
no further occasion to assume a tenderness (Child 129–131): 336 words

Chapter 10

claim, hold, and treat a human being (Sunderland 47): 16 words
it classes men-stealers among murderers (Sunderland 140): 18 words
to take the *earner*, is a compound, life-long theft (Weld, *Bible*, 11): 29 words
ascend to the bosom of the Father and resume (S. Grimké 24–25): 385 words
for the argument from internal evidence is not only refuted (Patton 6): 23 words
then it misrepresents the character of God (Patton 7): 12 words
The Old Testament contains this explicit (Patton 5): 182 words
He surveys the church, and lo! thousands (Patton 5–6): 473 words
he took upon himself the form of a servant (S. Grimké 14): 34 words
Are we not virtually as a nation adopting (S. Grimké 28): 168 words
be divested, except by an act of gross injustice (S. Grimké 5): 37 words
Modest and self-possessed, with a voice of great ("Lucy Stone"): 23 words

Chapter 11

His smooth cheek hath a glossy hue (Key): 257 words

Chapter 13

ferocious, gaunt, and savage-looking animals ("A Visit"): 29 words
The big bee flies high / The little bee makes the honey ("Sentimental"): 24 words

Chapter 15

What social virtues are possible in a society (Martineau, *Society*, 2:313): 24 words
it is not slavery under which he groans (Tillinghast): 20 words

Chapter 16

Whoever denies this, his lips libel his heart (Weld, *American*, 7): 73 words
and the sounds from a thousand musical instruments ("Dismal"): 26 words
all my brethren, let us take a rest (Simpson): 336 words
You may place the slave where ("Emancipation"): 133 words

Chapter 18

Their good deeds have been consecrated only ("Free Colored"): 55 words
had his aliquot proportion of the injustice done (Stewart 7): 143 words
no longer apparently the same people (McDonogh 18): 73 words
they are like other men; flesh and blood (McDonogh 24–25): 260 words

Chapter 19

dreaded every moment lest the scene should change (Child 138–139): 37 words
Webster and family entered Edgartown, on a visit ("Quite"): 241 words

Chapter 20

That government is despotic where the rulers (Stevens 6–7): 599 words
The loss of a firm national character (Maxcy 18–19): 139 words

Chapter 21

On the last day of November, 1620 (Stewart 9–10): 450 words
The origin of American slavery is not lost (Scoble 97): 43 words
human sacrifices awakened the capacious mind (Hughes 13): 103 words
from Scripture, and it is a little remarkable ("Christianized" 78): 96 words
I dare not predict how far your example (Garrison, *Address*, 5–6): 39 words
Remember what a singular relation you sustain (Garrison, *Address*, 6–7): 94 words
Happy is that people whose God is the Lord (Garrison, *Address*, 8): 23 words

Get as much education as possible for yourselves (Garrison, *Address*, 10): 34 words
its doctrines odious, its means contemptible (Garrison, *Address*, 22): 10 words
because they are profligate and vicious (Garrison, *Address*, 22): 35 words
The most beautiful flowers soon fade, and droop (*Gleanings* 24): 51 words
as you love us and hope to meet us (McDonogh 26): 30 words
In the midst of the buoyancy of youth (Welch 108): 186 words
Peace to his ashes! he has fought the fight (Hughes 13): 68 words
True greatness consists in doing good (Purvis 8): 60 words

Chapter 22

"Are you an *Odd Fellow?*" "No *Sir!*" ("Smart Boy"): 57 words
I say boldly that no man living (Baines 10): 253 words
paradise is high percentum on factory ("Worshippers"): 76 words

Chapter 23

in a form unusually repulsive and deadly (Beard 214–215): 268 words
In the midst of disorder and confusion death heaped (Beard 216): 38 words
ate nor slept, nor separated from each other (Martineau, *Society*, 2:325): 18 words
There she stood, trembling, blushing, and weeping (Child 137): 27 words
accustomed to the fondest indulgence, surrounded (Child 137): 12 words
understand how great was her degradation ("Woes"): 29 words
This was a most singular spot, remote ("A Peep" 244): 49 words
For many days she had a confused consciousness (Child 139–140): 70 words
so carefully cherished, and so tenderly beloved (Child 141): 19 words
It tells not only its own story of grief ("Story"): 40 words

Chapter 24

The evils consequent on slavery are not lessened (Beard 19): 46 words
labouring under the sense of their personal (Beard 21): 22 words
heard the twang of the driver's whip (Beard 27): 32 words
Hunger, thirst, fatigue, and loss of sleep (Beard 167–168): 42 words
uncheered by the voice of kindness, alone, hopeless ("Pauline"): 15 words
Thus carnage was added to carnage (Beard 192–193): 23 words
and their bones, partly calcined by the sun (Beard 193): 36 words

Chapter 25

dusk of the evening previous to the day when she was (Gates): 672 words

Chapter 26

The wind blew strong, and swept the flames ("Mother"): 50 words
were trifling in comparison (Garrison, "Declaration," 198): 82 words
A traditionary freedom will not save us ("Shackford's"): 128 words

Chapter 28

beautiful monkish legend ("Translation"): 19 words
fountains of mingled ("Mother"): 21 words
bells there called ("Pauline"): 17 words

PLAGIARISM IN *MIRALDA*

Chapter 7

The Bible furnishes (Thornwell 108): 170 words
Her form was tall ("Charlotte" 275): 22 words
We must try (Allen 13): 220 words
True Christian love (*Gleanings* 50): 20 words

Chapter 9

government is despotic (Stevens 6–7): 389 words
might take refuge in the heathen temples of Theseus ("Character" 199): 56 words
grinding and absolute (Stevens 7): 17 words

Chapter 11

have broken up the true cross for pencils (Gilfillan, "Napoleon," 182): 37 words
muscles around her faultless mouth became convulsed ("Very Touching"): 58 words

Chapter 12

The full-orbed moon shed her soft refulgence over (Veritas 291): 23 words
golden kisses burnished the rich clusters of purple ("Dead Bride"): 29 words

Chapter 13

youth, wonderful beauty, and uncommon courage ("Heroism" 48): 13 words

Chapter 14

a weary heart gets no gladness out of sunshine (Thackeray 48): 18 words
distance into streaks of purest gold, and nature seemed (Todd 22): 17 words
What social virtues (Martineau, *Society*, 2:313), 24 words

Chapter 15

evils consequent (Beard 19): 157 words
For many days ("Pauline"): 14 words
Thus carnage (Beard 167–168): 65 words

Chapter 16

dusk of the evening (Gates): 618 words

Chapter 17

the foundation (Bowditch 56–57): 90 words

Chapter 18

luxuriant verdure that forms the constant garb of the tropics (Ballou 72): 13 words
The big bee ("Sentimental"): 23 words
here these faithful ("Hunting"): 447 words

Chapter 19

were trifling (Garrison, "Declaration," 198): 17 words
A traditionary ("Shackford's"): 104 words

Chapter 21

teeth that a Tuscarora might envy (Ballou 162): 27 words
The most beautiful (*Gleanings* 24): 48 words
In the midst (Welch 108): 184 words

Chapter 22

in a form (Beard 214–216): 154 words

Chapter 24

trembling, blushing (Child 137): 24 words
accustomed to the fondest (Child 137): 12 words

Chapter 25

mingling gloomily with the surges (Simms 2:124): 21 words
groaned with its own wild and ungovernable (Simms 2:139): 11 words
illuminated the black and boiling surges (Simms (2:142): 10 words
the priests and choristers, the deep and solemn (Tartt 73): 21 words

Chapter 26

splendor of the setting sun, lingering (Aguilar 91): 37 words
broad sheets ("Mother"): 17 words

Chapter 27

God's illuminated clock, set in the dark steeple of time (Willmott 218): 10 words

Chapter 29

the opportunity of softening it in the brook (Beggs 51): 45 words

Chapter 30

beaten by his valet in learning Italian (Willmott 45): 9 words
from the humour of Chaucer to the dreams (Willmott 136): 12 words

Chapter 31

either flying noiselessly over the graves (Aguilar 361): 21 words
smiled at their own sparkling rays gleaming (Aguilar 382): 16 words

Chapter 32

beautiful monkish legend ("Translation"): 19 words
fountains of mingled ("Mother"): 22 words
hope gleamed up amidst its crushed and broken (Aguilar 396): 14 words
inward sunshine emanating from a mind (Strickland 86): 14 words

Chapter 33

the gleaming waters, the glistening stars (Aguilar 113): 22 words

Chapter 34

cardinal truths of religion and freedom ("Ralph"): 35 words
generosity are, at best, poor guarantees (Brown and Young 12): 161 words
body, his muscles, his bones, his flesh (Brown and Young 5): 161 words
The breast that glows with indignation (D. Brown 5): 102 words
Fringed with hoary rocks and thick dark (Aguilar 245): 13 words
Fame is the recompense, not of the living (Thatcher 3–4): 85 words

Chapter 36

casts man down from that exaltation (A. Grimké 5–6): 236 words

PLAGIARISM IN *CLOTELLE* (1864 AND 1867)

Chapter 2

bones, muscles ("An Auction"): 41 words

Chapter 5

its small dimpled hands were slyly hid (Welby 25): 25 words

Chapter 7

once unshorn ("Prospects"): 10 words
poplars lift (de Kroyft 23): 36 words
Her form ("Charlotte," 275): 22 words
True Christian (*Gleanings* 50): 20 words

Chapter 11

true cross (Gilfillan, "Napoleon," 182): 37 words
muscles around ("Very Touching"): 58 words

Chapter 12

full-orbed moon (Veritas 291): 23 words
golden kisses ("Dead Bride"): 29 words

Chapter 13

youth, wonderful ("Heroism" 48): 13 words

Chapter 14

weary heart (Thackeray 48): 18 words
into streaks (Todd 22): 17 words
social virtues (Martineau, *Society*, 2:313): 24 words

Chapter 15

evils consequent (Beard 19): 157 words
For many days ("Pauline"): 14 words
Thus carnage (Beard 167–168): 65 words

Chapter 16

dusk of the evening (Gates): 618 words

Chapter 18

luxuriant verdure (Ballou 72): 13 words
The big bee ("Sentimental"): 23 words
here these faithful ("Hunting"): 76 words

Chapter 19

were trifling (Garrison, "Declaration," 198): 15 words

Chapter 21

might envy (Ballou 162): 27 words
The most beautiful (*Gleanings* 24): 48 words
In the midst (Welch 108): 184 words

Chapter 22

in a form (Beard 214–216): 304 words

Chapter 24

trembling, blushing (Child 137): 24 words
accustomed to the fondest (Child 137): 12 words

Chapter 25

mingling gloomily (Simms 2:124): 21 words
groaned with (Simms 2:139): 11 words
illuminated the black (Simms (2:142): 10 words
the priests (Tartt 73): 21 words

Chapter 26

splendor of (Aguilar 91): 37 words
broad sheets ("Mother"): 17 words

Chapter 27

God's illuminated (Willmott 218): 10 words

Chapter 31

either flying (Aguilar 361): 21 words
smiled at (Aguilar 382): 16 words

Chapter 32

beautiful monkish legend ("Translation"): 19 words
fountains of mingled ("Mother"): 22 words

hope gleamed (Aguilar 396): 14 words
inward sunshine (Strickland 86): 14 words

Chapter 35

Fringed with (Aguilar 245): 13 words
Fame is (Thatcher 3–4): 85 words

PLAGIARISM IN *ST. DOMINGO*

poured untold treasures into France (Beard 16): 16 words
tolerated, if they did not encourage (Beard 21–22): 32 words
white enough to make them hopeful and aspiring (Beard 21): 13 words
Right is the most dangerous of weapons (Lamartine 313): 16 words
The oath of the Tennis Court (Beard 54): 12 words
The shout of battle was the only answer (Jay, *Inquiry*, 172): 46 words
blood bubbled silently in the hearts (Lamartine 316–317): 12 words
They fraternised with them, they became (Lamartine 327–328): 86 words
constituted the glory of Mirabeau (Whittier, "Lamartine's"): 10 words
Then was it that the mulattoes appealed (Beard 58): 111 words
Refusing to apply to France for aid (Beard 60): 59 words
placed themselves under the standard of royalty (Beard 61): 23 words
a chevalier of the order of Saint Louis (Beard 64–65): 23 words
crime was repaid with crime; vengeance followed (Beard 66): 8 words
an inward and prophetic genius revealed to him (Lamartine 36): 19 words
Truly did the flames of the French revolution (Beard 71): 40 words
there were whites who wore the black cockade (Beard 82): 44 words
the Rhine, and the Nile resounded with the exploits (Beard 157): 12 words
whose valor had disputed the laurel with Toussaint (Beard 157): 20 words
barbarous eloquence lay in expressive signs (Beard 167–168): 46 words
the French shall march here only over ashes (Beard 163): 43 words
That soul, when once the soul of a man (Martineau, *Hour*, 1:272): 62 words
forests of arrows will darken the sun-light (Cormenin 76–77): 20 words
Why have so many ships traversed the ocean (Beard 183–184): 112 words
In no place was the slaughter so terrible (Beard 190): 55 words
even in the repulsive remains of carnage (Beard 193): 22 words
five hundred gibbets, on which he hanged (Beard 253–254): 20 words
We have sworn to show no mercy (Beard 288): 132 words
nature annually rewarded the toil (Thornton 1:3): 23 words
His very name became a tower of strength (Beard 279): 17 words
Both born in a humble position, they raised (Beard 281–282): 128 words
rising from the depths of the ocean (Beard 296–297): 21 words

PLAGIARISM IN *THE ESCAPE*

Act 1 Scene 3

plunge amid its rolling, foetid shades (Schmucker 89–90): 140 words
It was a glorious moonlight night in autumn (Schmucker 93): 83 words

Act 3 Scene 4

My heart pants and my soul is moved (Pacini 4): 21 words
Thou who canst rend the veil of centuries. (Pacini 16): 8 words
Passions, and conscience, like another man (Knowles 44): 30 words

Act 5 Scene 1

Conceive of a mind, a living soul (Whipple 189): 98 words

Act 5 Scene 4

where is the invention / of this growing age (G. Taylor): 154 words

PLAGIARISM IN *THE BLACK MAN*

"The Black Man and His Antecedents"

generally received opinion of the most eminent (*God's* 94): 106 words
Volney assumes it as a settled point that (Armistead 122): 16 words
indicated the greatness which she was destined to attain (Blyden 13): 19 words
No nation has ever been found, which (Blyden 12–13): 123 words
slaves in that island have built some 220 chapels ("Jamaica"): 137 words
As with the eagle, so with man (Brooke 22): 76 words

"Benjamin Banneker"

nearer to the foot of the oppressor (D. Brown 17): 25 words
the inspirations of ambition, of hope, of health (D. Brown 37): 44 words
was endowed by Nature with all those excellent (Johnson 1:26): 80 words
that quality without which judgment is cold (Johnson 1:223): 23 words
He knew every branch of history, both natural (Johnson 3:305): 41 words
Like the golden sun that has sunk beneath (D. Brown 39): 32 words
believed in the divinity of reason (Lamartine 137): 41 words
He had faith in liberty, truth, and virtue (Lamartine 140): 8 words
laboured incessantly, lived irreproachably, and died (Doran 1:124): 12 words

"Nat Turner"

Biography is individual history, as distinguished (D. Brown 3): 33 words

"Madison Washington"

expressive countenance paints and reflects every (Cormenin 231): 28 words
dignified, calm, and unaffected features announced (Lamartine 231): 8 words
skin marbled with the animation of life, and veined (Lamartine 265–266): 24 words
He was an instrument of enthusiasm, whose value (Lamartine 233): 14 words
perfect preparation for the grand alternative ("Hero-Mutineers" 206): 29 words

"Henry Bibb"

In one of Casimir de la Vigne's dramas ("Unknown Painter" 177–178): 132 words
with as much calmness as if it had been (*God's* 91): 18 words
manly and heroic bearing excited the sympathy (*God's* 91): 15 words
wearing an expression of almost superhuman courage (*God's* 91): 51 words

"Crispus Attucks"

principle that taxation and representation (Goodrich, *History*, 1106): 77 words

"Dessalines"

rapidly through several intermediate grades (J. Brown 2:157): 36 words
entirely ignorant of learning, as the utmost (J. Brown 2:157): 17 words
His complexion was a dingy black; his eyes (J. Brown 2:158): 33 words
Hunger, thirst, fatigue and loss of sleep (Beard 167–168): 56 words
The lively green of the sugar-cane ("Notes" 153): 27 words
adroit, stern, savage man (Beard 246): 23 words
six military divisions, each to be under the command (J. Brown 2:146): 214 words
faith in religion was established by law (J. Brown 2:147): 20 words
Scorning effeminacy, he seemed ambitions to inure ("Parallel"): 31 words
wears out the blood that marked his course ("Parallel"): 37 words
Military talents have been ascribed to (J. Brown 2:158): 17 words

"Ira Aldridge"

general ear charmed, or the general tongue arrested (Doran 1:80): 61 words
were princes of the Foulah (Armistead, "Concluding," 156–158): 698 words

"Joseph Cinque"

in the month of August, 1839, there appeared (*African Captives* 2): 337 words
The schooner proved to be the *Amistad* (*African Captives* 2): 234 words
a man of great intelligence, and natural ability (*God's* 86–87): 195 words

"Alexandre Dumas"

Near Lisle, Dumas, with four men (Armistead, "Concluding," 140): 166 words
During this time he has published (Armistead, "Concluding," 141): 215 words

"Phillis Wheatley"

The interesting countenance and humble (Armistead, *Tribute*, 333): 36 words
As Phillis grew up to womanhood (Armistead, *Tribute*, 334–335): 121 words

"Henry Highland Garnet"

the son of an African Chief, stolen (Armistead, *Tribute*, 510–513): 89 words

"Alexander Crummell"

the grave Thucydides to the rhapsodical Lycophron ("Life and Policy" 4): 18 words

"Alexander Petion"

haughty mulattoes had been long dissatisfied (J. Brown 161): 21 words
Petion was a quateroon, the successor (J. Brown 165–166): 123 words
hotly pursued in his flight, finding it necessary (J. Brown 200–201): 344 words
Assuming no pretensions to personal or official (J. Brown 202): 110 words

"Frederick Douglass"

he was kindly received, and heartily welcomed (*God's* 111): 54 words
His vast and well-developed forehead (Cormenin 200–201): 30 words
lofty reason, natural and without pretension (Cormenin 146): 23 words
issuing from the depth of the soul (Cormenin 129): 13 words
He has taken lessons from the best ("New Publications"): 45 words

"Charles Reason"

A poem signifies design, method, harmony ("Poetry"): 167 words
poetry is to give pleasurable emotions ("Poetry"): 39 words

"Charlotte Forten"

Along with the brilliancy of style and warmth (*Memoirs* 539): 23 words
The gifts of nature are of no rank ("John Clare" 241): 42 words
muse delighted occasionally to catch the sunshine (Moir 47): 11 words

"William H. Simpson"

Taste has, frequently, for its object ("Cultivation" 480): 52 words
In Venice, the paintings of Titian (Hillard 1:52): 46 words

"Jean Pierre Boyer"

received in Paris the advantages of European (Beard 309): 218 words
the possession of what Christophe had exhausted (J. Brown 246): 31 words

"James McCune Smith"

History, antiquities, bibliography, translation (Moir 90): 23 words
the result of choice study, of nice observation (Moir 53): 29 words
law of labor is equally binding on genius ("Genius"): 102 words

"Edwin Bannister"

Talent is strength and subtlety of mind ("Talent" 144–145): 84 words

"Leonard J. Grimes"

the gloom, the high, dull, cold, stone walls ("The Slaver" 67): 45 words

"President Geffrard"

son of a general who had shown himself humane (Ludlow 523): 389 words
Just then, the emissaries of a conspiracy (Ludlow 523–524): 103 words

"George Vashon"

found her there. The same excellence appertains (Moir 32): 28 words

"William J. Wilson"

ennobles the sentiments, enlarges the affections (*Memorials* 390): 13 words
a quaintly curious felicity of diction (Moir 211): 17 words
from our torpidity and coldness to a sense (*Memorials* 390): 12 words

"John Mercer Langston"

The end of all eloquence is to sway men (Headley xv): 84 words
a deep and majestic stream, he moved steadily (Headley xxiii): 24 words
like a man under oath, though without ("New Publications"): 57 words
profound without being hollow (Cormenin 108): 8 words
in vigor of thought, in imagery of style (Cormenin 113): 17 words
He is a good writer who embodies in his works (Headley xvi–xvii): 72 words

"Joseph Jenkins"

stretch forth my affections (Aga 11): 80 words
My pride was raised (Aga 18): 110 words

"William Douglass"

his figure is prepossessing—a great thing (Ritchie 72): 79 words

"J. Theodore Holly"

He aims more at what he says than how he says it (Ritchie 55): 31 words

"James Pennington"

Henry Diaz, extolled in all the histories (Edgar 44–46): 129 words

"A Man Without a Name"

The sky was clear, the wind had hushed (Stratton 118–119): 24 words
the sweet chant of the feathered songsters (*Banvard* 16–17): 89 words

"Sir Edward Jordan"

A vessel of war was brought up ("Black Companion" 20): 71 words

"Captain Cailloux"

Night fell; the lovely southern night (Aguilar 117): 63 words

PLAGIARISM IN *THE NEGRO IN THE AMERICAN REBELLION*

Chapter 1

sapped the strength and rottened the virtue (Alger 23): 10 words
the first act in the drama of the American (Livermore 115–117): 491 words
A single passage from Mr. Bancroft's *History* (Livermore 124): 34 words
Prince, the valiant negro who seized that officer (Livermore 143): 92 words
There is abundant evidence of the fidelity (Livermore 158): 113 words
Colonel Greene was surprised and murdered (Livermore 159): 43 words
large numbers of negroes were enrolled (Livermore 199–200): 134 words

Chapter 2

The details of the plan, however, were not (Higginson 734): 374 words

Chapter 4

expressive countenance (Cormenin 231): 28 words
dignified, calm (Lamartine 231): 8 words
skin marbled (Lamartine 265–266): 24 words
instrument of enthusiasm (Lamartine 233): 14 words
perfect preparation ("Hero-Mutineers" 206): 29 words
Right is the most (Lamartine 313): 16 words

Chapter 5

In the earlier days of the Anti-Slavery movement ("Mobocracy" 17): 297 words
Think of a religious kidnapper! (Parker, *Nebraska*, 66): 93 words
One of the bitterest fruits of slavery in our land ("Progressive"): 95 words
On that occasion, the sons of free (Giddings): 126 words
"Dred-Scott decision" added fresh combustibles (Hall 7): 156 words

Chapter 6

for the bold attempt of John Brown (*Annual* 75–76): 387 words
let no one who glories in the revolutionary (Wheelock 189–90): 158 words

Chapter 7

Prosperity had made him giddy ("Causes" 522): 320 words
Weak as were the Southern people ("Causes" 521): 96 words

Chapter 11

Another public journal spoke of that achievement (Nell): 131 words
It is probably well known that the free ("Colored People"): 248 words

Chapter 12

New Orleans, however, though captured ("General" 186): 370 words
Gen. Butler gave orders that all negroes ("Butler"): 90 words

Chapter 13

loss of life, and always in the destruction (Clark 4): 29 words
At two o'clock on the morning of the same (Clark 5–8): 858 words
men were permitted to return to their homes (Clark 9–10): 146 words

Chapter 19

The iron hand of prejudice in the Northern ("Why Should"): 163 words

Chapter 20

The regiment was formed in a hollow square ("Presentation"): 171 words
Thence they march out of the Common ("March"): 100 words
They marched in good time, and wheeled ("Departure"): 84 words
All attempts to express the feelings ("March"): 158 words
On reaching the wharf at a quarter before ("Departure"): 161 words

Chapter 23

Night fell (Aguilar 117): 63 words

Chapter 27

from General Gilmore to evacuate the island (*Annual Report* 901–902): 123 words
eleven o'clock of Friday evening until four ("Letter of Edward" 215): 403 words
When about one hundred yards from the fort ("From Morris"): 166 words
When John Brown was led out of the Charlestown ("Colonel"): 847 words

Chapter 29

armed with Spencer rifles, which fire eight times (Arichold 8:415–416): 498 words
knapsacks, haversacks, canteens (Stephens): 278 words
Massachusetts went in first, with a cheer (G. B. 8:411): 158 words

Chapter 31

We have gleaned the facts of the fight ("Fort Pillow"): 1034 words
atrocities committed almost exceed belief ("More"): 151 words
Fitch says he saw twenty white ("Fort Pillow"): 132 words

Chapter 33

Honey Hill is about two and a half ("Battle of Honey Hill, S.C." 211): 170 words
But shall we weep for the sleeping (Mon. 97): 86 words

Chapter 35

on his beat in the streets of Norfolk ("Selected Miscellany"): 127 words
A Virginia rebel, who has issued a book ("Comical"): 179 words
We knew it; we prayed for de day (Nichols 161–162): 127 words
officers of the army, among them Gen. Slocum ("General"): 533 words
During the skirmishing, one of our men ("Negro Woman"): 159 words

Chapter 36

The sky (Stratton 118–119): 24 words
the sweet chant (*Banvard* 16–17): 89 words

Chapter 38

extraordinary bends of the wonderful ("Fourth of July Celebration"): 686 words
On the grounds in front of the residence ("Fourth of July"): 543 words

Chapter 39

A correspondent of the Cleveland "Leader" ("Bravery"): 54 words

Chapter 40

President Lincoln fell a sacrifice (Currie 200–201): 81 words
over the enemies of his country, while the peals (Bryant 188): 20 words

PLAGIARISM IN *THE RISING SON*

Chapter 1

It is said that the king of Ethiopia (W. Taylor 15): 236 words
entrepot of trade between the north and south (W. Taylor 51–53): 83 words
organized a regular army, and thus laid (W. Taylor 3): 62 words
drawn by two horses, and generally contained (W. Taylor 3–4): 35 words
Great attention was paid to the breeding (W. Taylor 16–17): 32 words
short sword, a helmet, and a shield (W. Taylor 18): 21 words
Coats of mail were used only by the principal (W. Taylor 20): 21 words
swords, battle-axes, maces, and clubs (W. Taylor 21): 11 words
After describing Arabia as "a land exhaling (Sears 39): 243 words
Homer wrote at least eight hundred years (Sears 38): 224 words
to a people whose color was peculiar, fixed (Edgar 17–18): 79 words
The German translation of Luther has Negroland (Edgar 19): 147 words
Hence, from the allusion of Jeremiah (Edgar 19): 45 words
are not constitutionally different from the rest (Edgar 23): 55 words
For if Cain was the progenitor of Noah (Edgar 22): 114 words
What was true of the Ethiopians (Edgar 47–48): 75 words

Chapter 2

Leaving a large force in Africa (Goodrich, *History*, 618): 154 words
French historians has often led them to compare ("Hannibal" 756–757): 765 words
rise to an expression still in vogue (Goodrich, *History*, 619): 130 words
Hannibal, notwithstanding his late reverses (W. Taylor 78): 148 words
equal to that of Hannibal in crossing (Goodrich, *Famous*, 154–155): 57 words
The more determined of the combatants (Abbott 290): 34 words
The city was given up to pillage (Goodrich, *Lights*, 125): 89 words
The sequel of the history of Carthage (Goodrich, *Lights*, 122): 24 words
No relics are to be seen of the grandeur (Goodrich, *Lights*, 126): 26 words

Chapter 3

South African explorer Carl Mauch visited the ruins ("Ruins"): 350 words

Chapter 5

from the grim worshippers of Odin (Sears 36): 10 words
There is a decided coincidence between (Armistead 13): 40 words

quaffing libations from human skulls (Sears 47–48): 68 words
multitudes of the native Irish were driven (Prichard 2:349): 181 words

Chapter 6

brought the subject of Mohammedanism prominently (Blyden 62–65): 666 words
settlement of modern times, sheltering forty thousand (Griffith): 249 words

Chapter 7

According to Bruce, who traveled in Africa (Edgar 19): 24 words
Quard, on the borders of Western Amhara (*American Year-Book*): 274 words

Chapter 8

the Timanis, the Susus, and the Veys (Wilson 90): 80 words
cultivate the soil to some extent (Wilson 91): 96 words
no more than might be said of every heathen tribe (Wilson 90): 22 words
have recently invented an alphabet for writing (Wilson 95–96): 132 words
wife is not placed on a footing of social equality (Wilson 182): 48 words
Sometimes they go forth in a body (Wilson 180–181): 160 words
death of the king it is not uncommon (Wilson 203): 42 words
the deyabo, a set of professional men (Wilson 133–135): 247 words
are unsurpassed for their cunning and shrewdness (Wilson 251–255): 311 words

Chapter 9

During the period when this traffic was carried (Wilson 349): 70 words
All those who have investigated the subject (Wilson 435): 78 words
Christianity does not invoke the aid of the sword (Wilson 446): 64 words
It begins every year in the month of August ("Slave Trade"): 968 words

Chapter 10

The interior presents a country inviting (Roberts 113): 304 words
The banks of the St. Paul's, St. John's (Warner 361): 61 words
Liberia is gradually growing in the elements ("National Progress" 43): 112 words
not less than six hundred tons of cam-wood (Roberts 114): 44 words
resound to the thunder of the locomotive (Clark 72–73): 46 words

Chapter 11

its mountains, the tropical luxuriance of its plains (Elliott 4): 23 words
white enough (Beard 21): 13 words
Right is the most (Lamartine 313): 16 words

The oath (Beard 54): 12 words
tolerated, if (Beard 21–22): 32 words
blood bubbled (Beard 316–17): 13 words
constituted the glory (Whittier, "Lamartine's"): 10 words
trembled; terror urged them to violence (Lamartine 327–328): 19 words
denying its prerogatives, and refusing the civic oath (Beard 58): 113 words
A young creole of good exterior (Beard 63): 117 words
raged with all the heat of a tropical climate (Beard 71): 30 words
commission retired from the burning city (Beard 71): 27 words

Chapter 13

Hunger, thirst (Beard 167–168): 19 words
By his activity and singular fierceness (J. Brown 2:157): 35 words
a savage, a slave, a soldier, a general (Beard 168): 21 words
The mulattoes, alarmed at the prospect (J. Brown 2:10): 99 words
Rigaud began the war by surprising Leogane (J. Brown 2:11–12): 247 words
Rigaud, reduced in his means of defence (J. Brown 2:15–16): 98 words

Chapter 14

adroit, stern (Beard 246): 23 words
Despotism and sensuality have often been (Beard 251): 60 words
in his impetuous and terrible march (Beard 253): 39 words
The numerous executions which began (Beard 257): 70 words
Children, women, and old men (Beard 257): 23 words
In no place was the slaughter so terrible (Beard 190): 43 words
even in the repulsive remains of carnage (Beard 193): 16 words

Chapter 15

While the cause of independence, forced (Beard 267–268): 73 words
window, high up on the side, looking out (Phillips, "Touissant"): 30 words
All communication with the outer world (Beard 269): 18 words
Endowed by nature with high qualities of mind (J. Brown 2:212): 135 words
an austere sobriety which bordered (J. Brown 2:26): 13 words
It was his custom to set off in a carriage (J. Brown 2:27): 125 words
No person knew better than he the art (J. Brown 2:27): 15 words
confined to the boundaries of St. Domingo (Rainsford 259): 28 words
tower of strength (Beard 279): 17 words

Chapter 16

assured the natives of the essential goodness (Beard 284): 17 words
independence of Saint Domingo is proclaimed (Beard 287–288): 73 words
Having, by a show of mildness, gained (Beard 291): 52 words
The title of majesty was conferred (Beard 299–301): 529 words

framers of the constitution under which Dessalines (Beard 303–304): 51 words
the mulattoes of Hayti despised the (Beard 304): 79 words
The regular army of Dessalines was composed (J. Brown 2:150): 216 words
This ferocious manifesto was intended (J. Brown 2:152–154): 981 words
Many of the great chiefs in the black (J. Brown 2:154–155): 392 words
Always violent and sanguinary, when there (J. Brown 2:159): 192 words
victorious mulattoes followed up their success (J. Brown 2:159): 77 words

Chapter 17

The ambitious and haughty mulattoes (J. Brown 2:161): 21 words
a quateroon, the successor of Rigaud (J. Brown 2:165–166): 114 words
In this contest the impetuosity (J. Brown 2:161–162): 327 words
The successes of Christophe in his late (J. Brown 2:162–165): 653 words
The struggle between the two presidents (J. Brown 2:177–178): 379 words
When Petion had been left at peace (J. Brown 2:188–190): 1025 words
Christophe, like Dessalines, had been (J. Brown 2:180–182): 882 words
On the 4th of April the Council (J. Brown 2:183): 295 words
finished these creations of his new monarchy (J. Brown 2:185–186): 173 words

Chapter 18

now enthroned as the sovereign of the North (J. Brown 2:191–192): 529 words
Conscious of his military superiority (J. Brown 2:192–193): 506 words
Petion conducted the defence with considerable (J. Brown 2:194): 206 words
The siege of Port au Prince had now continued (J. Brown 2:196–198): 843 words

Chapter 19

Christophe had now discovered the too palpable (J. Brown 2:199–200): 380 words
Petion dared not to tax his subjects (J. Brown 2:206): 126 words
The army of the monarchy was in all things (J. Brown 2:209): 197 words
Upon ordinary occasions Christophe assumed (J. Brown 2:215–216): 297 words
Christophe, though a pure African, was not (J. Brown 2:213–214): 291 words
Political offences were never left unpunished (J. Brown 2:211): 199 words
Petion had long been despondent (J. Brown 2:230–231): 442 words
Assuming no pretensions to personal or official (J. Brown 2:202): 70 words
Petion was subtle, cautious (J. Brown 2:201): 45 words

Chapter 20

new president was peaceably acknowledged (J. Brown 2:231): 35 words
Boyer, finding himself tranquilly seated (J. Brown 2:233–234): 397 words
Having accomplished the objects of his visit (J. Brown 2:235–236): 313 words

Chapter 21

Christophe, who now might be denominated (J. Brown 2:237–238): 561 words
Christophe was attacked, while at mass (J. Brown 2:239–241): 996 words
With a mind little capable of continuous thought (Beard 311): 73 words

Chapter 22

The authorities of Santo Domingo were clearly (J. Brown 2:248–250): 544 words
At length a secret agent of the minister (J. Brown 2:251): 148 words
At length, in 1825, after the recognition (Beard 312): 48 words
Boyer returned to Hayti in Leclerc's expedition (Beard 309): 48 words
the possession of what Christophe had exhausted (J. Brown 2:246): 32 words

Chapter 23

He had done little more than enter (Beard 315–316): 132 words

Chapter 24

He became a soldier at the early age of fifteen ("General"): 304 words
It may be set down as a truism, that slavery (Holly 327): 165 words

Chapter 26

Terror immediately seized the individual who beheld (Phillipo 248); 55 words
Dreams and visions constituted fundamental articles (Phillipo 273–274): 180 words
Brazil has given the death-blow (untitled, *Friends' Intelligencer*, 169–170): 472 words

Chapter 30

cavaliers—gentlemen-adventurers aspiring to live (Greeley 1–2): 76 words
It is very common at this day to speak (Greeley 2): 636 words

Chapter 31

prepared and used by the Reverend Samuel Phillips (Moore 137): 38 words
In 1641, the Massachusetts Colony passed the following (Coffin 8–9): 86 words

Chapter 32

On the 6th of May, 1720, the negroes (Coffin 11–12): 260 words
In August, 1730, an insurrection of blacks (Coffin 13–15): 431 words
In the year 1800, the city of Richmond (Coffin 24–25): 131 words

Chapter 33

The Boston Massacre, March 5, 1770, may justly (Livermore 115–117): 443 words
clear account of the condition of the army (Livermore 124): 33 words
Prince, the valiant negro who seized that officer (Livermore 143): 43 words
the "Battle of Rhode Island," on the 29th of August, (Livermore 158): 14 words
When Colonel Greene was surprised and murdered (Livermore 159): 43 words

Chapter 35

Lest this demonstration of 'public opinion' (Weld, *Slavery*, 156–157): 141 words

Chapter 36

His plans showed some natural generalship (Higginson 732): 99 words
The details (Higginson 734): 374 words

Chapter 38

A more marked testimonial would not (Phillips, "Letters"): 52 words

Chapter 39

in the month (*African Captives* 2): 337 words
The schooner (*African Captives* 2): 234 words
great intelligence (*God's* 86–87): 195 words

Chapter 42

Long be memorable (*Annual Report* 75–76): 133 words
free colored population ("Colored People"): 248 words

Chapter 45

The first intimation that the commanding ("Another Account" 7:15): 68 words
From eleven ("Letter of Edward L. Pierce"): 403 words
When about ("From Morris Island"): 130 words
The Fifty-Fourth ("From Morris Island"): 36 words
When inquiry ("Colonel"): 115 words

artillery was very harmless, but their musketry fearful (Arichold): 485 words
an aide came riding up to the Colonel (Stephens): 166 words
The Fifty-Fourth (G. B.): 158 words
After the rebels ("Fort Pillow Disaster"): 239 words
Honey Hill ("Battle of Honey Hill, S.C."): 170 words
The Thirty-second United States colored troops ("Batlle of Honey Hill"): 807 words

Chapter 48

Amid the moral and political darkness ("Third"): 20 words
heroism of this small body of proscribed (*Proceedings* 150): 32 words
face indicates perseverance that will not falter (Bungay 118): 13 words

Chapter 50

CRISPUS ATTUCKS
principle that (Goodrich, *History*, 1106): 77 words

PHILLIS WHEATLEY
As Phillis (Armistead, *Tribute*, 334–335): 121 words

BENJAMIN BANNEKER
nearer to (D. Brown 17): 25 words
the inspirations (D. Brown 37): 44 words
was endowed (Johnson 1:26): 80 words
that quality (Johnson 1:223): 23 words
He knew every (Johnson 3:305): 41 words
Like the golden (D. Brown 39): 32 words
believed in the divinity (Lamartine 137): 41 words
He had faith (Lamartine 140): 8 words
laboured incessantly (Doran 1:124): 12 words

FREDERICK DOUGLASS
he was kindly (*God's* 111): 54 words
His vast (Cormenin 200–201): 30 words
lofty reason (Cormenin 146): 23 words
issuing from (Cormenin 129): 13 words
He has taken ("New Publications"): 45 words

ALEXANDER W. WAYMAN
There is harmonious blending of the poetical (Bungay 29–30): 74 words

CHARLES REASON
poem signifies ("Poetry"): 167 words
Poetry is ("Poetry"): 41 words

WILLIAM J. WILSON
ennobles the sentiments (*Memorials* 390): 13 words
a quaintly curious (Moir 211): 17 words
from our torpidity (*Memorials* 390): 12 words

JOHN MERCER LANGSTON
The end (Headley xv): 84 words
a deep (Headley xxiii): 24 words
like a man ("New Publications"): 57 words

JAMES MCCUNE SMITH
History, antiquities (Moir 90): 23 words
law of labor ("Genius"): 102 words

ALEXANDER CRUMMELL
the grave ("Life and Policy"): 18 words

HENRY HIGHLAND GARNET
the son (Armistead, *Tribute*, 510–513): 89 words

EDMONIA LEWIS
The highest art is that which rises above ("Relation of Art" 36): 175 words

PHILIP A. BELL
vivid imagination over the productions of his pen (Bungay 106): 24 words

WILLIAM H. SIMPSON
It is a compliment to a picture to say (Hillard 1:51): 20 words
Taste has ("Cultivation" 480): 52 words
In Venice (Hillard 1:151): 33 words
The Venetian painters were evidently diligent (Hillard 1:151): 14 words
It is very easy to transcribe the emotions (Hillard 1:152): 46 words

EDWIN BANNISTER
Talent is ("Talent" 215–216): 84 words

IRA ALDRIDGE
the general ear charmed, or the general tongue arrested (Doran 1:80): 61 words

FANNY JACKSON
as freely as water from an unfailing fountain (Bungay 21): 15 words
The organ of benevolence is prominently developed (Bungay 22): 17 words

JOSEPH CLINTON
countenance mild, benignant and thoughtful (Bungay 74): 37 words
The outbursting and overwhelming effusions (Bungay 73): 34 words

BENJAMIN TANNER
viewed through the prism of his rich imagination (Bungay 302): 29 words

SINGLETON T. JONES
brilliant with unmeasured poetry (Bungay 18): 15 words
drives home a truth by solid argument (Bungay 61–62): 24 words
like a shock from an electric battery (Bungay 61): 13 words

HENRY GARLAND MURRAY
He possesses the true *vivida vis* of eloquence (Bungay 140): 8 words

ELIJAH W. SMITH
rich melody of his musically-embodied thoughts (Redding, "Keats," vii): 8 words
mankind and things around him in harmony (Redding, "Shelley," 242): 16 words
expression of his features was mild and good (Redding, "Shelley," 245): 22 words

PLAGIARISM IN *MY SOUTHERN HOME*

Chapter 1

Among the beautiful (Child 115): 51 words

Chapter 2

one circumstance (Bowditch 47): 287 words

Chapter 6

terminating in a long, slim head, and peaked bill (Parsons 136–137): 109 words
The big bee ("Sentimental"): 24 words

Chapter 7

Now it writhed in serpent coils (Craik 172): 20 words

Chapter 8

'tis Tabor ("Hunting"): 29 words
Some few scrapings and rasping of cowhide boots ("'Hard-Shell'"): 1,282 words

Chapter 10

dusk of the evening (Gates): 618
The room was horrible in its darkness ("Kentucky Love Story"): 25 words

Chapter 12

Congo Square takes its name, as is well ("Congo"): 615 words

Chapter 14

two dollars per annum on all colored male inhabitants ("Tax"): 154 words

Chapter 17

so frail that they must be fenced about ("Negro Equality"): 181 words

Chapter 18

the South, desiring no doubt to be fully ("Alabama"): 96 words
The principal business houses of the city ("Alabama"): 228 words
looking at the many gaudy articles of wearing ("Alabama"): 394 words

Chapter 19

Nothing has been left undone to cripple (Garrison, "Preface"): 37 words

Chapter 22

a girl with a rich brown skin ("Alabama"): 185 words
Great excitement is just now taking hold ("Colored Race"): 410 words

Chapter 25

ample and cogent machinery to produce the necessary ("Negro Exodus"): 670 words

Chapter 28

must never be forgotten, that whatever degree (King): 74 words
utmost possible exaltation of life into approximations ("Annual Meeting"): 49 words
etherealised and refined in the alembic of genius (Moir 2): 22 words
fascinating powers of language—eloquence, wit, humor (Newell 108): 18 words
to imbue our minds with broader and better views (P. Wright 161): 26 words
It is said, never a shadow falls (P. Wright 160–161): 67 words
Ask the Dutch Boor whence comes his contempt (Knox 39): 44 words

Chapter 29

those builders unequalled in ancient or modern (Knox 123): 10 words
For fourteen centuries they lorded it over (Knox 82): 41 words
Civilization, or the social condition of man (Knox 47): 18 words
quickness of apprehension (Johnson 1:26): 26 words
That quality (Johnson 1:223): 23 words

APPENDIX B

Bibliography of Plagiarized Works

Abbott, Jacob. *History of Hannibal the Carthaginian*. New York: Harper, 1849. Google Books. [*Rising Son*]

Account of the Principal Pleasure Tours in England and Wales, An. London: Baldwin, Cradock, and Joy, 1822. Google Books. [*American Fugitive*]

"Address." *The Parlour Magazine of the Literature of All Nations* (May 3, 1851): 1–2. Print. [*Three Years*]

African Captives, The. New York: n.p., 1839. Slavery and Anti-Slavery. [*Black Man, Rising Son*]

Aga, Selim. *Incidents Connected with the Life of Selim Aga*. Aberdeen: published for the author, 1846. Documenting the American South. [*American Fugitive, Black Man*]

Aguilar, Grace. *Home Scenes and Heart Studies*. New York: Appleton, 1853. Google Books. [*Miralda, Black Man, Clotelle, Negro in the American Rebellion*]

"Alabama: 'Nigger Day' in a Country Town." *New York Times* (November 30, 1874): 1. America's Historical Newspapers. [*My Southern Home*]

Alger, William. *The Genius and Posture of America*. Boston: Daily Bee, 1857. Internet Archive. [*Negro in the American Rebellion*]

Allen, George. *Resistance to Slavery Every Man's Duty*. Boston: Crosby and Nichols, 1847. Google Books. [*Clotel, Miralda*]

American Year-Book and National Register for 1869, The. Ed. David N. Camp. 2 vols. Hartford: Case, 1869. Google Books. [*Rising Son*]

"Annual Meeting of the Friends of Human Progress." *Liberator* (June 21, 1861): 100. Slavery and Anti-Slavery. [*My Southern Home*]

Annual Report of the American Anti-Slavery Society. New York: American Anti-Slavery Society, 1861. Slavery and Anti-Slavery. [*Negro in the American Rebellion*]

Annual Report of the Adjutant-General of the Commonwealth of Massachusetts. Boston: Wright and Potter, 1864. Google Books. [*Negro in the American Rebellion*]

"Another Account." In *The Rebellion Record: A Diary of American Events*, 11 vols., ed. Frank Moore, 7:15. New York: Van Nostrand, 1866. Google Books. [*Negro in the American Rebellion, Rising Son*]

Arichhold, A. P. "Action of the Colored Troops." In *The Rebellion Record*, 8:415–416. Google Books. [*Negro in the American Rebellion*]

Armistead, Wilson. "Concluding Chapter of Additional Evidence." In *God's Image in Ebony*, ed. Henry Gardiner Adams, 133–163. London: Partridge and Oakey, 1854. Google Books. [*Black Man*]

——. *A Tribute for the Negro*. Manchester: Irwin, 1848. Google Books. [*Black Man, Rising Son*]

"Auction, An." *New York Evangelist* (April 29, 1847): 1. American Periodicals Series. [*Narrative, Clotel, Clotelle*]

Ayrshire Directory, The. Ayr: Ayr Advertiser Office, 1851. Internet Archive. [*Three Years*]

Baines, Edward. "Testimony and Appeal on the Effects of Total Abstinence." *British Friend* 40 (January 1853): 8–11. Google Books. [*Clotel*]

Ballou, Maturin M. *History of Cuba; or, Notes of a Traveller in the Tropics*. Boston: Phillips, Sampson, 1854. Google Books. [*Miralda, Clotelle*]

Banvard; or, The Adventures of an Artist. London: Golbourn, 1848. Google Books. [*Black Man, Negro in the American Rebellion*]

"Battle of Honey Hill, The." *Liberator* (December 16, 1864): 203. American Periodicals Series. [*Rising Son*]

"Battle of Honey Hill, S. C., The" *Liberator* (December 30, 1864): 211. American Periodicals Series. [*Negro in the American Rebellion, Rising Son*]

Beard, John R. *The Life of Toussaint L'Ouverture*. London: Ingram, Cooke, 1853. Google Books. [*Clotel, Miralda, St. Domingo, Black Man, Rising Son*]

Beggs, Thomas. *Three Lectures on the Moral Elevation of the People*. Leicester: Cook, 1843. Google Books. [*Miralda*]

Bigland, John. *Letters on the Study and Use of Ancient and Modern History*. Philadelphia: Whitehall, 1806. Google Books. [*American Fugitive*]

Black, Adam, and Charles Black. *Black's Picturesque Tourist of Scotland*. Edinburgh: Black, 1842. Google Books. [*Three Years*]

"A Black Companion of the Bath." *Anti-Slavery Reporter* 9 (January 1861): 19–22. Google Books. [*Black Man*]

Blyden, Edward Wilmot. *Liberia's Offering*. New York: Gray, 1860. Google Books. [*Black Man*]

——. "Mohammedanism in Western Africa." *Methodist Quarterly Review* 53 (January 1871): 62–78. Google Books. [*Rising Son*]

Bowditch, William I. *Slavery and the Constitution*. Boston: Wallcut, 1849. Google Books. [*Clotel, Miralda, My Southern Home*]

"Bravery of the Negro Troops." *New York Evening Post* (June 27, 1864). [*Negro in the American Rebellion*]

Breckenridge, Robert. *Memoranda of Foreign Travel*. Philadelphia: Whetham, 1839. Google Books. [*Three Years*]

Brettell, Thomas. *A Topographical and Historical Guide to the Isle of Wight*. London: Leigh, 1840. Google Books. [*Three Years*]

Brown, David Paul. *Eulogium Upon Wilberforce*. Philadelphia: Collins, 1834. Google Books. [*Three Years, Black Man, Rising Son*]

[Brown, John, and John C. Young]. *An Address to the Presbyterians of Kentucky, Proposing a Plan for the Instruction and Emancipation of Their Slaves*. Newburyport, Mass.: Whipple, 1836. Google Books. [*Miralda*]

Brown, Jonathan. *The History and Present Condition of St. Domingo*. 2 vols. Philadelphia: Marshall, 1837. Google Books. [*Black Man, Rising Son*]

Brooke, Samuel. *Slavery and the Slave-Holder's Religion*. Cincinnati: Brooke, 1846. Slavery and Anti-Slavery. [*Black Man*]

Bryant, William Cullen. "The Death of the President." *Littel's Living Age* (April 29, 1865): 188. Google Books. [*Negro in the American Rebellion*]

Bungay, George W. *Crayon Sketches and Off-Hand Takings*. Boston: Stacy and Richardson, 1852. Google Books. [*Rising Son*]

Burritt, Elihu. "The Last Hour of the Anti-Corn Law League." In *Miscellaneous Writings*, 36–42. Worcester, Mass.: Drew, 1850. [*Three Years*]

"Butler and Phelps." *New York Tribune* (August 26, 1862): 3. America's Historical Newspapers. [*Negro in the American Rebellion*]

Carlisle, Lord (George William Frederick Howard). *Two Lectures on the Poetry of Pope, and on His Own Travels in America*. Leeds: Baines and Newsome, 1851. Google Books. [*Three Years*]

Carter, James. *A Visit to Sherwood Forest*. London: Longman, 1850. Google Books. [*Three Years*]

"Causes of the Rebellion, The." *Continental Monthly* 2 (November 1862): 513–524. Google Books. [*Negro in the American Rebellion*]

Channing, William Ellery. *Slavery*. Boston: Munroe, 1836. Google Books. [*Memoir*]

"Character and Modifications of Slavery." *Tait's Edinburgh Magazine* 20 (April 1853): 191–199. Google Books. [*Miralda*]

"Charlotte Corday." *Eclectic Magazine of Foreign Literature* 17 (June 1849): 275–276. Google Books. [*Clotel, Miralda, Clotelle*]

Child, Lydia Maria. "The Quadroons." In *The Liberty Bell*, ed. Maria Weston Chapman, 115–141. Boston: Massachusetts Anti-Slavery Fair, 1842. Google Books. [*Clotel, Clotelle, Memoir, My Southern Home*]

"Christianized Sensibility vs. Christianity." *New York Evangelist* (April 15, 1847): 58. American Periodicals Series. [*Clotel*]

Clark, Peter. *The Black Brigade of Cincinnati*. Cincinnati: Boyd, 1864. Internet Archive. [*Negro in the American Rebellion*]

Clark, Thomas. "Address of Rt. Rev. Thomas M. Clark, D.D." *African Repository* 43 (March 1867): 67–81. Google Books. [*Rising Son*]

Clarke, Henry Greene. *The British Museum: Its Antiquities and Natural History*. London: Clarke, 1850. Google Books. [*Three Years*]

Coffin, Joshua. *An Account of Some of the Principal Slave Insurrections*. New York: American Anti-Slavery Society, 1860. Google Books. [*Rising Son*]

"Colonel Robert Gould Shaw." *National Anti-Slavery Standard* (August 8, 1863): 1. Slavery and Anti-Slavery [*Negro in the American Rebellion, Rising Son*]
"Colored People of New Orleans, The." *Liberator* (March 11, 1864): 11. [*Negro in the American Rebellion, Rising Son*]
"Colored Race, The." *Donahoe's Magazine* 1 (1879): 457. Google Books. [*My Southern Home*]
"Comical Black Soldier, A." *Flag of Our Union* (December 15, 1866): 797. American Periodicals Series. [*Negro in the American Rebellion*]
"Congo Dance, The." *Boston Journal* (November 8, 1879): 6. [*My Southern Home*]
Cormenin, Louis-Marie de Lahaye. *The Orators of France*. New York: Baker and Scribner, 1847. Google Books. [*Three Years, St. Domingo, Black Man, Rising Son*]
Corry, John, and John Evans. *The History of Bristol, Civil and Ecclesiastical*. Bristol: Sheppard, 1816. Google Books. [*Three Years*]
Corson, John. *Loiterings in Europe*. New York: Harper, 1848. Google Books. [*Three Years*]
Cox, William. *Crayon Sketches*. 2 vols. New York: Conner and Cooke, 1833. Google Books. [*Three Years*]
"Cultivation of Taste." *Southern Literary Messenger* 8 (July 1842): 480–481. Google Books. [*Black Man, Rising Son*]
Craik, Dinah Marie Muloch. "The Rosicrucian—A Tale of Cologne." *Dublin University Magazine* 29 (February 1847): 161–174. Google Books. [*My Southern Home*]
Cunningham, Allan. Note to "Highland Mary." In *Works of Robert Burns*, ed. Allan Cunningham. London: Bohn, 1850. Google Books. [*American Fugitive*]
"Curious Funeral Service." *Wellsborough* (Pa.) *Eagle* (May 7, 1845): 1. Access Newspaper Archive. [*Clotel*]
Currie, Gilbert E. "Assassination of Abraham Lincoln." *American Mining Gazette* 2 (April 1865): 198–203. Google Books. [*Negro in the American Rebellion*]
Cursory Observations on the Churches of Bristol, by an Occasional Visitor. 2nd ed. Bristol: Mirror Office, 1843. Internet Archive. [*Three Years*]
Danforth, Joshua N. *Gleanings and Groupings from a Pastor's Portfolio*. New York: Barnes, 1851. Google Books. [*Three Years*]
Davis, Edward M. *Extracts from the American Slave Code*. Philadelphia: n.p., 1845. Slavery and Anti-Slavery. [*Narrative*]
"Dead Bride, The." *Macon Weekly Telegraph* (November 30, 1852): 4. America's Historical Newspapers. [*Miralda, Clotelle*]
de Kroyft, Helen. *A Place in Thy Memory*. New York: Trow, 1851. Google Books. [*Clotel, Clotelle*]
"Departure of 54th Regiment of Massachusetts Volunteers." *Liberator* (June 5, 1863): 91. Slavery and Anti-Slavery. [*Negro in the American Rebellion*]
"Dismal Swamp, The." *New York Commercial Advertiser* (July 7, 1848): 1. America's Historical Newspapers. [*Clotel*]
Dix, John Ross. *Pen and Ink Sketches of Poets, Preachers, and Politicians*. London: Bogue, 1846. Google Books. [*Three Years*]

Dixon, William Hepworth. *William Penn: An Historical Biography*. Philadelphia: Blanchard and Lea, 1851. Google Books. [*Three Years*]

Doran, John. *"Their Majesties' Servants": Annals of the English Stage*, 2 vols. London: Allen, 1860. Google Books [*Black Man, Rising Son*]

Edgar, Cornelius Henry. *The Curse of Canaan Rightly Interpreted*. New York: Baker and Godwin, 1862. Google Books. [*Black Man, Rising Son*]

Elliott, Charles Wyllys. *St. Domingo, Its Revolution and Its Hero*. New York: Dix, 1855. Google Books. [*Rising Son*]

"Emancipation in Maryland." *Liberator* (August 15, 1845): 130. Slavery and Anti-Slavery. [*Clotel*]

"Fine Arts in the Crystal Palace." *Illustrated Exhibitor* (June 21, 1851): 49–55. Google Books. [*Three Years*]

"Fort Pillow Disaster, The." *Philadelphia Inquirer* (April 20, 1864): 3. America's Historical Newspapers. [*Negro in the American Rebellion, Rising Son*]

Foster, Stephen S. *Brotherhood of Thieves*. Boston: Anti-Slavery Office, 1844. Google Books. [*Narrative, Three Years*]

"Fourth of July Celebration by the Miscegenations." *Richmond Daily Dispatch* (August 11, 1864). Perseus Digital Library. [*Negro in the American Rebellion*]

"Fourth of July at the House that Jeff. Built." *Liberator* (July 29, 1864). [*Negro in the American Rebellion*]

Fox, George. *History of Pontrefact, in Yorkshire*. Pontrefact: Fox, 1827. Google Books. [*Three Years*]

"Free Colored Veterans, The." *New Orleans Daily Picayune* (January 9, 1851): 2. America's Historical Newspapers. [*Clotel*]

"From Morris Island." *New York Tribune* (July 30, 1863). Newspapers.com. [*Negro in the American Rebellion, Rising Son*]

Galignani's New Paris Guide. Paris: Galignani, 1848. Google Books. [*Three Years*]

Garrison, William Lloyd. *An Address, Delivered Before the Free People of Color, in Philadelphia, New-York, and Other Cities, During the Month of June, 1831*. 2nd ed. Boston: Foster, 1831. Slavery and Anti-Slavery. [*Clotel*]

——. "Declaration of the National Anti-Slavery Convention." *Liberator* (December 14, 1833): 198. Slavery and Anti-Slavery. [*Clotel, Miralda, Clotelle*]

——. Preface to *Narrative of the Life of Frederick Douglass*, by Frederick Douglass. Boston: Anti-Slavery Office, 1845. Google Books. [*My Southern Home*]

[Gates, Seth M.]. "Slavery in the District." *New York Evangelist* (September 8, 1842): 1. American Periodicals Series. [*Clotel, Miralda, Clotelle, My Southern Home*]

G. B. "Another Account." In *The Rebellion Record: A Diary of American Events*, 11 vols., ed. Frank Moore, 8:411. New York: Van Nostrand, 1866. [*Negro in the American Rebellion, Rising Son*]

"General Butler in New Orleans." *The Spectator* (February 13, 1864): 185–186. [*Negro in the American Rebellion*]

"General Geffrard, Ex-President of Hayti." *Semi-Weekly Wisconsin* (April 17, 1867): 2. Newspapers.com. [*Rising Son*]

"General Sherman and the Negroes." *Liberator* (April 7, 1865): 1. Slavery and Anti-Slavery. [*Negro in the American Rebellion*]

"Genius and Labor." *Merry's Museum* 42 (July 1861): 77. Google Books. [*Black Man, Rising Son*]

Giddings, Joshua. "Letter from Joshua Giddings." *Liberator* (April 16, 1852): 62. Slavery and Anti-Slavery. [*Negro in the American Rebellion*]

Giles, Joel. *Practical Liberty: An Oration*. Boston: Eastburn's, 1848. Google Books. [*Three Years*]

Gilfillan, George. "Edward Irving." *Eclectic Review* 8 (July 1854): 1–13. Google Books. [*American Fugitive*]

——. "Lord Byron." In *Lectures Delivered Before the Young Men's Christian Association*, 409–438. London: Nisbet, 1852. Internet Archive. [*American Fugitive*]

——. "Napoleon." *Eclectic Magazine of Foreign Literature* 23 (June 1851): 181–188. Google Books. [*Miralda, Clotelle*]

Gleanings from Pious Authors. Ed. James Montgomery. 1846. Repr. Philadelphia: Longstreth, 1855. Google Books. [*Clotel, Miralda, Clotelle*]

God's Image in Ebony. Ed. Henry Gardiner Adams. London: Partridge and Oakey, 1854. Google Books. [*Black Man, Rising Son*]

Goodrich, Samuel. *Famous Men of Ancient Times*. Boston: Rand, 1843. Google Books. [*Rising Son*]

——. *A History of All Nations*. Auburn: Derby and Miller, 1851. Google Books. [*Black Man, Rising Son*]

——. *Lights and Shadows of African History*. Boston: Bradbury, Soden, 1844. Google Books. [*Rising Son*]

Greeley, Horace. *A History of the Struggle for Slavery Extension or Restriction in the United States*. New York: Dix, Edwards, 1856. Google Books. [*Rising Son*]

Griffith, George Bancroft. "Origin of Easter Day, and Easter Customs." *Potter's American Monthly* 10 (April 1878): 308. Google Books. [*Rising Son*]

Grimké, Angelina. *An Appeal to the Women of the Nominally Free States*. Boston: Knapp, 1838. Internet Archive. [*Miralda*]

[Grimké, Sarah]. *An Address to Free Colored Americans*. New York: Dorr, 1837. Slavery and Anti-Slavery. [*Clotel*]

Guide to the Glasgow and Ayrshire Railway. Ayr: McCormick and Gemmell, 1841. Google Books. [*American Fugitive*]

Hall, Newman. *The American War: A Lecture for Working Men*. Boston: American Tract Society, 1862. Google Books. [*Negro in the American Rebellion*]

"Hannibal." *Blackwood's Edinburgh Magazine* 57 (June 1845): 752–765. Google Books. [*Rising Son*]

"'Hard-Shell' Sermon, A." *Springfield Republican* (November 13, 1874): 3. America's Historical Newspapers. [*My Southern Home*]

"Hartley Coleridge." *The National Magazine* 1 (July 1852): 71–72. Google Books. [*Three Years*]

Hazlitt, William. *The Spirit of the Age; or, Contemporary Portraits*. London: Colburn, 1825. Google Books. [*Clotel*]

Headley, Joel Tyler. "An Essay on the Rise and Fall of Eloquence in the French Revolution." In Cormenin, *The Orators of France*, xv–xxx. Google Books. [*Black Man, Rising Son*]

"Hero-Mutineers, The." *New York Evangelist* (December 25, 1841): 206. American Periodicals Series. [*Black Man, Negro in the American Rebellion*]

"Heroism of Elizabeth Cazotte." In *Noble Deeds of Woman; or, Examples of Female Courage and Virtue*, ed. Elizabeth Starling, 47–51. Boston: Phillips, Sampson, 1853. Google Books. [*Miralda, Clotelle*]

Higginson, Thomas Wentworth. "Denmark Vesey." *Atlantic Monthly* 7 (June 1861): 728–744. Google Books. [*Negro in the American Rebellion, Rising Son*]

Hillard, George Stillman. *Six Months in Italy*. Boston, Ticknor, Reed & Fields, 1853. Google Books. [*Black Man, Rising Son*]

Historical, Antiquarian, and Picturesque Account of Kirkstall Abbey, An. London: Longman, 1827. Google Books. [*Three Years*]

History of Kirkstall Abbey, Near Leeds, Yorkshire. Leeds: Heaton, 1837. Google Books. [*Three Years*]

Holly, J. Theodore. "Thoughts on Hayti." *Anglo-African Magazine* 1 (October 1859): 327–329. Slavery and Abolition. [*Rising Son*]

Home and Grave of Byron, The. London: Longman, n.d. Google Books. [*Three Years*]

Hughes, Benjamin F. *Eulogium on the Life and Character of William Wilberforce*. New York: Office of *The Emancipator*, 1833. Slavery and Anti-Slavery. [*Clotel*]

"Hunting Robbers with Bloodhounds." *Utica Daily Observer* (September 25, 1848): 1. Old Fulton NY Postcards. [*Clotel, Miralda, Clotelle, My Southern Home*]

[Hutson, William F.]. "The *History of the Girondists*, or Personal Memoirs of the Patriots of the French Revolution." *Southern Presbyterian Review* 2 (1848): 387–413. Google Books. [*Clotel*]

"Introduction." *Illustrated Exhibitor* (June 7, 1851): 1–3. Google Books. [*Three Years*]

Irving, Washington. *Abbotsford and Newstead Abbey*. London: Murray, 1835. Google Books. [*Three Years*]

——. *The Sketch-Book of Geoffrey Crayon*. 2 vols. London: Murray, 1822. Google Books. [*Three Years*]

J. A. J. "The Ancient Egyptians, Negroes." *The Friend* (November 19, 1836): 52–53. Google Books. [*Black Man*]

"Jamaica." *American Presbyterian Review* 3 (July 1861): 588. Google Books. [*Black Man*]

Jay, William. *Inquiry Into the Character and Tendency of the American Colonization and American Anti-Slavery Societies*. New York: Williams, 1837. Google Books. [*Three Years, St. Domingo*]

"John Clare, the Northamptonshire Poet." *Eliza Cook's Journal* 4 (February 1851): 241. Google Books. [*Black Man*]

Johnson, Samuel. *The Works of Samuel Johnson*. 2 vols. New York: Dearborn, 1832. Google Books. [*Black Man, Rising Son, My Southern Home*]

"Kentucky Love Story, A." *Boston Weekly Globe* (January 21, 1879): 7. Newspapers.com [*My Southern Home*]

Key, Thomas G. "My Little Nig." *Liberator* (December 27, 1844): 208. American Periodicals Series. [*Clotel*]

King, John. *The American Family Physician*. Cincinnati: Longley, 1857. Google Books. [*My Southern Home*]

Knowles, James Sheridan. *Love: A Play*. London: Moxon, 1840. Google Books. [*Escape*]

Knox, Robert. *The Races of Men: A Fragment*. Philadelphia: Lea and Blanchard, 1850. Google Books. [*My Southern Home*]

Laing, Samuel. *Notes of a Traveler on the Social and Political State of France*. London: Longman, 1842. Google Books. [*Three Years*]

Lamartine, Alphonse de. *History of the Girondists*. Trans. H. T. Ryde. 3 vols. London: Bohn, 1848. Google Books. [*St. Domingo, Black Man, Negro in the American Rebellion, Rising Son*]

"Late Thomas Hood, The." *London Times* (July 20, 1854): 10. Gale News Vault. [*American Fugitive*]

"Letter of Edward L. Pierce." In *The Rebellion Record: A Diary of American Events*, 11 vols., ed. Frank Moore, 7:215–216. New York: Van Nostrand, 1866. Google Books. [*Negro in the American Rebellion, Rising Son*]

"Life and Policy of Pitt, The." *Westminster Review* 78 (July 1862): 1–39. Google Books. [*Black Man, Rising Son*]

Livermore, George. *An Historical Research Respecting the Opinions of the Founders of the Republic on Negroes as Slaves, as Citizens, and as Soldiers*. Boston: John Wilson, 1862. Google Books. [*Negro in the American Rebellion*]

"Lucy Stone." *Anti-Slavery Advocate* 1 (January 1853): 29. Slavery and Abolition. [*Clotel*]

Ludlow, J. M. "Geffrard, President of Hayti." *Good Words* 3 (December 1862): 522–527. British Periodicals. [*Black Man*]

Macaulay, Thomas Babington. *The History of England, from the Accession of James II*. 3 vols. London: Longman, 1849. Google Books. [*Three Years*]

"March of the Dark Brigade, The." *The Independent* (June 4, 1863): 4. American Periodicals Series. [*Negro in the American Rebellion*]

Martineau, Harriet. *The Hour and the Man*. 3 vols. London: Moxon, 1841. Google Books. [*St. Domingo*]

———. *Society in America*. 3 vols. London: Saunders and Otley, 1837. Google Books. [*Clotel, Miralda, Clotelle*]

Maxcy, Milton. *An Oration, Delivered in the Dutch Church in Schenectady*. Albany, N.Y.: Whiting, 1803. Google Books. [*Clotel*]

McDonogh, John. *Letter of John McDonogh, on African Colonization*. New Orleans: Commercial Bulletin, 1842. Slavery and Anti-Slavery. [*Clotel*]

"Memoirs of Celebrated Characters." *London Literary Gazette* (June 10, 1854): 539–541. Google Books. [*Black Man*]

Memorials of Early Genius; and Achievements in the Pursuit of Knowledge. London: Nelson, 1848. Google Books. [*Three Years, Black Man, Rising Son*]

Miller, Hugh. *Scenes and Legends of the North of Scotland*. London: Johnstone and Hunter, 1850. Google Books. [*Three Years*]

"Mobocracy in the Senate." In *Annual Reports of the American Anti-Slavery Society*, 16–24. New York: Anti-Slavery Society, 1859. Google Books. [*Negro in the American Rebellion*]

Moir, David Macbeth. *Sketches of the Poetical Literature of the Past Half-Century*. Edinburgh: Blackwood, 1851. Google Books. [*Three Years, Black Man, Rising Son*]

Mon. Untitled article. *Weekly Anglo-African* (May 21, 1864). In *Voices of the 55th: Letters from the 55th Massachusetts Volunteers, 1861–1865*, ed. Noah Trudeau. Dayton, Ohio: Morningside House, 1996. [*Negro in the American Rebellion*]

Moore, George H. "Slave Marriages in Massachusetts." *The Historical Magazine* 15 (February 1869): 135–137. Google Books. [*Rising Son*]

"Mother, The." *Albany Evening Journal* (January 10, 1849): 2. *America's Historical Newspapers*. [*Clotel, Miralda, Clotelle*]

"Monument to Thomas Hood, The." *London Daily News* (July 19, 1854): 5. Newspaper Archive. [*American Fugitive*]

"More of the Fort Pillow Butchery." *New York Tribune* (April 21, 1864): 1. Old Fulton NY Postcards. [*Negro in the American Rebellion*]

"National Progress." *African Repository* 43 (February 1867): 43–44. Google Books. [*Rising Son*]

"Negro Equality." *Liberator* (May 22, 1863): 1. American Periodicals Series. [*My Southern Home*]

"Negro Exodus, The." *Chicago Daily Tribune* (June 25, 1879): 9. Newspapers.com. [*My Southern Home*]

"Negro Woman Shot, A." *Liberator* (April 7, 1865): 1. American Periodicals Series. [*Negro in the American Rebellion*]

Nell, William Cooper. "The War, and Colored American Auxiliaries." *Liberator* (September 6, 1861): 96. [*Negro in the American Rebellion*]

New Guide for Strangers and Residents in the City of York, A. York: Hargrove, 1844. Google Books. [*Three Years*]

New Guide to the Museum, Palace, and Gardens of Versailles, A. Versailles: Klefer, 1847. Google Books. [*Three Years*]

"New Publications." *New York Daily Tribune* (May 15, 1855): 6. Old Fulton NY Postcards. [*Black Man, Rising Son*]

Newell, Daniel. "The Influence of Light Literature Upon the Family Circle." *Christian Family Magazine* 2 (January 1843): 105–112. Google Books. [*My Southern Home*]

Nichols, George Ward. *The Story of the Great March*. New York: Harper, 1865. Google Books. [*Negro in the American Rebellion*]

"Notes of Life in Hayti: The Ill-Fated City." *Knickerbocker* 20 (August 1842): 153–160. Google Books. [*Black Man*]

"Oration Over the Tomb of Hood." *London Daily News* (July 19, 1854): 5. British Newspaper Archive. [*American Fugitive*]

Pacini, Giovanni. *Saffo: A Lyrical Tragedy in Three Acts.* Boston: Eastburn's Press, 1847. [*Escape*]

Palfrey, John G. *Papers on the Slave Power.* Boston: Merrill, Cobb, 1846. Slavery and Anti-Slavery. [*Clotel*]

"Parallel Between Bonaparte and Wellington." *Knickerbocker* 19 (January 1842): 1–18. Google Books. [*Black Man*]

Parker, Theodore. *The Boston Kidnapping.* Boston: Crosby, 1852. Slavery and Anti-Slavery. [*Rising Son*]

——. *The Nebraska Question.* Boston: Mussey, 1854. Slavery and Anti-Slavery. [*Negro in the American Rebellion*]

Parsons, Charles Grandison. *Inside View of Slavery; or, A Tour Among the Planters.* Boston: Jewett, 1855. Google Books. [*My Southern Home*]

Patton, William Weston. *Slavery, the Bible, Infidelity: Pro-slavery Interpretations of the Bible.* Hartford: Burleigh, 1847. Google Books. [*Clotel*]

"Pauline." *British and Foreign Anti-Slavery Reporter* (July 1, 1846): 102–103. Google Books. [*Clotel, Miralda, Clotelle*]

"Peep Into an Italian Interior, A." *Chambers' Edinburgh Journal* (April 16, 1852): 241–245. Google Books. [*Clotel*]

Phillippo, James Munsell. *Jamaica, Its Past and Present State.* London: Snow, 1843. Google Books. [*Rising Son*]

Phillips, Wendell. "Letters from Wendell Phillips," *National Anti-Slavery Standard* (April 27, 1867): 1. Slavery and Anti-Slavery. [*Rising Son*]

——. "Toussaint L'Ouverture." *Liberator* (April 3, 1863): 56. Slavery and Anti-Slavery. [*Rising Son*]

Planta, Edward. *A New Picture of Paris.* London: Leigh, 1816. Google Books. [*Three Years*]

"Poetry and the Drama." *The Critic* (December 1, 1853): 626. Google Books. [*Black Man, Rising Son*]

"Popular Enlightenment." *People's and Howitt's Journal* 4 (1851): 276–278. Print. [*Three Years*]

Prichard, James Cowles. *Researches Into the Physical History of Mankind.* London: Sherwood, Gilbert, and Piper, 1837. Google Books. [*Rising Son*]

Proceedings of the Anti-Slavery Society. New York: American Anti-Slavery Society, 1864. Slavery and Anti-Slavery. [*Rising Son*]

"Progressive Friends, The." *National Anti-Slavery Standard* (June 12, 1858): 1. Slavery and Anti-Slavery. [*Negro in the American Rebellion*]

"Prospects of Slavery." *New York Daily Times* (April 19, 1853): 1. American Periodicals Series. [*Clotel, Clotelle*]

Purvis, Robert. *A Tribute to the Memory of Thomas Shipley.* Philadelphia: Merrihew and Gunn, 1836. Slavery and Anti-Slavery. [*Clotel*]

"Quite a Blunder." *Emancipator and Republican* (August 16, 1849): 1. American Periodicals Series. [*Clotel*]

Rainsford, Marcus. *An Historical Account of the Black Empire of Hayti.* London: Cundee, 1805. Google Books. [*Rising Son*]

"Ralph W. Emerson and Charles Sumner." *Liberator* (January 16, 1846): 10. Slavery and Anti-Slavery. [*Three Years, Miralda*]

"Relation of Art to Nature, The." *Cornhill Magazine* 14 (July 1866): 28–36. Google Books. [*Rising Son*]

Redding, Cyrus. "Memoir of John Keats." In *The Poetical Works of Coleridge, Shelley, and Keats*, v–vii. Philadelphia: Howe, 1831. [*Rising Son*]

——. "Memoir of Percy Bysshe Shelley." In *The Poetical Works of Coleridge, Shelley, and Keats*, 241–247. Philadelphia: Howe, 1831. [*Rising Son*]

Ritchie, James Ewing. *The London Pulpit*. London: Tweedie, 1858. Google Books. [*Black Man*]

Roberts, Joseph Jenkins. "Address of Hon. Joseph J. Roberts," *African Repository* 45 (April 1869): 103–117. [*Rising Son*]

"Ruins of Zimbaoe in South Africa, The." *Littel's Living Age* 113 (June 1872): 512. Google Books. [*Rising Son*]

Schmucker, Samuel Mosheim. *The Yankee Slave Driver; or, The Black and White Rivals*. Philadelphia: Evans, 1858. Google Books. [*Escape*]

Scoble, John. "American Slavery." *Anti-Slavery Reporter* (July 1, 1846): 97. Slavery and Anti-Slavery. [*Clotel*]

Scottish Tourist, and Itinerary, The. Edinburgh: Stirling and Kenney, 1830. Google Books. [*Three Years*]

Scribner, Isaac. *Review of the Rev. U. C. Burnap's Sermon on Bible Servitude*. Lowell, Mass.: Pillsbury, 1844. Google Books. [*Three Years*]

Sears, E. H. "The African Race." *Christian Examiner* 41 (July 1846): 33–48. Google Books. [*Rising Son*]

"Selected Miscellany," *Springfield Republican* (April 20, 1864): 6. America's Historical Newspapers. [*Negro in the American Rebellion*]

"Sentimental." *Boston Daily Bee* (January 24, 1849): 1. America's Historical Newspapers. [*Clotel, Miralda, Clotelle, My Southern Home*]

"Shackford's Lecture on the War with Mexico." *North Star* (March 10, 1848): 1. Slavery and Anti-Slavery. [*Clotel, Miralda*]

"Shocking Affair—Desperate Courage of a Slave." *Liberator* (May 11, 1849): 76. Slavery and Anti-Slavery. [*Clotel*]

Sigourney, Lydia. *Pleasant Memories of Pleasant Lands*. Boston: Munroe, 1842. Google Books. [*Three Years*]

Simms, William Gilmore. "The Plank." In *Martin Faber: The Story of a Criminal; and Other Tales*. 2 vols. New York: Harper, 1847. Google Books. [*Miralda, Clotelle*]

Simpson, J. Mac. C. "The Slaveholder's Rest." *Liberator* (November 23, 1849): 188. American Periodicals Series. [*Clotel*]

"Slave Trade, The." *Charleston Daily News* (October 23, 1872): 1. Chronicling America. [*Rising Son*]

"Slaver: A Tale of Our Own Times, The." *Graham's American Monthly Magazine* 31 (August 1847): 61–71. American Periodicals Series. [*Black Man*]

"Smart Boy." *Rural Repository* (June 6, 1846): 111. Google Books. [*Clotel*]

Spence, Elizabeth. *Summer Excursions.* London: Longman, 1809. Google Books. [*American Fugitive*]

Stanton, Henry Brewster. *Sketches of Reforms and Reformers.* New York: Wiley, 1849. Google Books. [*Three Years*]

Stephens, George. Untitled letter. *Weekly Anglo-African* (March 26, 1864). Repr. *A Voice of Thunder: A Black Soldier's Civil War,* ed. Donald Yacovone, 295–300. Urbana: University of Illinois Press, 1997. [*Negro in the American Rebellion, Rising Son*]

Stevens, Thaddeus. *Speech of Mr. Thaddeus Stevens, of Pennsylvania, in the House of Representatives.* Washington D.C.: n.p., 1850. Slavery and Anti-Slavery. [*Clotel, Miralda*]

Stewart, Alexander. "Education." In *Materials for Thinking, Extracted from the Works of the Learned of All Ages.* London: Chidley, 1846. Google Books. [*American Fugitive*]

Stewart, Alvan. *A Legal Argument Before the Supreme Court of the State of New Jersey.* New York: Finch and Weed, 1845. Google Books. [*Clotel*]

"Story of a Slave Mother." *Pennsylvania Freeman* (November 18, 1852): 186. Slavery and Anti-Slavery. [*Clotel*]

Stranger's Guide Through the City of York, The. York: Bellerby's, 1832. Google Books. [*Three Years*]

Stratton, Royal B. *Captivity of the Oatman Girls.* New York: Stratton, 1858. Google Books. [*Black Man, Negro in the American Rebellion*]

"Street Exhibitions in London." *Chambers' Edinburgh Journal* (March 15, 1834): 51. Google Books. [*Three Years*]

Strickland, Agnes. "White Thorne Farm." In *The Keepsake of Friendship,* 85–110. Boston: Fuller, 1849. Google Books. [*Miralda, Clotelle*]

Sunderland, La Roy. *Anti-Slavery Manual.* 3rd ed. New York: Benedict, 1839. Slavery and Anti-Slavery. [*Clotel*]

"Talent and Genius." In *Acton; or, the Circle of Life,* 154–155. New York: Appleton, 1849. Google Books. [*Black Man, Rising Son*]

Tappan, Lewis. *Address to the Non-Slave Holders of the South.* New York: Benedict, 1843. Google Books. [*Narrative*]

[Tartt, William Macdowall]. "The Widow of Antwerp." In *The Keepsake of Friendship,* 316–322. Boston: Fuller, 1849. Google Books. [*Miralda, Clotelle*]

"Tax on Colored Population." *Boston Daily Atlas* (February 25, 1846): 2. America's Historical Newspapers. [*My Southern Home*]

Taylor, George. "The Underground Railway." *Liberator* (June 19, 1857): 100. Slavery and Anti-Slavery. [*Escape*]

Taylor, William Cooke. *The Student's Manual of Ancient History.* New York: Appleton, 1845. Google Books. [*Rising Son*]

Thackeray, William Makepeace. *The English Humourists of the Eighteenth Century.* London: Smith, Elder, 1853. Google Books. [*Miralda, Clotelle*]

[Thatcher, Benjamin B.]. Preface to *The Poetical Works of Mrs. Felicia Hemans.* Philadelphia: Ash, 1835. Google Books. [*Miralda, Clotelle*]

"Third Decade of the American Anti-Slavery Society." *Liberator* (December 18, 1863): 202. Slavery and Anti-Slavery. [*Rising Son*]

Thornton, Edward. *History of the British Empire in India.* 4 vols. London: Allen, 1842. [*St. Domingo*]

[Thornwell, James]. "The Religious Instruction of the Black Population." *Southern Presbyterian Review* 1 (December 1847): 89–120. Google Books. [*Clotel, Miralda*]

Tillinghast, W. "Chattel and Wages Laborers." *Liberator* (April 20, 1849): 61. Slavery and Anti-Slavery. [*Clotel*]

[Todd, John]. "Natural Bridge in Virginia." In *Town's Fourth Reader*, by Salem Town, 54–58. Cincinnati: Derby, Bradley, 1845. Google Books. [*Miralda, Clotelle*]

"Transept, The." *Illustrated Exhibitor* (June 7, 1851): 9–12. Google Books. [*Three Years*]

"Translation of St. Catherine, The." *People's Journal* 2 (1847): 255. Google Books. [*Clotel, Miralda, Clotelle*]

"Unknown Painter, The." *Chambers' Edinburgh Journal* (June 30, 1838): 177–178. Proquest. [*Black Man*]

Untitled article. *Friends' Intelligencer* (May 18, 1867): 169–170. Google Books. [*Rising Son*]

Untitled article. *London Times* (February 27, 1850): 4. Gale News Vault. [*Three Years*]

Veritas. "The Diamond and the Cinder." In *The Odd-Fellow's Offering.* New York: Walker, 1854. Google Books. [*Miralda, Clotelle*]

"Very Touching." *Kentucky Garland* 1 (October 1854): 60. Google Books. [*Miralda, Clotelle*]

"Views of the Benevolent Society of Alexandria." *Alexandria Gazette* (June 22, 1827): 2. America's Historical Newspapers. [*Clotel*]

"Visit to a Kennel of Blood-hounds, Kept for the Purpose of Hunting Slaves, A." *London Nonconformist* (December 29, 1847): 912. Access Newspaper Archive. [*Clotel*]

Wait, Benjamin. *Letters from Van Dieman's Land.* Buffalo: Wilgus, 1843. Google Books. [*Narrative*]

Wakefield, Priscilla. "On Variety and Inconsistency of Character." In *Variety: or, Selections and Essays*, 119–125. London: Parke, 1809. Google Books. [*American Fugitive*]

Warner, Daniel. "Address of President Warner." *African Repository* 43 (December 1867): 353–365. Google Books. [*Rising Son*]

Welby, Amelia. "Lines Written on Seeing an Infant Sleeping on Its Mother's Bosom." In *Poems*, 25–27. Boston: Tompkins, 1845. Google Books. [*Clotelle*]

[Welch, Jane S.]. "Jairus's Daughter." *New England Offering* 1 (August 1848): 108. Google Books. [*Clotel, Miralda, Clotelle*]

Weld, Theodore Dwight. *American Slavery as It Is.* New York: American Anti-Slavery Society, 1839. Google Books. [*Clotel, Rising Son*]

——. *The Bible Against Slavery*. New York: American Anti-Slavery Society, 1838. Google Books. [*Clotel*]

Wheelock, Edwin M. "Harper's Ferry and Its Lesson." *Liberator* (November 18, 1859): 184. Slavery and Anti-Slavery. [*Negro in the American Rebellion*]

Whipple, Edwin P. *Lectures on Subjects Connected with Literature and Life*. Boston: Ticknor, Reed, and Fields, 1850. Google Books. [*Escape*]

Whitter, John G. "The Great Slave Market," *Emancipator and Republican* (November 23, 1843): 120. America's Historical Newspapers. [*Clotel*]

——. "Lamartine's History of the Girondins." *National Era* (November 4, 1847): 1. Proquest [*St. Domingo, Rising Son*]

"Why Should the Negro Fight?" *Liberator* (August 8, 1862): 32. Slavery and Anti-Slavery. [*Negro in the American Rebellion*]

Willett, Mark. *An Excursion from the Source of the Wye*. Chepstow: Evans, 1820. Google Books. [*Three Years*]

Willis, Nathaniel Parker. *Inklings of Adventure*. 2 vols. New York: Saunders and Otley, 1836. Google Books. [*Three Years*]

——. *Letters from Under a Bridge*. London: Virtue, 1840. Google Books. [*Three Years*]

——. *Pencillings By the Way*. New York: Morris and Willis, 1844. Google Books. [*Three Years*]

——. *Rural Letters*. New York: Baker and Scribner, 1849. Google Books. [*Three Years*]

Willmott, Robert. *Pleasures, Objects, and Advantages of Literature*. London: Bosworth, 1851. Google Books. [*Miralda, Clotelle*]

Wilson, John Leighton. *Western Africa*. New York: Harper, 1856. [*Rising Son*]

"Woes of Slavery, The." *Pennsylvania Freeman* (November 18, 1852): 186. Slavery and Anti-Slavery. [*Clotel*]

"Worshippers of Mammon." *Anti-Slavery Bugle* (April 10, 1846): 4. Chronicling America. [*Clotel*]

Wright, George Newenham. *An Historical Guide to the City of Dublin*. London: Baldwin, Cradock, and Joy, 1825. Google Books. [*Three Years*]

Wright, P. B. "Valedictory Address." *Eclectic Medical Journal* 28 (April 1868): 160–162. Google Books. [*My Southern Home*]

Wright, Thomas. *History and Antiquities of the Town of Ludlow*. Ludlow: Procter and Jones, 1826. Google Books. [*American Fugitive*]

Notes

Introduction

1. Roland Barthes, *The Pleasure of the Text*, trans. Richard Miller (New York: Farrar, Straus, and Giroux, 1975), 19.

2. The story was first reported in "An Adventure," *Boston Daily Advertiser* (September 28, 1871): 1.

3. William Wells Brown, *The Rising Son* (Boston: Gray, 1874), 26–33.

4. Some of the implausibilities of the account were pointed out by the *New York Herald*: "It appears from the narrative that Brown was captured by a party of [Klansmen]," the *Herald* writes, "and was on his way to a convenient hanging tree, when he opportunely came across a man in delirium tremens, of course a dear friend of the Ku Kluxers. They directed that he save the life of this man, and he proceeded to do so, injecting morphine by the hypodermic process, and doing other things so wonderful and relieving the man of his pains so rapidly that the Ku Kluxers thought he was an emissary of the devil. . . . It was quite a miraculous escape; but everybody is not required to place implicit confidence in the truth of the story" ("Dr. William Wells Brown," *New York Herald* [September 28, 1871]: 6).

5. Bliss, for Barthes, "come[s] only with the *absolutely new*, for only the new disturbs (weakens) consciousness." In certain texts, he goes on to say, "words *glisten*, they are distracting, incongruous apparitions—it matters little if they are pedantic; thus, I personally take pleasure in this sentence of Leibnitz: '. . . as though pocket watches told time by means of a certain *horodeictic* faculty, without requiring springs, or as though mills ground grain by means of a *fractive* quality, without requiring anything on the order of millstones.'" The antithesis of the glistening word, he goes on to say, is the stereotype, "the word repeated without any magic, any enthusiasm, as though it were natural, as though by some miracle this recurring word were adequate on each occasion" (Barthes, *Pleasure*, 40, 42).

6. William Wells Brown, "Speech at Anniversary of the New York Anti-Slavery Society" (1856), in *Clotel and Other Writings*, ed. Ezra Greenspan (New York: Library of America, 2014), 913–914. All subsequent references to the works included in this edition—the 1847 *Narrative*, *Clotel*, *The American Fugitive in Europe*, *The*

Escape, *The Black Man*, *My Southern Home*, and selected speeches and public letters—will appear parenthetically in the text with the abbreviation *C*. Because the versions of *Clotel* and *The Black Man* in this edition do not include the introductory memoirs—"Narrative of the Life and Escape of William Wells Brown" and "Memoir of the Author"—those memoirs will be cited separately.

7. J. Saunders Redding, *To Make a Poet Black* (1939; repr., Ithaca, N.Y.: Cornell University Press, 1988), xxix. Redding's verdict on Brown could not be farther from my own: "Brown was driven by the necessity for turning out propaganda in a cause that was too close to him for emotional objectivity and reasonable perspective," he declares. "He was simply a man of slightly more than ordinary talents doing his best in a cause that was his religion" (26, 25).

8. See, for instance, the analyses of the "moments of aesthetic excess" in Harriet Jacobs's writing (Theo Davis, "Harriet Jacobs's 'Excrescences': Aesthetics and Politics in *Incidents in the Life of a Slave Girl*," *Theory and Event* 13 [2010]); the perplexingly unmotivated "fabrications" in James Williams's *Narrative* (Lara Langer Cohen, *The Fabrication of American Literature: Fraudulence and Antebellum Print Culture* [Philadelphia: University of Pennsylvania Press, 2012], 123); the "Englishy English" fixations of black abolitionists overseas (Elisa Tamarkin, *Anglophilia: Deference, Devotion, and Antebellum America* [Chicago: University of Chicago Press, 2008], 179); the "surplus fascination" of the beautiful slave girl in Brown (Gustavus Stadler, *Troubling Minds: The Cultural Politics of Genius in the United States, 1840–1890* [Minneapolis: University of Minnesota Press, 2006], 81); and the "extravagant, superabundant structure" of black panoramic exhibitions (Daphne Brooks, *Bodies in Dissent: Spectacular Performances of Race and Freedom, 1850–1910* [Durham, N.C.: Duke University Press, 2006], 82).

9. For an especially impressive recent effort to open up the field, see Lara Langer Cohen and Jordan Alexander Stein, eds., *Early African American Print Culture* (Philadelphia: University of Pennsylvania Press, 2012).

10. I am excluding from this list of major publications his compilation of antislavery songs, *The Anti-Slavery Harp* (1848), and two pamphlets: *St. Domingo* (1854) and *Memoir of William Wells Brown* (1859). I am also leaving out two works that are not officially included in the list of Brown's publications but should be: Josephine Brown's *Biography of an American Bondman* (1856) and William Craft's *Running a Thousand Miles to Freedom* (1860). As I have recently argued, Brown is extremely likely to have written most of *Biography* himself and to have cowritten *Running* with Craft. See Sanborn, "The Plagiarist's Craft: Theatricality and Fugitivity in *Running a Thousand Miles for Freedom*," *PMLA* 128 (2013): 907–922.

11. Frederick Douglass, *Narrative of the Life of Frederick Douglass* (1845; repr., New York: Penguin, 1982), 86–87.

12. Brown, "Narrative of the Life and Escape of William Wells Brown," in *Clotel; or, The President's Daughter* (London: Partridge & Oakey, 1853), 28–29.

13. For related readings of these two passages, see Hildegard Hoeller, *From Gift to Commodity: Capitalism and Sacrifice in Nineteenth-Century American Fiction* (Durham: University of New Hampshire Press, 2012), 121–122; and Ivy G. Wilson,

Specters of Democracy: Blackness and the Aesthetics of Politics in the Antebellum U.S. (New York: Oxford University Press, 2011), 37–38.

14. Wilson (*Specters*, 38, 37) similarly discusses this scene in relation to a "graffiti aesthetic," pointing out that "whereas the tutorial scene in Douglass's *Narrative* intimates the allure of rhetoric as an art and political form, the analogous moment in Brown's narrative signals a particular preoccupation with visual culture."

15. For more on this crucial Derridean concept, see Asja Szafraniec, *Beckett, Derrida, and the Event of Literature* (Stanford, Calif.: Stanford University Press, 2007), 78–83; and Samuel Weber, *Benjamin's -abilities* (Cambridge, Mass.: Harvard University Press, 2008), 5–6, 116–117.

16. Jonathan Elmer, *Reading at the Social Limit: Affect, Mass Culture, and Edgar Allan Poe* (Stanford, Calif.: Stanford University Press, 1995), 64.

17. Gillian Beer, *Darwin's Plots: Evolutionary Narrative in Darwin, George Eliot, and Nineteenth-Century Fiction* (Cambridge: Cambridge University Press, 1983), 163.

18. Donald Barthelme, "Introduction to 'Paraguay,'" in *Writer's Choice*, ed. Rust Hills (New York: McKay, 1974), 25.

19. Ralph Ellison, *Invisible Man* (1952; repr., New York: Vintage, 1995), 153.

1. Plagiarama!

1. William Wells Brown, *Narrative of the Life of William W. Brown* (1847), in *Clotel and Other Writings*, ed. Ezra Greenspan (New York: Library of America, 2014), 26. All subsequent references to the works included in this edition—the 1847 *Narrative, Clotel, The American Fugitive in Europe, The Escape, The Black Man, My Southern Home*, and selected speeches and public letters—will appear parenthetically in the text with the abbreviation *C*. Benjamin Wait, *Letters from Van Dieman's Land* (Buffalo: Wilgus, 1843), 124.

2. Stephen S. Foster, *Brotherhood of Thieves* (Boston: Anti-Slavery Office, 1844), 23.

3. "An Auction," *New York Evangelist* (April 29, 1847): 1.

4. William Wells Brown, *Narrative of William W. Brown*, 2nd ed. (1848; repr. Mineola, N.Y.: Dover, 2003), 54–55; Robert Purvis, *A Tribute to the Memory of Thomas Shipley* (Philadelphia: Merrihew and Gunn, 1836), 16.

5. Brown, *Narrative of William W. Brown*, 2nd ed., 64–65, 74; Edward M. Davis, *Extracts from the American Slave Code* (Philadelphia: Davis, 1845), 1, 4.

6. Brown, *Narrative of William W. Brown*, 2nd ed., 75; Lewis Tappan, *Address to the Non-Slave Holders of the South* (New York: Benedict, 1843), 17.

7. Louis-Marie de Lahaye Cormenin, *The Orators of France* (New York: Baker and Scribner, 1847), 113, 108; Joel Tyler Headley, "An Essay on the Rise and Fall of Eloquence in the French Revolution," in Cormenin, *Orators*, xxiii.

8. Cormenin, *Orators*, 245.

9. Alphonse de Lamartine, *History of the Girondists*, trans. H. T. Ryde, 3 vols. (New York: Harpers, 1847), 1:265.

10. Two of the best recent studies of plagiarism in the nineteenth century are Robert Macfarlane, *Original Copy: Plagiarism and Originality in Nineteenth-Century Literature* (New York: Oxford University Press, 2007); and Tilar J. Mazzeo, *Plagiarism and Literary Property in the Romantic Period* (Philadelphia: University of Pennsylvania Press, 2006).

11. For discussions of Crafts's use of Dickens, see Hollis Robbins, "Blackening *Bleak House*: Hannah Crafts's *The Bondwoman's Narrative*," in *In Search of Hannah Crafts: Critical Essays on* The Bondwoman's Narrative, ed. Henry Louis Gates Jr. and Hollis Robbins (New York: Basic Civitas Books, 2004), 71–86; and Gill Ballinger, Tim Lustig, and Dale Townshend, "Missing Intertexts: Hannah Crafts's *The Bondwoman's Narrative* and African American Literary History," *Journal of American Studies* 39 (2005): 207–237.

12. Thomas Mallon, *Stolen Words: Forays Into the Origins and Ravages of Plagiarism* (New York: Penguin, 1989), 136.

13. "The normal response to [plagiarism]," writes Peter Shaw, "tends to be an instinctive recoil accompanied by a shudder of uneasiness or an uncomfortable feeling in the pit of the stomach" ("Plagiary," *The American Scholar* 51 [1982]: 334). For recent examples of this response, see Lizzie Widdicombe's account of the case of Quentin Rowan, whose plagiarisms of spy novels resemble Brown's plagiarisms of passages from travel narratives and sentimental fictions ("The Plagiarist's Tale," *The New Yorker* [February 13, 2012]).

14. Erika Renée Williams, "A Lie of Omission: Plagiarism in Nella Larsen's *Quicksand*," *African American Review* 45, nos. 1–2 (2013): 205, 206.

15. Ibid., 206, 213. See also Beverly Haviland's reading of Nella Larsen's plagiarism as an "act of literary suicide" ("Passing from Paranoia to Plagiarism: The Abject Authorship of Nella Larsen," *Modern Fiction Studies* 43 [1997]: 295) and Robert Hemenway's description of Zora Neale Hurston's plagiarism as "an unconscious attempt at academic suicide" (*Zora Neale Hurston: A Literary Biography* [Urbana: University of Illinois Press, 1980], 99).

16. Although it is sometimes imagined that mid-nineteenth-century Americans and Britons were at ease with plagiarism, that is not in fact the case. Throughout the digital archive, one discovers passages such as these: "Plagiarism appears to us to be the most degraded form which felony can assume" ("Eminent Modern Writers," *The Idler* 2 [January 1856]: 96). "I feel that this vice is so low, so contemptible that I can scarcely touch it" (Thomas Montgomery, *Literary Societies, Their Uses and Abuses* [Albany: Gray, Sprague, 1853], 14–15). Similar sentiments appeared in the abolitionist press. "How contemptible does a writer appear when detected in a palpable and intentional plagiarism! One will thereafter read him in doubt and suspicion; denying him the credit of *every* good idea and eloquent expression" (untitled, *Liberator* [August 9, 1850]: 128). "The word 'Lectures' awakens associations of inanity and tediousness, pompous displays of superficial knowledge, oracular utterances of commonplaces, and literary larcenies, in comparison with which henroost robbery is reputable" (John G. Whittier, "Literary Notices," *National Era* (November 1, 1849): 175.

17. Herman Melville, *Moby-Dick* (1851; repr. New York: Norton, 2001), 227.

18. Obama offered these comments during a campaign appearance in Virginia on July 13, 2013. For a transcript, see http://www.factcheck.org/2012/07/you-didnt-build-that-uncut-and-unedited/.

19. Paul St. Amour, *The Copywrights: Intellectual Property and the Literary Imagination* (Ithaca, N.Y.: Cornell University Press, 2003), 37.

20. Ibid., 40. The "praise of modern writers should be measured by the merit that appears upon the face of their pages, without reference to the sources whence the notions may have been drawn," writes the author of an 1842 newspaper article on plagiarism. "As we pass up along the backward chain of authors we find invention retreating before us indefinitely, till at the head of the line we catch Prometheus stealing all the fire of inspiration from heaven. The fact is, that in all cases the praise of a thing is due not to the first faint conceiver of it, but to the last complete applier of it" ("Plagiarism," *New-York Mirror* [January 15, 1842]: 18). Such arguments appeared less frequently than the condemnations of plagiarism that I cite above, but they were not at all uncommon in the periodical literature of the 1840s and 1850s. See, for example, "The Philosophy of Plagiarism," *Hood's Magazine and Comic Miscellany* 3 (1845): 465–468; [Horace Binney Wallace], "Plagiarism," *Morris's National Press* (March 14, 1846): 2; [Frederick Saunders], "Literary Larcenies," *United States Magazine, and Democratic Review* 19 (September 1846): 203–208; A. M. W., "Plagiarism: An Apology for the Last Comer," *American Review* 4 (August 1849): 139–150; A. Mitchell, "Plagiarism," *Knickerbocker* 43 (April 1854): 331–336; and "Plagiarism: Especially That of Coleridge," *Eclectic Magazine* 32 (August 1854): 485–488.

21. Herman Melville, *Billy Budd, Sailor*, ed. Harrison Hayford and Merton J. Sealts Jr. (Chicago: University of Chicago Press, 1962), 56.

22. Charlotte Forten-Grimké, *The Journals of Charlotte Forten-Grimké*, ed. Brenda Stevenson (New York: Oxford University Press, 2004), 330.

23. Kathy Acker, "Dead Doll Humility," *Postmodern Culture* 1, no. 1 (September 1990).

24. See Douglas Shepard, "Nathanael West Rewrites Horatio Alger, Jr.," *Satire Newsletter* (Fall 1965): 13–28; and Gary Scharnhorst, "From Rags to Patches, or *A Cool Million* as Alter-Alger," *Ball State University Forum* 21 (1980): 58–65.

25. West, *A Cool Million*, in *Novels and Other Writings* (New York: Library of America, 1997), 135.

26. Ibid., 157.

27. Edward Everett, "An Address Delivered at Lexington," in *Orations and Speeches on Various Occasions*, 2 vols. (Boston: Little and Brown, 1850): 1:554.

28. Martha Finley, *Elsie's Girlhood* (New York: Dodd, Mead, 1872), 142–143.

29. West, *Cool Million*, 157.

30. Ibid., 213. The parallel passages from *Joe's Luck* may be found in Shepard, "Nathanael West," 19–27.

31. Although there has been some attention to Hopkins's plagiarism from Brown in *Hagar's Daughter* (Lois Brown, *Pauline Elizabeth Hopkins: Black Daughter of*

the Revolution [Chapel Hill: University of North Carolina Press, 2008], 346; Holly Jackson, "Another Long Bridge: Reproduction and Reversion in *Hagar's Daughter*," in *Early African American Print Culture*, ed. Lara Langer Cohen and Jordan Alexander Stein [Philadelphia: University of Pennsylvania Press, 2012], 192–202) and in her nonfictional writings for *The Colored American Magazine* (Ira Dworkin, "Introduction," *Daughter of the Revolution: The Major Nonfiction Works of Pauline E. Hopkins*, ed. Ira Dworkin [New Brunswick, N.J.: Rutgers University Press, 2007], xxxvii–xxxix), the extensive plagiarism in *Of One Blood*, along with the intermittent plagiarism in *Winona*, has gone unnoticed.

32. Henry Louis Gates Jr., *The Signifying Monkey: A Theory of African-American Literary Criticism* (New York: Oxford, 1988), xxvi.

33. H. Rider Haggard, *She: A History of Adventure* (London: Longmans, 1887), 98; Rudyard Kipling and Wolcott Balestier, "The Naulahka," *Century Illustrated Monthly Magazine* 43 (1892): 669.

34. John Hartley Coombs, ed., *Dr. Livingstone's Seventeen Years' Exploration and Adventure in the Wilds of Africa* (Philadelphia: Lloyd, 1857), 134.

35. As Gill Ballinger, Tim Lustig, and Dale Townshend have observed, "for Gates and other critics, intertextuality tends to be construed in terms of an individual writer's response, either to a previous writer (Walker and Hurston, Ellison and Wright), or to a collective and monological discourse of power (Douglass and the language of slavery)." As a result, they rightly note, "the concept of intertextuality . . . has remained an attenuated one for many critics of African American literature" ("Missing Intertexts," 234). The haunting of voices in Hopkins is an especially useful example of a kind of intertextuality that moves beyond the standard model of "signifyin(g)."

36. Pauline Hopkins, *Of One Blood; or, The Hidden Self* (New York: Washington Square Press, 2004), 21–22.

37. Ibid., 40.

38. The sentence reads as follows: "The young man bowed over her hand, murmuring some indistinct words of rapture and thanks, feeling the glamour of her presence and beauty like a man who has been poring over a poem, losing himself in it, until it has become, as it were, a part of himself" ("Alixe," *Frank Leslie's Popular Monthly* 16 [1883]: 726).

39. Hopkins, *Of One Blood*, 67.

40. The opening of the sentence reads as follows: "A weird baritone, vailed, as it were, rising and falling upon every wave of the soprano of Lady Beatrice, and reaching the ear apparently from some strange distance. . . ." ("The Haunted Voice," *Frank Leslie's Popular Monthly* 18 [1884]: 670).

41. For more on Hopkins's plagiarism in *Of One Blood*, including a list of the passages she appropriated and bibliographic information on the sources from which she appropriated them, see Geoffrey Sanborn, "The Wind of Words: Plagiarism in *Of One Blood*," *J19* 3 (2015): 67–87.

42. William Hunt, "Preface," *The American Biographical Sketch Book* (New York: Nafis and Cornish, 1849), 5.

43. Henry Gardiner Adams, preface to *God's Image in Ebony* (London: Partridge and Oakey, 1854), ii.

44. Hunt, preface, 7–8; William Cobbett, *Advice to Young Men* (New York: Doyle, 1833), 165; John Randolph, *Letters to a Young Relative* (Philadelphia: Carey, Lea, and Blanchard, 1834), 236; Benjamin Disraeli, *Henrietta Temple*, 3 vols. (London: Colburn, 1837), 1:102.

45. The relevant passages may be found by searching the following phrases: "the crimes and miseries of mankind" (Clarkson); "hapless victims of this revolting system" (Phillippo); "petty philosophy follows in the train" (Watson); "more degraded in the scale of humanity" (Garrison); "fostered with unremitting assiduity" (Nourse); "his flesh marble, and his sinews iron" (Moodie); "a good life is the soundest orthodoxy" (Whittemore); "has his mercantile agents in England" (Thome and Kimball); "with skins of the darkest hue" ("Biographic Sketches"); "the unblushing knavery of trade" (Child); and "instrument to chase away the mass" (Williams). The passages from Nourse and Moodie may only be found on the database Slavery and Anti-Slavery; the rest may be found on Google Books.

46. William Wells Brown, *Miralda; or, The Beautiful Quadroon* (1860–1961; repr. Marlborough: Adam Mathew Publications, 2003), 65–66.

47. "Very Touching," *Kentucky Garland* 1 (October 1854): 60. The many versions of this filler paragraph that were published in American newspapers between 1854 and 1860 may be found by searching phrases like "faultless mouth became convulsed," "anon she met my ardent," and "drooping lashes, the muscles" on Google Books, Internet Archive, Newspapers.com, Old Fulton NY Postcards, America's Historical Newspapers, American Periodical Series, Chronicling America, and the American Antiquarian Society's Historical Periodicals Collection.

48. Brown, *Rising Son*, 93–94. The original passage may be found in George Bancroft's "Origin of Easter Day, and Easter Customs," *Potter's American Monthly* 10 (1878): 308.

49. Washington Irving, *The Sketch-Book of Geoffrey Crayon*, 2 vols. (London: Murray, 1822): 1:120–121.

50. "Prospects of Slavery," *New York Daily Times* (April 19, 1853): 1; Helen de Kroyft, *A Place in Thy Memory* (New York: Trow, 1851), 23.

51. David Macbeth Moir, *Sketches of the Poetical Literature of the Past Half-Century* (Edinburgh: Blackwood, 1851), 211; *Memorials of Early Genius: and Achievements in the Pursuit of Knowledge* (London: Nelson, 1848), 390.

52. William Wells Brown, *The Rising Son*, 2nd ed. (Boston: A. G. Brown, 1876), 553; Cyrus Redding, "Memoir of Percy Bysshe Shelley," in *The Poetical Works of Coleridge, Shelley, and Keats* (Philadelphia: Howe, 1831), 245; Redding, "Memoir of John Keats," in *The Poetical Works of Coleridge, Shelley, and Keats* (Philadelphia: Howe, 1831), vi.

53. Acker, "Dead Doll Humility." See also the sentence in the biography of Benjamin Banneker that is built from sentences in David Paul Brown's *Eulogium Upon Wilberforce* ("Like the golden sun that has sunk beneath the western horizon, he has sunk into the grave, life's dark and inevitable horizon, but still throws

upon the world which he sustained and enlightened in his career, the reflected beams of his departed glory") and Samuel Johnson's *The Lives of the English Poets* ("[Samuel Butler is] a man whose name can only perish with his language").

54. The source texts are as follows: David Paul Brown, *Eulogium Upon Wilberforce* (Philadelphia: Collins, 1834); Samuel Johnson, *The Works of Samuel Johnson*, 2 vols. (New York: Dearborn, 1832); Lamartine, *History of the Girondists*; and John Doran, *Their Majesties' Servants*, 2 vols. (London: Allen, 1860).

55. Cormenin, *Orators*, 231.

56. Brown, *Three Years in Europe* (London: Gilpin, 1852), 256.

57. Lamartine, *History*, 1:233.

58. Mallon, *Stolen Words*, 236–237.

59. Ibid., 237.

60. See, for instance, ibid., 25, 47.

61. Terry Eagleton, *Figures of Dissent: Critical Essays on Fish, Spivak, Žižek, and Others* (London: Verso, 2003), 238–239.

62. Ibid., 239.

63. Brown, *Three Years*, 259–260.

64. Cormenin, *Orators*, 200–201.

65. Ibid., 146, 129, 255.

66. Frederick Douglass, "Letter from William W. Brown," *Frederick Douglass' Paper* (June 10, 1853). The sentence was almost certainly written by Julia Griffiths, Douglass's close friend, who was the secretary of the Rochester Ladies' Anti-Slavery Society.

67. "The Duke of Wellington's Funeral," *British Banner* (November 17, 1852): 7. Newspaper Archive.

68. The article in the *Globe* was reprinted under the title "Mr. Disraeli's Plagiarism" in the *London Morning Chronicle* (November 17, 1852): 6.

69. Untitled article, *Caledonian Mercury* (November 18, 1852): 1. "How fallen is this famous Chancellor now, and irrecoverably fallen!" lamented the *Fife Herald*, in representatively bombastic tones. "This literary suicide affects the whole literary order, and causes every member of it to hang his head in grief and shame" ("Stop Thief!" *Fife Herald* [November 25, 1852]: 3).

70. Untitled article, *London Times* (November 22, 1852): 4.

71. Untitled article, *London Morning Chronicle* (November 23, 1852): 1.

72. Untitled article, *London Daily News* (November 23, 1852): 1.

73. "Mr. Disraeli's Plagiarism," *Sheffield and Rotherham Independent* (November 27, 1852): 2.

74. For analyses of these and other plagiarisms in *Clotel*, see Lara Langer Cohen, "Notes from the State of Saint Domingue: The Practice of Citation in *Clotel*," in Cohen and Stein, eds., *Early African American Print Culture*, 161–177; Dawn Coleman, *Preaching and the Rise of the American Novel* (Columbus: Ohio State University Press, 2013), 174–196; and Geoffrey Sanborn, "'People Will Pay to Hear the Drama': Plagiarism in *Clotel*," *African-American Review* 45, nos. 1–2 (2012): 65–82. See also my edition of *Clotel*, which is forthcoming from Broadview Press.

75. "Shackford's Lecture on the War with Mexico," *North Star* (March 10, 1848): 1.

76. Quoted in Brown, *Rising Son*, 23–24.

2. The Spirit of Capitalization

1. Nathaniel Uring, *A History of the Voyages and Travels of Captain Nathaniel Uring* (London: Wilkins, 1726), 120–121.

2. Among the places in which the anecdote was reprinted during Brown's lifetime are Samuel Gardner Drake, *The Book of the Indians of North America* (Boston: Drake, 1833); *Joe Miller's Jests* (London: Whittaker, 1836), 107; and James Wimer, *Events in Indian History* (Lancaster, Penn.: Hills, 1841), 495–496, all of which are available on Google Books. The remainder of the references may be found by searching words and phrases like "Governor" "whipping," "Indian," and "head work" on Google Books, America's Historical Newspapers, and American Periodicals Series.

3. "The Indian; or, Self-Interest," in *The Common-place Book of Humorous Poetry* (London: Tegg, 1826), 310–313.

4. Samuel Drake, "Uring's Notices of New-England—1709," *Collections of the New Hampshire Historical Society* 3 (1832): 150.

5. "Head Work," *The Family Magazine* (July 20, 1833): 112.

6. William Wells Brown, *Narrative of the Life of William W. Brown* (1847), in *Clotel and Other Writings*, ed. Ezra Greenspan (New York: Library of America, 2014), 28–29. All subsequent references to the works included in this edition—the 1847 *Narrative*, *Clotel*, *The American Fugitive in Europe*, *The Escape*, *The Black Man*, *My Southern Home*, and selected speeches and public letters—will appear parenthetically in the text with the abbreviation *C*.

7. William Andrews, *To Tell a Free Story: The First Century of Afro-American Autobiography, 1760–1865* (Urbana: University of Illinois Press, 1988), 145, 147, 149.

8. Rafia Zafar, *We Wear the Mask: African Americans Write American Literature, 1760–1870* (New York: Columbia University Press, 1997), 83.

9. The *locus classicus* of this argument is Raymond Hedin's "The American Slave Narrative: The Justification of the Picaro," *American Literature* 53 (1982): 630–645.

10. Andrews, *To Tell a Free Story*, 166.

11. Zafar, *We Wear the Mask*, 87. See also Daphne Brooks's argument that Brown's depiction of his "savvy but nonetheless mean-spirited ruse" is calculated to provoke "the disdain of his pious abolitionist audience" (introduction to *The Great Escapes: Four Slave Narratives* [New York: Barnes and Noble, 2007], xxvii, xxviii).

12. Tess Chakkalakal makes a similar point about *Clotel*, arguing that it "reveals an author struggling to be free of his personal experience" (*Novel Bondage: Slavery, Marriage, and Freedom in Nineteenth-Century America* [Urbana: University of Illinois Press, 2011], 30).

13. William Lloyd Garrison, *An Address Delivered Before the Free People of Color, in Philadelphia, New-York, and Other Cities* (Boston: Foster, 1831), 6–7.

14. Any such history would have to include, in addition to Brown's works, Jacob D. Green's *Narrative of the Life of J. D. Green* (Huddersfield: Fielding, 1864), which includes a remarkably Brown-like account of tricking someone into getting whipped on his behalf; Henry Watson's *Narrative of Henry Watson* (Boston: Bela Marsh, 1848), in which Watson reproduces Bishop Meade's much-reproduced sermon to slaves and makes the geographically and chronologically impossible claim to have witnessed it; Lewis and Milton Clarke's *Narratives of the Sufferings of Lewis and Milton Clarke* (Boston: Bela Marsh, 1846), which often lifts off into sportiveness; and the nonsatirical comedy of many black abolitionist lectures, such as an 1851 lecture by Henry Bibb in Milwaukee, which ended with Bibb "in the middle of a hen-coop, into which he had pitched, head foremost, after leaping a high board fence, fleeing from a slave trader, in . . . St. Louis" (*Milwaukee Daily Free Democrat* [July 10, 1851]: 2).

15. Zora Neale Hurston, *Their Eyes Were Watching God* (1937; repr. New York: Harper & Row, 1990), 48.

16. It is important to remember, in this context, that most abolitionists were not New England Brahmin. "If we may judge by their occupations and property status," writes Edward Magdol in *The Antislavery Rank and File* (New York: Praeger, 1986), the vast majority of abolitionists were "women and men in the lower and middle ranks of American society" (151). In the areas of Massachusetts and New York that Magdol studies, the signers of antislavery petitions and members of abolitionist societies "tended to be the most mobile, least propertied, and most economically expectant in the population" (64). They were earners rather than proprietors, renters or boarders rather than owners, and after the shifting of the abolitionist base in the 1840s, when the Whigs departed, "leaving a vacuum that ex-Democrats [began] to fill," they were, in John G. Whittier's words, "bolder, freer, and less influenced by conservatism" (cited in Magdol, *The Antislavery Rank and File*, 106). The same is likely to have been true of the merely curious drop-ins at abolitionist lectures. Throughout the 1840s and 1850s, "the lecture-going public was . . . made up of people who perceived themselves in motion, in a state of preparation or expectation," writes Donald Scott. "Life appeared to them less a matter of settling into an established niche than a process of continuing self-construction" ("The Popular Lecture and the Creation of a Public in Mid-Nineteenth-Century America," *Journal of American History* 66 [1980]: 801).

17. In making this claim, I am adjusting the angle of my argument away from the perspective that I took up in chapter 1. Whereas I argued there that much of the plagiarism in Brown's work suggests something about Brown himself, or at least about his preferences as a writer, I am suggesting here that the instances of capitalization in Brown's work primarily indicate his sense of his *audience's* preferences. In some of those instances, Brown may very well have shared his audience's preferences; in other instances, he may not have. It is one of the basic conditions of reading Brown's work that one can never finally decide between those two options, never be entirely sure how personally invested he is in the shows he puts on. The private-

joke plagiarisms—shows in which, until now, Brown himself was the only audience—are, in other words, an outlying case, offering a highly unusual means of access to Brown's personal tastes.

18. "Public Reception of Wm. W. Brown in the Metropolis of England," *Liberator* (November 2, 1849): 1. Attacking slavery while admiring enterprise and industry, as Brown does here, may seem logically incoherent, given the degree to which slavery and the culture of modernity were intertwined. As Nyong'o Tavia points out, however, "the uneven ground of history ensures that social struggles are usually pitched not in terms of opposing discourses but in competitions over a single vernacular and improvisations upon a common repertoire" (*The Amalgamation Waltz: Race, Performance, and the Ruses of Memory* [Minneapolis: University of Minnesota Press, 2009], 103). Instead of opposing the vernacular of racial modernity, Brown learned how to speak it fluently; instead of turning his back on the repertoire of white American stories, he riffed endlessly on its contents.

19. *Commonwealth* (May 4, 1867): 2.

20. Severn Teackle Wallis, "Barnum and Mrs. Stowe," *Metropolitan Magazine* 3 (April 1855), reprinted in *Writings of Severn Teackle Wallis*, 4 vols. (Baltimore: Murphy, 1896), 2:70, 2:83–84.

21. Neil Harris, *Humbug: The Art of P. T. Barnum* (Boston: Little, Brown, 1973), 57, 56.

22. Ian Watt, *The Rise of the Novel: Studies in Defoe, Richardson, and Fielding* (Berkeley: University of California Press, 1957), 180.

23. Catherine Gallagher, "The Rise of Fictionality," in *The Novel: History, Geography, and Culture*, ed. Franco Moretti (Princeton, N.J.: Princeton University Press, 2006), 346, 347.

24. James W. Cook, *The Arts of Deception: Playing with Fraud in the Age of Barnum* (Cambridge, Mass.: Harvard University Press, 2001), 28.

25. "Town and Rural Humbugs," *The Knickerbocker* 45 (March 1855): 237.

26. P. T. Barnum, *The Life of P. T. Barnum, Written by Himself* (1855; repr. Urbana: University of Illinois Press, 2000), 225.

27. Ibid., 171.

28. In *Funny Stories by Phineas T. Barnum* (London: Routledge, 1890), which reproduces many of the anecdotes in the 1855 autobiography, Barnum acknowledges, in a preface, that they may be something other than authentic. "Although many of the incidents related in the present volume came under my own eyes . . . there are, doubtless, more or less funny anecdotes given herein which, while not new to all my readers, are probably so to a large majority of them—and as 'chestnuts' to a few are fresh meat to the many, I have not hesitated to insert funny and witty stories without being absolutely certain that they are original" (iv–v).

29. Thomas M. Eddy, "Barnum," *Ladies Repository* 15 (March 1855): 170. The anecdote to which he refers may be found in "Editor's Table," *Knickerbocker* 39 (May 1852): 482–483.

30. Eddy, "Barnum," 175.

31. Ibid., 170, 174; emphasis in original.

32. John Passmore Edwards, *Uncle Tom's Companions* (London: Edwards, 1852), 97.

33. Ibid., 104.

34. Brown, *A Description of William Wells Brown's Original Panoramic Views of the Scenes in the Life of an American Slave* (1850), reprinted in *The Black Abolitionist Papers*, vol. 1: *The British Isles, 1830–1865*, ed. C. Peter Ripley [Chapel Hill: University of North Carolina Press, 1985], 198.

35. Brown, *Three Years in Europe* (London: Gilpin, 1852), 97–104.

36. "Review of *Three Years in Europe*," *London Athenaeum* (October 2, 1852): 1056; "A Wild Cat Bank," *Cork Examiner* (October 13, 1852): 4; "Wild Cat Banks," *Bristol Mercury* (October 16, 1852): 1; "Wild Cat Banks," *New York Times* (February 8, 1853): 6; "Three Years in Europe," *Frederick Douglass's Paper* (November 19, 1852): 1; Brown, *Clotel*, 31; Josephine Brown, *Biography of an American Bondman* (Boston: Wallcut, 1856), 46–50; William Wells Brown, *Memoir of William Wells Brown* (Boston: Anti-Slavery Office, 1859), 25–29.

37. Richard Dyer, *White* (New York: Routledge, 1997), 31.

38. Lara Langer Cohen, *The Fabrication of American Literature: Fraudulence and Antebellum Print Culture* (Philadelphia: University of Pennsylvania Press, 2012), 100; Peter Brooks, *Reading for the Plot: Design and Intention in Narrative* (New York: Vintage, 1985), 38.

39. Karen Halttunen, *Confidence Men and Painted Women: A Study of Middle-Class Culture in America, 1830–1870* (New Haven, Conn.: Yale University Press, 1982), 197; John G. Cawelti, *Apostles of the Self-Made Man: Changing Concepts of Success in America* (Chicago: University of Chicago Press, 1965).

40. Johnson Jones Hooper, *Some Adventures of Captain Simon Suggs* (1845; repr. Nashville, Tenn.: Sanders, 1993), 12.

41. Ibid., 12–13.

42. Ibid., 13.

43. Ibid., 19.

44. Michel de Certeau, *The Practice of Everyday Life*, trans. Steven Rendall (Berkeley: University of California Press, 1984).

45. Hooper, *Some Adventures of Captain Simon Suggs*, 48.

46. Max Weber, *The Protestant Ethic and the Spirit of Capitalism*, trans. Talcott Parsons (New York: Scribner's, 1958), 17.

47. Ibid., 21.

48. Ibid., 58.

49. Ibid., 64.

50. Terence Whalen, "Introduction: P. T. Barnum and the Birth of Capitalist Irony," in Barnum, *The Life of P. T. Barnum*, xvi–xvii.

51. Thomas Chandler Haliburton, *Judge Haliburton's Yankee Stories* (Philadelphia: Lindsay and Blakiston, 1844), 45, 46; emphasis in original.

52. For the painting anecdote, see William Wells Brown, *The Black Man* (New York: Hamilton, 1863), 25–26; for the freight car anecdote, see *Clotel* (*C* 156–58) and *Negro in the American Rebellion*, 370–373; for the wet-sheets anecdote, see

Black Man, 28–30, and *Rising Son*, 13–16; for the church-pew anecdote, see *Negro in the American Rebellion*, 367–370; for the cemetery anecdote, see *My Southern Home* (*C* 766); for the flour-bag anecdote, see *Black Man*, 26–27, and *Rising Son*, 33–35; and for the communion-wine anecdote, see *Black Man*, 18, and *My Southern Home* (*C* 29–30).

53. Ralph Ellison, "Change the Joke and Slip the Yoke," in *Shadow and Act* (New York: Vintage, 1953), 54, 53–54.

54. Ibid., 54.

55. Ibid., 55.

56. Sigmund Freud, *Jokes and Their Relation to the Unconscious*, trans. James Strachey (New York: Norton, 1960), 120.

57. Ibid.

58. Ibid., 119–20.

59. Adam Phillips, *On Kissing, Tickling, and Being Bored: Psychoanalytic Essays on the Unexamined Life* (Cambridge, Mass.: Harvard University Press, 1993), 86.

60. Ibid.

61. See "Untitled," *Practical Christian* (March 2, 1844): 84, EBSCO; "Me and Massa," *The New Parley Library* (December 28, 1844): 239, Google Books; "Miscellaneous," *Cataract and Waterfall* (Worcester, Mass.) (February 7, 1844): 1, EBSCO; "Humorous," *Rhode Island Temperance Pledge* (May 22, 1847): 4, EBSCO; "Humorous," *Literary American* (New York) (December 1, 1849): 438, EBSCO; "Untitled," *Cleveland Plain Dealer* (January 9, 1850): 3, America's Historical Newspapers; "The Junk Locker," *Yankee Privateer* (February 25, 1854): 3, EBSCO; "All Sorts of Paragraphs," *Banner of Light* (August 1, 1863): 5, EBSCO; "Draught of the Seine," *Wilkes' Spirit of the Times* (May 29, 1864): 196, EBSCO; "Wit, Wisdom, and Humor," *Christian Advocate and Journal* (November 24, 1864): 371, EBSCO.

62. "Sentimental," *Boston Daily Bee* (January 24, 1849): 1. Brown had first used the anecdote in *Clotel* (*C* 129).

63. Brown, *Black Man*, 18.

64. Brown, *Negro in the American Rebellion*, 330.

65. Clayton Marsh, "Stealing Time: Poe's Confidence Men and the 'Rush of the Age,'" *American Literature* 77 (June 2005): 259.

66. Advertisement, *Poughkeepsie Daily Eagle* (March 11, 1862): 1.

67. "Daily Log Book," *Poughkeepsie Daily Eagle* (March 13, 1862): 2.

68. "Tour of William Wells Brown," *Liberator* (April 4, 1862): 54.

69. William Wells Brown, letter to Marius Robinson (November 29, 1857), reprinted in *Speak Out in Thunder Tones: Letters and Other Writings by Black Northerners, 1787–1865*, ed. Dorothy Sterling (New York: Doubleday, 1973), 127.

70. He probably had the same idea in Paterson, New Jersey, another city outside the usual abolitionist circuit, a few months earlier. On December 24, 1861, the *Paterson Daily Guardian* announced that "at three o'clock on Christmas Day . . . the celebrated WM. WELLS BROWN will give a humorous and highly entertaining lecture, calculated to send everybody away with a broad grin however ruefully

they appear on entering. Don't fail to hear this man; for he is no Artemus Ward"—a lecturer whose performance in Paterson had just been panned by the *Daily Guardian*—"but a regular genius in his way and worth your while to study as a character." Accompanying the article is a "programme of the entertainment," headlined "Great Attractions at Continental Hall," which promises not only an afternoon's worth of "classical, humorous, and sentimental recitations by the celebrated Elocutionist and Orator, Wm. Wells Brown" but an evening concert, "comic and sentimental," whose "intervals . . . will be filled by Mr. Brown, with his unequalled attractive powers" ("Christmas Festivities," *Paterson Daily Guardian* [December 24, 1861]: 3).

71. For an excellent history of black anticolonizationists, see Ousmane Power-Greene, *Against Wind and Tide: The African American Struggle Against the Colonization Movement* (New York: New York University Press, 2014).

72. The *St. John's Public Ledger* reprints the anecdote from the *Spirit of the Times*, emphasizing, in a prefatory note, that it is "*not* from *Uncle Tom's Cabin*" ("A Pious Nigger," *St. John's Public Ledger* [November 23, 1852]: 2; emphasis in original).

73. *Miralda*, 83–85; *Clotelle*, 42–43.

74. "'Tis a sweet night:—the very stars look out / From their bright places with a joyous sheen" (T. W. R., "Sonnet," in *The Odd-Fellows' Offering* [New York: Walker, 1854], 255).

75. Richard Dyer, *Only Entertainment* (New York: Routledge, 1992), 20.

76. Melville, *The Confidence-Man* (1857; repr. New York: Penguin, 1990), 218.

77. Ibid.

78. "Ashamed of His Relatives," *Morning Star* (June 20, 1860): 45, EBSCO.

79. I take the phrase "joyless reformism" from the psychoanalytic theorist Joel Whitebook. "One essential source for visions of a better society—visions that could be debated in a just public sphere—is the psychic imaginary and its refashioning of the contents of cultural tradition," Whitebook writes. "Without the input of the imaginary, any such debate, while possibly just, is in danger of being empty" (*Perversion and Utopia: A Study in Psychoanalysis and Critical Theory* [Cambridge, Mass.: MIT Press, 1995], 89).

80. Kennell Jackson, "Introduction: Traveling While Black," *Black Cultural Traffic: Crossroads in Global Performance and Popular Culture*, Harry J. Elam Jr. and Kennell Jackson, eds. (Ann Arbor: University of Michigan Press, 2005), 30.

81. "A Word to Our People," *Anglo-African Magazine* 1 (September 1859): 297.

82. Elizabeth Grosz, *The Nick of Time: Politics, Evolution, and the Untimely* (Durham, N.C.: Duke University Press, 2004), 98.

83. Barnum, *The Life of P. T. Barnum*, 296.

84. Phillips, *On Flirtation: Psychoanalytic Essays on the Uncommitted Life* (Cambridge, Mass.: Harvard University Press, 1994), 41.

85. Harriet Beecher Stowe, *Uncle Tom's Cabin* (1852; repr. New York: Norton, 2010), 404; emphasis in original.

3. The Aesthetic of Attractions

1. "The Anniversaries," *New York Herald* (May 9, 1849): 1.

2. The quotation is from Thomas Allston Brown, *A History of the New York Stage*, 3 vols. (New York: Dodd, Mead, 1903), 1:423. Among the "various entertainments of a light order" at the Minerva Rooms, Brown writes, was an 1847 performance by the Sable Harmonists (1:423). References to the other performances or exhibitions may be found in "Music and Musical Intelligence," *Anglo-American* (December 19, 1846): 214; "Tenth Semi-Annual Concert," *The Golden Rule and Odd-fellows Family Companion* 8 (1848): 127; Peter E. Palmquist and Thomas R. Kailbourn, *Pioneer Photographers from the Mississippi to the Continental Divide* (Stanford, Calif.: Stanford University Press, 2005), 284; and Ezekiel Porter Belden, *New-York: Past, Present, and Future* (New York: Putnam, 1849), 21–23.

3. "Anniversaries," 1.

4. Brown frequently opened and closed his lectures with songs. A year earlier, at the "crowdedly attended" annual meeting of the American Anti-Slavery Society in Convention Hall on Wooster Street, he had, according to a reporter for the *New York Sun*, opened the proceedings with "I Am a Slave No More," which was "encored twice in true theatrical style." He obligingly offered up "The Little Blind Boy," which was "cheered, and encored, like the former" ("Selections," *National Anti-Slavery Standard*, 18 May 1848, 1).

5. "Anniversaries," 1.

6. Mary Potter Thacher Higginson, *Thomas Wentworth Higginson: The Story of His Life* (Boston: Houghton, Mifflin, 1914), 97.

7. "Anniversaries," 1. In the same issue of the *New York Herald*, a petition signed by Herman Melville, Washington Irving, and other literati urged the English actor Charles Macready to go ahead with a repeat performance of *Macbeth*, in spite of the rough treatment Macready had received from a nativist crowd during the first performance. The next day, outside the Astor Opera House, ten blocks away from the Minerva Rooms, at least twenty-five people were killed and over 120 injured in clashes between nativists and the state militia, in what became known as the Astor Place Riot. It is quite possible that some of the members of Brown's audience participated in the protest that led to that event.

8. W. Caleb McDaniel, "The First and the Fourth: Abolitionist Holidays, Respectability, and Radical Interracial Reform," *American Quarterly* 57 (2005): 129.

9. "Anniversaries," 1.

10. Ibid.

11. I offer this account of Brown's speech in part as a means of counteracting the widespread assumption that "two kinds of performances, embodying distinct class projections, ran on very different tracks through the cultural landscape of the antebellum North"—that "minstrel circuits connected the urban theaters of the Northeast and the far West, whereas slave narrators performed on the lecture circuits of organized reform" (Ann Fabian, *The Unvarnished Truth: Personal Narratives in Nineteenth-Century America* [Berkeley, University of California

Press, 2000], 110). It is worth noting, in this context, that this rough-and-tumble speech was recorded not in any of the usual abolitionist venues, but in the *New York Herald*, which was, as a rule, "utterly unscrupulous in its attacks upon the abolitionists, in misrepresentation of their conduct, and in efforts (too often successful) to instigate to acts of violence and outrage against them" ("The American Press," *Anti-Slavery Advocate* 2 [October 1853]: 102).

12. Samuel May Jr. to John Bishop Estlin (May 21, 1849), quoted in Larry Gara, "The Professional Fugitive in the Abolition Movement," *Wisconsin Magazine of History* 48 (1965): 203.

13. John Bishop Estlin to Samuel May Jr. (May 2, 1851), reprinted in *British and American Abolitionists: An Episode in Transatlantic Understanding*, ed. Clare Taylor (Edinburgh: Edinburgh University Press, 1974), 377. Two months earlier, the following advertisement had appeared in a British newspaper: "**ARRIVAL OF THE THREE FUGITIVE SLAVES** *FROM AMERICA*. WM. WELLS BROWN & WM. CRAFT, Fugitive Slaves from the United States, will deliver LECTURES on AMERICAN SLAVERY, in the ATHENAEUM LECTURE ROOM, on TUESDAY AND WEDNESDAY evenings, MARCH 11 and 12, to commence each evening at Half-past Seven o'Clock. ELLEN CRAFT, the White Slave, who effected her own escape and that of her husband by assuming men's apparel and travelling above a thousand miles through the Slave States, will also be present. WILLIAM CRAFT will narrate the manner in which himself and wife escaped. During the Lectures, Mr. BROWN will exhibit and explain his splendid PANORAMIC VIEWS OF SLAVERY, Painted on 2,000 feet of Canvas" (*Carlisle Journal*, [March 7, 1851]: 2).

14. Wallace Stevens, "The Motive for Metaphor," in *The Collected Poems of Wallace Stevens* (New York: Knopf, 1955), 288.

15. The turn-of-the-century cinema of attractions is, for Gunning, just one manifestation of the aesthetic of attractions, an aesthetic that emerged from a mid-nineteenth-century "channeling of visuality towards the production of desire essential for the creation of a consumer culture" (Tom Gunning, "The Whole Town's Gawking: Early Cinema and the Visual Experience of Modernity," *Yale Journal of Criticism* 7 [1994]: 194). "While the impulse to *curiositas* may be as old as Augustine, there is no question that the nineteenth century sharpened this form of 'lust of the eyes' and its commercial exploitation," he writes. "Expanding urbanization with kaleidoscopic succession of city sights, the growth of consumer society with its new emphasis on stimulating spending through visual display, and the escalating horizons of colonial exploration with new peoples and territories to be categorized and exploited all provoked the desire for images and attractions" (Tom Gunning, "An Aesthetic of Astonishment: Early Film and the (In)credulous Spectator," in *Viewing Positions: Ways of Seeing Film*, ed. Linda Williams [New Brunswick, N.J.: Rutgers University Press, 1995], 125).

16. Tom Gunning, "Attractions: How They Came Into the World," in *The Cinema of Attractions Reloaded*, ed. Wanda Strauven (Amsterdam: Amsterdam University Press, 2006), 36. Even in early cinema, however, attractions are not entirely independent of narrative. "While I define attractions in opposition to narrative structure," Gunning writes, "in actual practice these two different modes of spec-

tator address often interact within a single film" (Gunning, "Whole Town's Gawking," 191).

17. Tom Gunning, *D. W. Griffith and the Origins of American Narrative Film* (Urbana: University of Illinois Press, 1993), 66.

18. Charles Baudelaire, "The Painter of Modern Life," in *My Heart Laid Bare and Other Prose Writings* (London: Soho, 1986), 37.

19. Michael Berthold, "Cross-Dressing and Forgetfulness of Self in William Wells Brown's *Clotel*," *College Literature* 20 (1993): 27.

20. Glenda Carpio, *Laughing Fit to Kill: Black Humor in the Fictions of Slavery* (New York: Oxford University Press, 2008), 38.

21. Ezra Greenspan, *William Wells Brown: An African American Life* (New York: Norton, 2014), 495.

22. "Wm. Wells Brown," *Anti-Slavery Bugle* (February 7, 1857): 2.

23. "Wm. Wells Brown," *Liberator* (August 1, 1856): 124.

24. Other respondents felt the same way. "The 'pictures' of slaves bound for the market, the sale of slaves, the city of New Orleans, W. W. Brown caught, &c., were . . . diverting," writes a viewer of one of Brown's panoramic exhibitions, "and the highly spiced anecdotes *a la* Baron Munchausen, with which his description of them was interspersed, afforded excellent entertainment—alternately moving to demonstrations of sympathetic indignation and incontinent laughter" ("Slavery in the United States," *Carlisle Journal* [March 14, 1851]: 2). "Until the close of the lecture or rather series of recitations and experiences, those gathered were kept in a state of anticipated suspense as to what was next coming!" exclaims a reporter covering one of Brown's 1861 appearances in Paterson, New Jersey. "The lecture was so full of hits and amusing reflections on affected and hypocritical foibles, that the crowd were kept in a grin from the opening to the close of the affair" ("The Lecture of Wm. Wells Brown," *Paterson Daily Guardian* [December 13, 1861]: 3).

25. Robert Lewis, "Introduction: From Celebration to Show Business," in *From Traveling Show to Vaudeville: Theatrical Spectacle in America, 1830–1910*, ed. Robert Lewis (Baltimore, Md.: Johns Hopkins University Press, 2003), 9.

26. "Places of Public Amusement," *Putnam's Magazine* 3 (February 1854): 148–149.

27. George W. Bungay, *Crayon Sketches and Off-Hand Takings* (Boston: Stacy and Richardson, 1852), 61.

28. Ibid., 62.

29. Brown, *Rising Son*, 531.

30. William Wells Brown, "Speech at Annual Meeting of the American Anti-Slavery Society" (1862), in *Clotel and Other Writings*, ed. Ezra Greenspan (New York: Library of America, 2014), 947–948. All subsequent references to the works included in this edition—the 1847 *Narrative*, *Clotel*, *The American Fugitive in Europe*, *The Escape*, *The Black Man*, *My Southern Home*, and selected speeches and public letters—will appear parenthetically in the text with the abbreviation *C*.

31. Samuel Brooke, *Slavery and the Slave-Holder's Religion* (Cincinnati: published for the author, 1846), 22.

32. Ibid., 22.

33. William Lloyd Garrison, *An Address Delivered Before the Free People of Color* (Boston: Foster, 1831), 22; *Gleanings from Pious Authors*, ed. James Montgomery (1846; repr. Philadelphia: Longstreth, 1855), 24.

34. Theodore Weld, *American Slavery as It Is* (New York: American Anti-Slavery Society, 1839), 7; "The Dismal Swamp." *New York Scientific American* (July 22, 1848): 350.

35. Tom Gunning, "The Cinema of Attraction[s]: Early Film, Its Spectator, and the Avant-Garde," in *The Cinema of Attractions Reloaded*, ed. Wanda Strauven (Amsterdam: Amsterdam University Press, 2006), 387.

36. Gunning, "Aesthetic," 123; Gunning, "Attractions," 37. The essential feature of "an aesthetic of attractions, whether of the cinema, the sensational press, or the fairground" is, for Gunning, that its "hold on spectators depends on arousing and satisfying visual curiosity through a direct and acknowledged act of display, rather than following a narrative enigma within a diegetic site into which the spectator peers invisibly" (Tom Gunning, " 'Now You See It, Now You Don't': The Temporality of the Cinema of Attractions," *Velvet Light Trap* 32 [Fall 1993]: 6). I am extending Gunning's argument in a new direction by applying it to fictional and nonfictional texts, but as his allusion to "the sensational press" and his evocations of the arguments of Roland Barthes and Peter Brooks should suggest, Gunning prepares the way for this expansion of his claims.

37. The passage beginning "It was on the eve of a presidential election" and ending "I am a son of Mr. John Gosling" (*C* 172) consists almost entirely of set-up lines and punch lines. At least one of these gags, the one that ends the sequence, is copied from a newspaper's filler article ("Smart Boy," *Rural Repository* [June 6, 1846]: 111).

38. The number consists of a comic anecdote about the secretive tippling of nominal teetotalers (*C* 173–175).

39. The minister's melodramatically anaphoric declamation ("*I have known . . . I have known . . . I have known . . .*" [*C* 175–176]) is copied, italics and all, from a magazine article (Edward Baines, "Testimony and Appeal on the Effects of Total Abstinence," *The British Friend* 40 [January 1853]: 10).

40. The counteranecdote runs from "It is indeed wonderful" to "whiskey, blacking, and all" (*C* 176).

41. The Southerner's response reproduces a filler article excerpted from a speech by Parker Pillsbury ("Worshippers of Mammon," *Anti-Slavery Bugle* [April 10, 1846]: 4).

42. The "account of a grand bull fight" that the minister reads is transcribed from "Sunday Amusements in New Orleans," *New York Weekly Herald* (April 9, 1853): 114.

43. Zora Neale Hurston, *Their Eyes Were Watching God* (1937; repr. New York: Harper & Row, 1990), 59.

44. For an analysis of gags—"atemporal bursts of violence and/or hedonism that are as ephemeral and as gratifying as the sight of someone's pie-smitten face"—see Donald Crafton, "Pie and Chase: Gag, Spectacle, and Narrative in Slapstick Comedy," in *The Cinema of Attractions Reloaded*, ed. Wanda Strauven (Amsterdam: Amsterdam University Press, 2006), 355–364. For a Gunning-influenced reading

of the structural function of numbers in musicals, see Pierre-Emmanuel Jaques, "The Associational Attractions of the Musical," in *The Cinema of Attractions Reloaded*, ed. Wanda Strauven (Amsterdam: Amsterdam University Press, 2006), 281–288.

45. John Ernest, *Resistance and Reformation in Nineteenth-Century African-American Literature: Brown, Wilson, Jacobs, Delany, Douglass, and Harper* (Oxford: University of Mississippi Press, 1995), 23; M. Giulia Fabi, "The 'Unguarded Expressions of the Feelings of the Negroes': Gender, Slave Resistance, and William Wells Brown's Revisions of *Clotel*," *African American Review* 27 (1993): 640; Eva Allegra Raimon, *The 'Tragic Mulatta' Revisited: Race and Nationalism in Nineteenth-Century Antislavery Fiction* (New Brunswick, N.J.: Rutgers University Press, 2004), 68, 70.

46. Russ Castronovo, *Fathering the Nation: American Genealogies of Slavery and Freedom* (Berkeley: University of California Press, 1995), 32.

47. Gunning, "'Now You See It,'" 6.

48. Ibid., 7–8.

49. Gunning, "Aesthetic," 117, 116.

50. Mark Twain, letter to Olivia Langdon Clemens (November 27, 1871), in *Mark Twain's Letters*, vol. 4: *1870–1871*, ed. Victor Fischer and Michael B. Frank (Berkeley: University of California Press, 1995), 498; emphasis in original. For more on Twain's performative aesthetics—drawn, like Brown's, from masculine subcultures but geared far more than Brown's toward the reinscription of the lines between white men and their others—see Randall Knoper, *Acting Naturally: Mark Twain in the Culture of Performance* (Berkeley: University of California Press, 1995).

51. Gunning, "Aesthetic," 129.

52. For an excellent reading of the figure of the phantasmagoria in Benjamin's writings, see Kevin Hetherington, *Capitalism's Eye: Cultural Spaces of the Commodity* (New York: Routledge, 2007). "Benjamin does not want to simply subject phantasmagoria to critique," Hetherington writes. "Rather, and this is what singles him out from the Marxist tradition, he wants to construct these phantasmagoria as dialectical images in order to reveal, and thereby redeem from capitalism, the genuine utopian quest for an experience of the world that humanity has which is expressed in such ideals as luxury, comfort, abundance, and ease" (94).

53. For a description of Brown's successful panorama and magic-lantern tours, see Greenspan, *William Wells Brown*, 239–249, 289, 310.

54. Wolfgang Schivelbusch, *The Railway Journey: The Industrialization of Time and Space in the Nineteenth Century* (Berkeley: University of California Press, 1977), 60.

55. For more on the development of such spaces, see Anne Friedberg, *Window Shopping: Cinema and the Postmodern* (Berkeley: University of California Press, 1993); and William Leach, *Land of Desire: Merchants, Power, and the Rise of a New American Culture* (New York: Vintage, 1993).

56. The allusion at the end of the sentence is to Mary Anne Doane's *The Emergence of Cinematic Time: Modernity, Contingency, and the Archive* (Cambridge, Mass.: Harvard University Press, 2002).

57. Edgar Allen Poe, "The Philosophy of Composition," in *Essays and Reviews* (New York: Library of America, 1984), 13; emphasis in original.

58. Robert Fanuzzi, *Abolition's Public Sphere* (Minneapolis: University of Minnesota Press, 2003), xv.

59. Ibid., xxi.

60. In a report on an antislavery fair in Waterloo, New York, Brown observes that "the mottos which were upon the walls were read again and again by those present" ("Waterloo Fair," *National Anti-Slavery Standard* [March 25, 1847]: 170). For other references to the mottoed flags on the walls at antislavery fairs, see Maria Weston Chapman, "The Twelfth National Anti-Slavery Bazaar," *Liberator* (January 23, 1846): 14; and M. G., "Description of the Pennsylvania Anti-Slavery Fair," *Anti-Slavery Advocate* 1 (February 1853): 35–36.

61. Stephen M. Best, *The Fugitive's Properties: Law and the Poetics of Possession* (Chicago: University of Chicago Press, 2004), 261.

62. Toni Morrison, *Beloved* (New York: Vintage, 2004), 288.

63. Kennell Jackson, "Introduction: Traveling While Black," in *Black Cultural Traffic: Crossroads in Global Performance and Popular Culture*, ed. Harry J. Elam Jr. and Kennell Jackson (Ann Arbor: University of Michigan Press, 2005), 4.

64. James Snead, "On Repetition in Black Culture," *Black American Literature Forum* 1 (Winter 1981): 150.

65. Paul Gilroy, *Against Race: Imagining Political Culture Beyond the Color Line* (Cambridge, Mass.: Harvard University Press, 2000), 201.

66. Bernard W. Bell, *The Afro-American Novel and Its Tradition* (Amherst: University of Massachusetts Press, 1987), 36.

67. Herman Melville, *Israel Potter*, in *Pierre, Israel Potter, The Piazza Tales, The Confidence-Man, Uncollected Prose, and Billy Budd, Sailor* (New York: Library of America, 1984), 479.

68. Henri Bergson, *Laughter: An Essay on the Meaning of the Comic* (1911; repr. Mineola, N.Y.: Dover, 2005), 10.

69. Adam Phillips, *Houdini's Box: The Art of Escape* (New York: Random House, 2001), 158.

70. Gunning, "Aesthetic," 118.

71. Robert Reid-Pharr, *Conjugal Union: The Body, The House, and the Black American* (New York: Oxford University Press, 1999), 19.

72. Untitled letter, *Liberator* (June 13, 1856): 95.

4. The Beautiful Slave Girl

1. A lengthier version of the article, attributed to "H. S. D.," first appeared in the *Utica Liberty Press* and was republished in the *National Anti-Slavery Standard* in early 1845. Because it was not as current as the *New York Evangelist* version, because it reads not "her emotions were too deep for tears" but "her emotion was too deep for tears," and because its description of the woman's appearance is less like the description in "A True Story of Slave Life" than the *New York Evange-*

list version is, it was probably not Brown's source. Its last paragraph, which was cut from all subsequent versions, reads as follows: "It is but just to remark, that the above sale never took place to our knowledge. But no thanks to slaveholders nor the system of American Slavery, that it has not. They have all the elements, and all that is lacking is the suitable circumstances" ("An Auction," *National Anti-Slavery Standard* [March 20, 1845]: 165). Although Brown probably encountered "An Auction" as a news item, in other words, it is in fact a work of fiction.

2. William Wells Brown, "A Lecture Delivered Before the Female Anti-Slavery Society of Salem at Lyceum Hall" (1847), in *Clotel and Other Writings*, ed. Ezra Greenspan (New York: Library of America, 2014), 871. All subsequent references to the works included in this edition—the 1847 *Narrative*, *Clotel*, *The American Fugitive in Europe*, *The Escape*, *The Black Man*, *My Southern Home*, and selected speeches and public letters—will appear parenthetically in the text with the abbreviation *C*.

3. William Wells Brown, "A True Story of Slave Life," *Anti-Slavery Advocate* 1 (December 1852): 23.

4. Ibid.

5. He was, of course, not alone. "For many, slave and free, the act of rape signified the slave trade and even slavery itself," writes Edward E. Baptist ("'Cuffy,' 'Fancy Maids,' and 'One-Eyed Men': Rape, Commodification, and the Domestic Slave Trade in the United States," in *The Chattel Principle: Internal Slave Trades in the Americas* [New Haven, Conn.: Yale University Press, 2004], 183). For studies of the abolitionist equation of slavery with sexual abuse, see Ronald Walters, "The Erotic South: Civilization and Sexuality in American Abolitionism," *American Quarterly* 25 (1973): 177–201; and Carol Lasser, "Voyeuristic Abolitionism: Sex, Gender, and the Transformation of Antislavery Rhetoric," *Journal of the Early Republic* 28 (2008): 83–114.

6. As Baptist points out, the very "idea of the slave commodity carried a frisson, an implication, of the power and pleasure—sadistic or sexual (or both)—that created the precious commodity thus consumed" ("'Cuffy,'" 178). The "fancy girl" was the quintessential embodiment of that frisson. "She was neither precisely black nor white and neither field labor nor house hand but rather the 'fancy' of the market for selling the right to rape a special category of women marked as unusually desirable," Baptist writes. "The history of rape, obvious to all though openly spoken of by few, was the remembered meaning of the fetish of the fancy maid in the white male mind" ("'Cuffy,'" 183, 188).

7. "Unwillingly," Baptist writes, "such women introduced a pornographic history, one that was obscene yet for that very reason more lusted after, into the parlors, bedrooms, and above all, the markets of the elite white man's world" ("'Cuffy,'" 187–188).

8. Brown, *Three Years in Europe* (London: Gilpin, 1852), 273–274.

9. William Wells Brown, *A Description of William Wells Brown's Original Panoramic Views of the Scenes in the Life of an American Slave* (1850), reprinted in *The Black Abolitionist Papers*, vol. 1: *The British Isles, 1830–1865*, ed. C. Peter Ripley (Chapel Hill: University of North Carolina Press, 1985), 200.

10. The value of the fancy girl "stems not simply from her whiteness and beauty," Gustavus Stadler writers, "but from the knowledge or knowingness . . . that she produces for the people who gaze at her. . . . Everyone is *familiar* with her as a type of slave laborer even if not with her particular 'mystery' " (*Troubling Minds*, 81; emphasis in original).

11. Ibid. The "spectacular rise in prices resulting from the interregional slave trade made human property one of the most costly, and therefore most valuable, forms of investment in the country," writes the historian Stephen Deyle. By 1860, the value of the slave population—conservatively estimated at $3 billion, or $86.7 billion in 2013 dollars—"was roughly three times greater than the total amount of all capital, North and South combined, invested in manufacturing, almost three times the amount invested in railroads, and seven times the amount invested in banks. It was also equal to about seven times the total value of all currency in circulation in the country" (*Carry Me Back: The Domestic Slave Trade in American Life* [New York: Oxford University Press, 2005], 59, 60).

12. Alice Walker, *In Search of Our Mother's Gardens: Womanist Prose* (New York: Harcourt Brace Jovanovich, 1983), 301.

13. Ann duCille, *The Coupling Convention: Sex, Text, and Tradition in Black Women's Fiction* (New York: Oxford University Press, 1993), 22, 23.

14. Gilles Deleuze, "Coldness and Cruelty," trans. Jean McNeil, in *Masochism* (New York: Zone, 1991), 31.

15. William Wells Brown, *Narrative of William W. Brown* (Boston: Anti-Slavery Office, 1848), 16.

16. Frederick Douglass, *My Bondage and My Freedom* (1855; repr. New York: Penguin, 2003), 69.

17. Solomon Northrup, *Twelve Years a Slave* (1853; repr. Baton Rouge: Louisiana State University Press, 1968), 196–198. Northrup's narrative was written with the aid of an upstate New York lawyer named David Wilson.

18. See in particular Jenny Franchot, "The Punishment of Esther: Frederick Douglass and the Construction of the Feminine," in *Frederick Douglass: New Literary and Historical Essays*, ed. Eric J. Sundquist (Cambridge: Cambridge University Press, 1990): 141–165; Deborah E. McDowell, "In the First Place: Making Frederick Douglass and the Afro-American Narrative Tradition," in *Critical Essays on Frederick Douglass*, ed. William L. Andrews (Boston: G. K. Hall, 1991): 192–214; and Jeannine DeLombard, " 'Eye-witness to the Cruelty': Southern Violence and Northern Testimony in Frederick Douglass's 1845 *Narrative*," *American Literature* 73 (June 2001): 245–275.

19. Karen Sánchez-Eppler, "Bodily Bonds: The Intersecting Rhetorics of Feminism and Abolition," *Representations* 24 (1988): 48. "Even if the use of the wounded body in anti-slavery efforts asked on-lookers and readers to gaze not too long upon the body itself," Jennifer James writes, the "risk of specularity is apparent: the body is at risk of being imagined in a permanent state of damage or injury" (" 'Civil' War Wounds: William Wells Brown, Violence, and the Domestic Narrative," *African American Review* 39 [2005]: 52).

20. J. Brown, *Biography of an American Bondman* (Boston: Wallcut, 1856), 7.

21. In the *Narrative*, he mentions the whippings of slaves named Patsey and Delphia, and in *The Escape*, Mrs. Gaines twice takes Hannah offstage, telling her that she will "whip her well," but in none of these cases is there anything like the prolonged, fixated attention to detail that one finds in the work of writers like Douglass and Northrup.

22. Brown, *Description*, 193–194, 200, 194.

23. "W. W. Brown in Ohio—the Underground Railroad," *National Anti-Slavery Standard* (April 7, 1855): 2.

24. Brown, *Clotelle*, 15.

25. "W. W. Brown in Ohio," 2.

26. Amelia Welby, "Lines Written on Seeing an Infant Sleeping on Its Mother's Bosom," in *Poems* (Boston: Tompkins, 1845), 25, 26.

27. Laura Mulvey, *Fetishism and Curiosity* (Bloomington: Indiana University Press, 1996), 5.

28. Ibid., 5.

29. Ibid., xiv.

30. Ibid., 12, 13.

31. Ibid., xiv.

32. Martha Schoolman, "Violent Places: *Three Years in Europe* and the Question of William Wells Brown's Cosmopolitanism," *ESQ* 58, no. 1 (2012): 4, 24.

33. William Farmer, "Fugitive Slaves at the Great Exhibition," *Liberator* (July 18, 1851): 4.

34. Michael A. Chaney, *Fugitive Vision: Slave Image and Black Identity in Antebellum Narrative* (Bloomington: Indiana University Press, 2008), 60.

35. Toni Morrison, *Playing in the Dark: Whiteness and the Literary Imagination* (Cambridge, Mass.: Harvard University Press, 1992), 11, 69.

36. Samuel Weber, *Theatricality as Medium* (New York: Fordham University Press, 2004), 191; emphasis in original.

37. Ibid.

38. "Pauline," *Anti-Slavery Reporter* (July 1, 1846): 103.

39. Brown, *Three Years*, 297.

40. Brown, "True Story," 23.

41. Brown, *Miralda*, 150; Brown, *Clotelle*, 73.

42. Brown, *Miralda*, 151; Brown, *Clotelle*, 74.

43. Brown, *Clotelle*, 9. The scene was presumably in *Miralda* as well, but the issue of the *Anglo-African Magazine* in which the first chapters of *Miralda* appeared has not survived.

44. "Pauline," 103.

45. Freud, "Fetishism," in *Sexuality and the Psychology of Love*, trans. James Strachey (New York: Simon and Schuster, 1963), 207.

46. *Narratives of the Sufferings of Lewis and Milton Clarke* (Boston: Bela Marsh, 1846), 75; Deleuze, "Coldness," 32.

47. Deleuze, "Coldness," 31. In a recent essay, Saidiya Hartman has made a similar effort to "revisit the scene of subjection without replicating the grammar of violence," to "imagine a *free state*" that is not "the time before captivity or slavery."

Her "critical fabulation" of the history of a slave girl named Venus necessarily begins, she writes, "in the wake of her disappearance and with the wild hope that our efforts can return her to the world. The conjunction of hope and defeat define this labor and leave open its outcome" ("Venus in Two Acts," *Small Axe* 12 [June 2008]: 4, 11, 14).

48. William Wells Brown, *Memoir of William Wells Brown* (Boston: Anti-Slavery Office, 1859), 20–21.

49. E. L. McCallum, *Object Lessons: How to Do Things with Fetishism* (Albany, N.Y.: SUNY Press, 1999), 140.

50. Ibid., 137, 141.

51. Ibid., 4, 5.

52. Brown, *Three Years*, 291; Brown, *Miralda*, 208; Brown, *Clotelle*, 95.

53. "The Translation of St. Catherine," *People's and Howitt's Journal* 2 (1847): 255.

54. Ibid.

55. Ibid.

56. There is a relationship, clearly, between the hovering state that I am describing here and the "unreal estate" that duCille identifies as Brown's preferred literary space: "a fictive realm of the fantastic and coincidental, not the farfetched or the fanciful." DuCille suggests, however, that when Brown mingles " 'the real' and 'the romantic,' " it is "usually for decidedly political purposes" (*The Coupling Convention*, 18). What I am trying to suggest here is that Brown's fetishistic repetitions tend to take him further away from the realm of "decidedly political purposes"—at least as those purposes have traditionally been understood—without ever entirely leaving that realm behind.

5. The Sound of Fame

1. William Wells Brown, *The Escape* (1858), in *Clotel and Other Writings*, ed. Ezra Greenspan (New York: Library of America, 2014), 424. All subsequent references to the works included in this edition—the 1847 *Narrative*, *Clotel*, *The American Fugitive in Europe*, *The Escape*, *The Black Man*, *My Southern Home*, and selected speeches and public letters—will appear parenthetically in the text with the abbreviation *C*. Samuel Mosheim Schmucker, *The Yankee Slave Driver; or, The Black and White Rivals* (Philadelphia: Evans, 1858), 93.

2. Giovanni Pacini, *Saffo: A Lyrical Tragedy in Three Acts* (Boston: Eastburn's Press, 1847), 4; James Sheridan Knowles, *Love: A Play* (London: Moxon, 1840), 3.1.227–231.

3. Edwin P. Whipple, *Lectures on Subjects Connected with Literature and Life* (Boston: Ticknor, Reed, and Fields, 1850), 189.

4. Ann duCille, "Where in the World Is William Wells Brown? Thomas Jefferson, Sally Hemings, and the DNA of African-American Literary History," *American Literary History* 12 (2000): 443–462.

5. Martin Puchner, *Stage Fright: Modernism, Anti-Theatricality, and Drama* (Baltimore, Md.: Johns Hopkins University Press, 2002), 109.

6. Ann duCille, *The Coupling Convention: Sex, Text, and Tradition in Black Women's Fiction* (New York: Oxford University Press, 1993), 25.

7. Lara Langer Cohen, "Notes from the State of Saint Domingue: The Practice of Citation in *Clotel*," in *Early African American Print Culture*, ed. Lara Langer Cohen and Jordan Alexander Stein (Philadelphia: University of Pennsylvania Press, 2012), 161.

8. Ibid., 164.

9. Elizabeth Bishop, "At the Fishhouses," in *The Complete Poems* (New York: Farrar, Straus & Giroux, 1979), 64.

10. William Hazlitt, "On the Living Poets," in *Lectures on the English Poets* (London: Taylor and Hessey, 1818), 283–284.

11. [Benjamin B. Thatcher], "Preface," in *The Poetical Works of Mrs. Felicia Hemans* (Philadelphia: Ash, 1835), 11; emphasis in original.

12. Andrew Bennett, *Romantic Poets and the Culture of Posterity* (Cambridge: Cambridge University Press, 1999), 5; Leo Braudy, quoted in ibid., 61.

13. Thatcher, "Preface," 11, 13, 20.

14. Bennett, *Romantic Poets*, 80.

15. Brown, *Miralda*, 234; Brown, *Clotelle*, 104.

16. Andrew Bennett, "Poetry and Ignorance," in *Romantic Generations: Text, Authority, and Posterity in British Romanticism*, ed. Lene Østermark-Johansen (Copenhagen: Museum Tusculanem Press, 2003), 83–84.

17. Grace Aguilar, *Home Scenes and Heart Studies* (New York: Appleton, 1853), 91; *Miralda*, 177/*Clotelle*, 84.

18. Aguilar, *Home Scenes and Heart Studies*, 382; *Miralda*, 206/*Clotelle*, 94.

19. Aguilar, *Home Scenes and Heart Studies*, 113; *Miralda*, 217. A differently rewritten version of the same sentence appears in *The Black Man* (*C* 667) and *The Negro in the American Rebellion*, 167.

20. William James, *The Principles of Psychology*, 2 vols. (New York: Holt, 1990), 1:245–246.

21. Nathaniel Parker Willis, *Pencillings by the Way* (New York: Morris and Willis, 1844), 149, 81; Nathaniel Parker Willis, *Letters from Under a Bridge* (London: Virtue, 1840), 111.

22. Nathaniel Hawthorne, *The Scarlet Letter* (1850; repr. New York: Norton, 2005), 126.

23. Sianne Ngai, *Ugly Feelings* (Cambridge, Mass.: Harvard University Press, 2005), 66. It should be said, however, that the final predicate in the anaphoric sequence in "An Appeal" actually derives from Stephen S. Foster, *Brotherhood of Thieves* (Boston: Anti-Slavery Office, 1844), 11.

24. Maurice Blanchot, *The Space of Literature*, trans. Ann Smock (Lincoln: University of Nebraska Press, 1982), 223; emphasis in original.

25. "Hunting Robbers with Bloodhounds," *Utica Daily Observer* (September 25, 1848): 1.

26. "A Peep Into an Italian Interior," *Chambers' Edinburgh Journal* (April 16, 1852): 244/*C* 183; "The Mother," *Albany Evening Journal* (January 10, 1849): 2/*C* 196.

27. Brown, *Clotelle*, 89–90.

28. John Guillory, *Cultural Capital: The Problem of Literary Canon Formation* (Chicago: University of Chicago Press, 1993), 93.

29. "Oration Over the Tomb of Hood," *London Daily News* (July 19, 1854): 5.

30. Lord Carlisle, *Two Lectures on the Poetry of Pope* (London: Simkin, Marshall, 1851), 8.

31. See Samuel Johnson, *The Works of Samuel Johnson* (New York: Dearborn, 1832), 2:252; "John Clare, the Northamptonshire Poet," *Eliza Cook's Journal* 4 (February 15, 1851): 241; "Poetry and the Drama," *The Critic* (December 1, 1853): 626; and David Macbeth Moir, *Sketches of the Poetical Literature of the Past Half-Century* (Edinburgh: Blackwood, 1851), 2.

32. [Robert Vaughan], "*Festus—A Poem*," *British Quarterly Review* 3 (May 1846): 390.

33. Edward Wilmot Blyden, *Liberia's Offering* (New York: Gray, 1860), 35.

34. Alexander Stewart, "Education," in *Materials for Thinking, Extracted from the Works of the Learned of All Ages* (London: Chidley, 1846), 325.

35. Blanchot, *The Space of Literature*, 42, 41.

36. Ibid., 27; emphasis in original.

37. Leo Bersani and Ulysse Dutoit, *Forms of Being: Cinema, Aesthetics, Subjectivity* (London: British Film Institute, 2004), 117.

38. Samuel Weber, *Theatricality as Medium* (New York: Fordham University Press, 2004), 27.

39. Herman Melville, *Moby-Dick* (1851; repr. New York: Norton, 2001), 406.

40. William Hazlitt, *The Spirit of the Age; or, Contemporary Portraits* (London: Colburn, 1825), 150, 151–152, 157.

41. Ibid., 154, 155.

42. Ibid., 155; emphasis in original.

43. Adam Phillips, *Promises, Promises: Essays on Psychoanalysis and Literature* (New York: Basic Books, 2001), 352.

44. "William Wells Brown," *Boston Evening Journal* (January 15, 1885): 4.

Index